自然拼读教学指南

PHONICS INSTRUCTIONAL GUIDE

本指南适用于在职英语学教师、职前英语教师、培训机构、家庭英语启蒙

陈岷婕/尹国杰 —— 著

经济管理出版社
ECONOMY & MANAGEMENT PUBLISHING HOUSE

图书在版编目（CIP）数据

自然拼读教学指南/陈岷婕，尹国杰著．—北京：经济管理出版社，2024.1
ISBN 978-7-5096-9597-5

Ⅰ.①自…　Ⅱ.①陈…②尹…　Ⅲ.①英语课—教学研究—中小学　Ⅳ.①G633.412

中国国家版本馆 CIP 数据核字(2024)第 037227 号

组稿编辑：杨国强
责任编辑：杨国强
责任印制：许　艳
责任校对：蔡晓臻

出版发行：经济管理出版社
（北京市海淀区北蜂窝 8 号中雅大厦 A 座 11 层　100038）
网　　址：www.E-mp.com.cn
电　　话：（010）51915602
印　　刷：唐山玺诚印务有限公司
经　　销：新华书店
开　　本：720mm×1000mm/16
印　　张：18.25
字　　数：333 千字
版　　次：2024 年 4 月第 1 版　　2024 年 4 月第 1 次印刷
书　　号：ISBN 978-7-5096-9597-5
定　　价：68.00 元

Preface (Foreword)

This phonics instructional guide is written by my former PhD student, Ms. Chen Min Jie, who is dedicated to promoting the effectiveness of English education compulsory education phase in mainland China. Based on extensive, in-depth reading of relevant literature, the national curriculum for English in compulsory education, and also her PhD research, she decided to write a guide for instruction in phonics. Such a guide will be extremely beneficial to pre-service EFL teachers, in-service EFL teachers as well as dedicated parents to help children with basic phonics decoding rules, as the decoding rules or the sound phonemes are the fundamental elements in the English language.

Given that, this guide first introduces basic knowledge related to phonics to make readers understand the importance of knowing phonics decoding rules and how phonics plays a role in promoting EFL learners' reading and spelling as well as reading comprehension ability. Then, the author introduces phonics decoding rules in chapter two, which is convenient for readers to get a comprehensive understanding of the specific rules. In the third chapter, phonics instruction guidelines are provided on the basis of a detailed description of the phonics instruction approaches. Additionally, the author also provides a sample teaching lesson for the readers' reference.

Last but not least, the author has compiled a phonics instruction reference word list in the sequence of specific phonemes and phonograms based on the required vocabulary in the national curriculum. Thus, this is a comprehensive phonics guide for pre-service EFL teachers, EFL teachers and parents. No other book compiles so much comprehensive information in such a usable form in both the English and Chinese languages. I am confident that such a guide will be indispensable to English teachers in China.

Associate Professor Dr. Goh Hock Seng
01-01-2024
Sultan Idris Education University, Malaysia

Brief Introduction to Goh Hock Seng:

Goh Hock Seng (Ph. D.) taught at Sultan Idris Education University, Malaysia, since it was established in 1997 before his retirement in 2022. His areas of academic expertise were TESL Methodology, Teacher Education, and Second Language Acquisition. He published widely in international journals and has also published a few books.

序

语音是英语学习的基础，良好的拼读能力对学习者学习单词读音、记忆词汇、提高读写能力有显著的促进作用。然而，目前小学阶段的英语课程中不再把传统的音标教学作为必修内容，大部分教科书中也不再涉及音标教学，部分学生到了中学阶段还不能很好地掌握英语语音和拼读的基本技能，给英语听、说、读、看、写的各种活动带来障碍，影响了整体的学习效果。

自然拼读（Phonics）在欧美国家的儿童语言学习中已有较长的历史，主要用于辅助母语国家儿童发展读写能力。后来国内英语教学引进这一工具，用于儿童英语语音和读写的启蒙。相对于传统的音标教学，自然拼读比较符合儿童的认知特点，上手学起来更容易，有助于维护学习者的学习兴趣，还可以有效促进英语学习的效率。

学习拼读需要遵循一定的规律，如需要学习者具备一定数量的听力词汇积累、熟悉词汇的意思，如果能与配套阅读材料一起使用效果会更好。目前市面上有不少国外引进的拼读材料，但存在内容繁琐又不太适合中国儿童英语学习需要的问题。

这本《自然拼读教学指南》对国外拼读教学体系和内容进行了创造性吸收和本土化改进，更适合中国学习者的英语学习。作者陈岷婕老师长期在高校从事英语教学相关工作，熟悉中国学习者英语学习的特点，对他们英语语音学习的特殊困难有较好的理解，使得这本书编写得非常有针对性。

本书的核心内容基于全国基础外语教育研究“十四五”规划重点课题“通过自然拼读与语音教学提升中国学生英语语言能力的行动研究”，探索通过自然拼读和语音教学提升中国学生英语语言能力的有效路径和方法。本书理论性与实践性兼顾，既可以帮助英语教师提高语音教学的认识和素养，又为教师教学提供了丰富多样的教学模式、教学技巧和实用材料。将传统的音标教学与自然拼读教学巧妙结合是本书的特色之一，便于教师更好地指导学生熟悉英语语音与拼写的对应关系、提高英文解码能力和读写能力，为学生后续的英语学习奠定良好的基础。本书内容科学性与趣味性兼顾，选材精到、编排系统、循序渐进、难易适中，是英语教学的好帮手。

陈力

2024 年 1 月于北京

陈力博士（教授）：人民教育出版社英语编审室编审，课程教材研究所研究员，人教版小学英语教科书副主编

Contents

Section 1　Phonics-Related General Knowledge

This section aims to help trainees master basic knowledge related to phonics:

Main Goals	This section aims to help trainees master: 1. the basic conception of phonics and phonics instructions. 2. basic knowledge of English sound systems related to phonics. 3. the basic connotations and skills of phonemic awareness.
Specific Objectives	The trainees are able to master: 1. the definition of phonics. 2. the definition of phonics instructions. 3. the definition of the SSP model of phonics instruction. 4. the benefits of the SSP model. 5. the relationship between phonics and reading. 6. the 44 speech sounds represented by graphemes. 7. terminologies related to phonics in sound systems. 8. the basic connotations of phonemic awareness. 9. phonemic awareness skills. 10. the development process of phonemic awareness.

1.1　What is Phonics

Phonics involves studying the correspondence between letters and sounds (International Literacy Association [ILA], 2018). It is necessary for both reading and writing.

1.2　What is Phonics Instruction

Phonics instruction teaches learners about the relationship between letters and sounds, as well as how to use this knowledge to recognise words while reading and spelling words. It is not a specialised method of instruction and there are numerous approaches to teaching it (Blevins, 2017; ILA, 2019).

1.3 What is Synthetic Phonics Instruction

Synthetic phonics is a teaching approach that enables beginners to quickly and proficiently acquire the ability to read. Correspondences between individual sounds (phonemes) and letters are first introduced to learners. Then, they are taught to combine various letter-sounds to form words.

1.4 What is the Systematic Synthetic Phonics Approach

The systematic synthetic phonics (SSP) approach entails teaching synthetic phonics methodically and systematically. It begins with the most superficial letter-sound relationship and progresses to the most complex letter combination (MMU, 2015).

1.5 What are the Benefits of the SSP Approach

Through the SSP approach, beginners can quickly develop into confident and self-sufficient readers. They will be capable of rapidly progressing from decoders to fluent readers. Furthermore, they will be able to read words they had never previously heard or seen (MMU, 2015).

1.6 What is the Correlation between Phonics and Reading

Why is it necessary for language beginners to learn phonics? This question elucidates the connection between phonics and early reading.

Reading, particularly early reading, is considered to have two levels. The first is reading at word level and the second is reading at text level (Carroll et al., 2011).

(1) Word-reading level: Phonics instruction assists readers in decoding words, which aids in word recognition. The more practice the reader has with word recognition, the more sight words he or she will acquire. Then, reading on a word level can be accomplished (Blevins, 2017).

(2) Text-reading level: Increased sight word exposure improves reading fluency. Attention and mental energy focus are shifted away from word identification and towards the context's meaning. As a result, reading comprehension is enhanced (Blevins, 2017; ILA, 2018, 2019).

1.7 Two Prerequisites of Phonics Instruction

Two critical prerequisites of phonics instruction ensure that all learners are prepared.

(1) Phonemic awareness: The ability to recognise that a word is composed of sounds and to manipulate sounds in spoken words (Blevins, 2017).

(2) Alphabetic recognition: Knowledge of the names and sounds of letters.

Both factors are significant predictors of early reading success (Blevins, 2017). Synthetic phonics instruction is the optimum option for EFL learners because it concurrently develops phonemic awareness.

1.8 The 44 Speech Sounds of English

English is a 26-letter alphabetic language. These letters, when combined in various ways, represent 44 distinct sounds. Among these, there are 25 consonant sounds and 19 vowel sounds, as illustrated below:

Tab. 1.1

Number	Consonant Sounds	Vowel Sounds
1	/b/ **b**at	/ai/ c**a**k**e**
2	/d/ **d**og	/ee/ f**ee**t
3	/f/ **f**an	/igh/ b**i**k**e**
4	/g/ **g**ate	/oa/ c**o**d**e**
5	/h/ **h**at	/yoo/ c**u**b**e**
6	/j/ **j**ump/**g**ym	/a/c**a**t
7	/k/**k**ite/**c**at	/e/ b**e**d
8	/l/ **l**eaf	/i/ f**i**sh
9	/m/**m**op	/o/ f**o**g
10	/n/**n**et	/u/d**u**ck
11	/p/ **p**ig	/uh/ **a**larm
12	/r/ **r**ap	/air/ ch**air**
13	/s/ **s**un/**c**ent	/ir/ b**ir**d
14	/t/ **t**op	/ar/ c**ar**
15	/v/ **v**ase	/or/ f**or**
16	/w/ **w**agon	/oi/ b**oy**

续表

Number	Consonant Sounds	Vowel Sounds
17	/y/ **y**o-**y**o	/ou/ h**ou**se
18	/z/ **z**oo	long /oo/ m**oo**n
19	/ch/ **ch**eese	short /oo/b**oo**k
20	/sh/ **sh**ark	
21	/zh/ trea**s**ure	
22	voiced /th/ **th**e	
23	unvoiced /th/ **th**umb	
24	/hw/ **wh**y	
25	/ng/ ri**ng**	

Note: Except for the schwa symbol /uh/, which is taken from Bear et al. (2020), *all the sound symbols within the slashes above and throughout this guide are taken from the Oxford Phonics Spelling Dictionary, hunt et al.* (2020).

1.9 What is a Consonant

The term "**consonant**" refers to any letter that is not a vowel (that is, not A, E, I, O or U) (Bear et al., 2020). When the term "consonants" or "consonant" is used in this guide, it refers to capitalised consonant letters.

1.10 What is a Consonant Sound

A **consonant sound** is typically the same as the consonant letter to which it corresponds.

When a sound is produced, airflow is partially or entirely interrupted (Blevins, 2017). In this guide, sounds are denoted by being placed within slashes to differentiate them from letters.

1.11 What is a Vowel

Vowels include A, E, I, O and U (Bear et al., 2020).

Vowel letters are used to represent or assist in the representation of vowel sounds.

Furthermore, throughout this guide, the term "vowels" is represented by the corresponding capitalised vowel letters such as A, E, I, O and U.

1.12 What is a Vowel Sound

When a **vowel sound** is made, the airflow is unobstructed. Vowel sounds are often represented by vowel letters (Blevins, 2017). Correspondingly, the consonants "W" and "Y" frequently function as vowels, as in the words "fly" and "happy". When the letter Y appears at the end of a word or syllable, it functions as a vowel. When combined with another vowel, as in the words "few", "how" and "slow", the letter W functions as a vowel. The letters W and Y do not represent distinct sounds as vowels (Blevins, 2017).

1.13 What is a Digraph (Letter Team/ Letter Pair)

A **digraph** is comprised of two letters that each represent a single sound. Bishop (1986) refers to this as a **letter team**, while Blevins (2017) refers to it as a **letter pair**.

There are consonant and vowel digraphs, for example, "SH" in "ship" and "O" in "ocean" (Bear et al., 2020). In English, this is referred to as a "spelling pattern" (Blevins, 2017). The terms "digraph", "letter team", "letter pair" and "spelling pattern" are used interchangeably in this guide.

1.14 What is a Vowel Digraph

The term "**vowel digraph**" refers to a vowel pair or vowel team that represents a single vowel sound, such as "-AI" in the word "rain" (Bear et al., 2020). It may also be referred to as a vowel team or vowel pair (Bishop, 1986; Blevins, 2017).

1.15 What is a Consonant Digraph

The term "**consonant digraph**" refers to a consonant team or pair that represents a single consonant sound, such as "SH", "CH", "TH", "WH", "PH", "GH" and "NG" (Bear et al., 2020; Bishop, 1986; Blevins, 2017).

1.16 What is a Diphthong

Diphthongs are vowel sounds produced by the mouth gliding (Bear et al., 2020; Blevins, 2017). In the English sound system, there are two diphthongs:

/oi/ as in the word "coil"

/ou/ as in the words "cow" or "house"

1.17 What is a Consonant Cluster

A **consonant cluster** occurs when two consonant letters are combined in a word while each letter retains its distinct sound.

The term "consonant cluster" refers to a blend's written form. This means the printed letters, such as "SL" in the word "sloth" (Blevins, 2017).

This is distinct from the term "digraph", which refers to two letters that represent the same sound.

1.18 What is a Consonant Blend

A **consonant blend** refers to the sound or phoneme (s) of a consonant cluster, for example, /sl/ in "sloth". The consonant blend draws attention to the spoken form, which means the sound (Blevins, 2017). For instance, the **consonant cluster** "SK" corresponds to the **consonant blend** /sk/ in the word "skip".

1.19 What is an Onset-Rime

The term "**onset-rime**" refers to the two components of a syllable. A "rime" is the vowel letter and everything following it in a syllable. Typically, the onset is a consonant, a consonant blend or a digraph preceding the rime.

More precisely, "**rime**" is a linguistic term that refers to a "word chunk" or "phonogram". For instance, in the word "tag", the rime unit is "AG" and the onset part is the letter "T". If a word contains two syllables, it must contain two distinct sets of onset and rimes. Certain words, such as "at", "up" and "out", lack an onset (Blevins, 2017).

1.20 What is a Phonogram

A **phonogram** is a letter or group of letters that represent a sound, syllable or collection of sounds without referring to any particular meaning (Blevins, 2017). This concept is frequently referred to as "word chunks" or "word families". Linguistically, a phonogram is also known as the rime in a word. For instance, the phonogram -AY consists of two letters representing the long-A sound /ai/ found in the words "ray" or "hay". The phonogram -ACK is composed of the sound /a/ and /k/ and it appears in words like "back", "hack", "attack" and "slack". Since they all end in "-ACK", they can be classified as a single word family (Blevins, 2017).

1.21 What is a Syllable

A **syllable** is known as the smallest unit of sound in a language in which a single vowel phoneme and consonant phoneme combination are pronounced. A single vowel phoneme can form a syllable by itself. Simply put, a syllable is a unit of spoken language that consists of a vowel followed or preceded by several consonants. Syllables are units of sound that are frequently discernible through the movement of the mouth (Bear et al., 2020).

1.22 What is an Open Syllable

An **open syllable** can be a syllable ending in a vowel or a stressed syllable ending in a vowel followed by a consonant (except the letter R) and a silent letter E. In an open syllable, the vowel letter usually stands for its long vowel sound, which sounds like its letter name. In other words, when a syllable ends in a long vowel sound, as in the word "ti-ger", the syllable "ti" is an **open syllable** (Bear et al., 2020).

1.23 What is a Closed Syllable

A closed syllable is the type of syllable that ends with a consonant letter. In other words, a closed syllable ends in a consonant sound or is "closed" by a consonant sound. A closed syllable in polysyllabic words contains a short vowel sound enclosed by two consonants, as in "rab-bit" (Bear et al., 2020).

1.24 What is a Stable Syllable

The term "**stable syllable**" is also used to refer to a "**final stable syllable**". Most frequently found in multisyllabic words, it has various configurations and is divided into two groups:

The first category occurs at the end of a word. This is the only type of syllable that does not contain a vowel sound, as in ta-ble, bri-dle, re-bel, loc-al, un-cle, chapel and me-dal. Many final stable syllables have a consonant, an "L" and an e at the end. These combinations are called "final" because they are found in the final position of a word. They are called "stable" because the pronunciation of each is comparatively reliable.

The second category is referred to as "other stable final syllables". This type of syllable occurs at the end of a word and can be taught using the terms "phonograms", "word chunks" or "word families". These syllables are -SION, -TION, -TURE, -SURE, -AGE, -CIOUS and -TIOUS, which can be found in words like "vision", "station", "nature", "composure", "bandage", "gracious" and "scrumptious".

1.25 Syllable Juncture Patterns

At the point where syllables meet, there is an alternating pattern of consonants (C) and vowels (V). For instance, the word "read" has the syllable pattern "CVVC" at the point where the syllables meet (Bear et al., 2020).

1.26 Four Basic One-Syllable Patterns in English

(1) Closed syllable patterns.

This is the most prevalent pattern, in which the syllable contains one vowel and ends with a consonant. The majority of words that employ this pattern contain "short vowel" sounds. There are thirteen distinct variats in total:

Tab. 1.2

Pattern	Example	Pattern	Example
CVCC	hand	CVCCC	match
CVC	cat	CVCCe	judge
CCVCC	fresh	CCVCCC	crutch
CCVC	trip	CCVCCe	grudge
CCCVCC	script	VCC	add
VC	in	CCCVC	scrap
VCCC	inch		

(2) Vowel team (digraph) patterns.

This is the second most frequently encountered pattern, with twelve variants:

Tab. 1.3

Pattern	Example	Pattern	Example
CVVC	heat	CCVVC	treat
CVVCC	reach	CVV	pay
CCVV	play	CVVCe	leave
CCVVCC	bleach	CCVVCe	freeze
CCCVVC	sprain	VVC	oat
VVCC	each	CCCVV	three

(3) Vowel-consonant-silent E patterns.

This is the third most frequently encountered pattern, with four distinct variants:

Tab. 1. 4

Pattern	Example	Pattern	Example
CVCe	race	CCCVCe	strike
CCVCe	shave	VCe	ate

(4) Open syllable patterns.

This is the fourth most frequently occurring pattern. There are only two variants: CCV for "she" and CV for "we".

Acquiring knowledge of those patterns can assist in determining the sound of vowels and teaching short or long vowel sounds during the phonics instruction process.

1. 27 What is Phonemic Awareness

Phonemic awareness is the recognition or understanding that a word is composed of a series of discrete sounds. Each sound is referred to as a phoneme. The capacity to recognise and manipulate sounds into spoken words is included in phonemic awareness (Blevins, 2017), which is also referred to as **phoneme awareness.**

1. 28 What is Phonological Awareness

Phonological awareness is an awareness of various speech sounds, such as syllables, rhymes and individual phonemes (Bear et al., 2020). It entails the capacity to break down spoken language into syllables or individual phonemes, the distinctive sounds of the language the student is learning to read. It can be acquired through singing, syllable tapping, rhyming and segmenting words into individual sounds (ILA, 2018).

1. 29 Phonemic Awareness and Phonological Awareness

Aspects of phonemic awareness are included in phonological awareness.

Phonological awareness is divided into two levels: superficial and deeper. The former entails determining the number of syllables in words, as well as identifying general rhymes and alliterations. Meanwhile, the deeper level is simply phonemic awareness, which young language learners can use to identify and manipulate words as phonemes

(ILA, 2019).

1.30 Phonemic Awareness Skills

(1) Rhyme: To identify rhymes between words, as in cat/hat, can/man and goat/coat.

(2) Alliteration: To identify alliterative word pairs, such as sun/sum and leaf/live.

(3) Assonance: To recognise similar sounds within words, such as the "ea" in "leaf", "bean" and "peach".

(4) Oral blending: To pronounce a word in its entirety when listening to the phonemes separately. Typically oral blending is classified into three sub-categories:

(A) Syllable blending: For example, note these word parts: ta... ble. Pronounce the word in its entirety: Table.

(B) Onset/rime blending: For example, note these word parts: /p/... an. Pronounce the word as a whole: Pan.

(C) Phoneme-by-phoneme blending: For example, note these word parts: /s/ /a/ /t/. Then pronounce the word as a whole: Sat.

(5) Oral segmentation: Oral segmentation contains three sub-skills:

(A) Oral segmenting syllables: Listen to the word "ta... ble" spoken syllable by syllable and keep track of the syllables.

(B) Onset/rime Segmentation: Note the word "pan". Pronounce the initial sound of the word first, followed by the remainder (/p/... an).

(C) Phoneme-by-phoneme segmentation (sound counting). For example, note the word "sat" and repeat it sound for sound (phoneme by phoneme). After that, count the phonemes.

(6) Phonemic manipulation: There are nine sub-skills of phonemic manipulation (Blevins, 2017):

(A) Initial sound substitution: For example, replace the first sound in the word "mat" with /s/ to get the word "sat".

(B) Final sound substitution: For example, replace the last sound in the word "mat" with /p/ to get the word "map".

(C) Vowel substitution: For example, replace the middle sound in "map" with /o/ to get the word "mop".

(D) Syllable deletion: For example, pronounce the word "baker" without "ba-"

to get the sound "-ker".

(E) Initial sound deletion: For example, pronounce the word "sun" without /s/ to get the sound "-un".

(F) Final sound deletion: For example, pronounce "hit" without the /t/ sound to get the sound "hi-".

(G) Initial phoneme in a blend deletion: For example, pronounce the word "step" without the sound /s/ to get the sound "-tep".

(H) Final phoneme in a blend deletion: For example, pronounce the word "best" without the sound /t/ to get the sound "bes-".

(I) Second phoneme in a blend deletion: For example, pronounce the word "frog" without the sound /r/ to get the sound "f-og".

1.31 The Development of Phonemic Awareness

Phonemic awareness can be taught and it can be developed fairly rapidly by practising the skills mentioned above.

Phonemic awareness can be developed and strengthened in EFL learners through systematic synthetic phonics instruction, because blending skills are practised alongside letter-sound relationships (Bald, 2007).

If phonemic awareness must be taught independently, children's literature such as rhyme books, alliteration books and phonemic manipulation would be beneficial, as would activities or word games relating to the abilities mentioned above (Blevins, 2017).

1.32 The Importance of Phonemic Awareness

Phonemic awareness is a prerequisite for phonics instruction to begin. Learners with a weak sense of phonemic awareness may have difficulty grasping the alphabetic principle. For example, they may have difficulties in discriminating sounds in words, be unable to segment sounds within words or not understand what is meant by the term "sound". Furthermore, language beginners must be able to segment a word like "sit" /s/-/i/-/t/ if they are to correctly spell the word.

Once learners have mastered the fundamentals of phonemic awareness, they can progress to early reading at word level. Reading, on the other hand, enhances phonemic awareness (Blevins, 2017).

Section 2 Phonics Decoding Rules

This section aims to help trainees master the most common phonics decoding rules.

Main Goals	This section aims to help trainees master: 1. common phonics decoding rules. 2. the most common phonograms.
Specific Objectives	The trainees will be able to master: 1. common decoding rules of vowel sounds. 2. common decoding rules of consonant sounds. 3. common phonograms.

This section introduces letter names and sounds. The English language contains 26 letters and 44 sounds. There are 25 consonant sounds and 19 vowel sounds among the 44 sounds. Categories are used to introduce vowels and consonants.

Consonant blends, digraphs of consonants, variant vowels and vowel teams (digraphs) are also introduced in this section. Finally, the term "word families" (also known as phonograms or word chunks) is introduced.

Note: In this guide, slashes with a letter, such as in /k/, refer to a sound, not to spellings or letters. For instance, the sound /k/ is represented by the letter K, as in "Kitten". Dashes are used before a word or spelling pattern, such as -CK or -Y, to indicate that the spelling pattern or letter is never in the initial position when representing the corresponding sound.

2.1 Vowel Sounds

2.1.1 Categories of Vowel Sounds

Vowel sounds can be divided into.

(A) Long vowel sounds.

(B) Short vowel sounds.

(C) Other vowel sounds (Blevins, 2017).

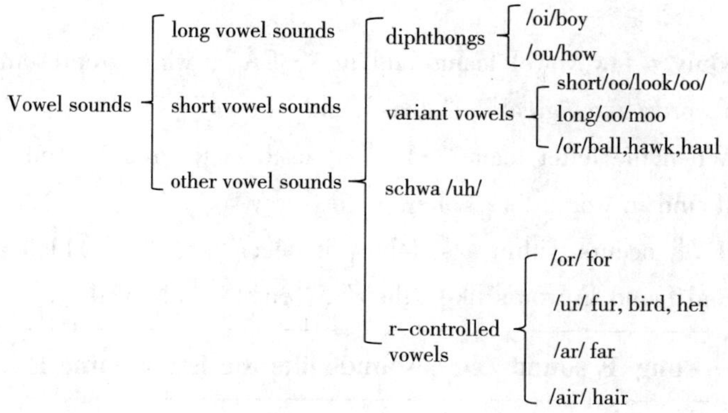

Fig. 2.1

2.1.2 Introduction to Two Special Vowel Letters

Before introducing the vowel sounds, two **special vowel letters** are introduced first. Two letters can be silent in words: One is the letter **E** and the other is the letter **U**.

Silent E: The letter E is frequently silent when it is the final letter in a word and there is another vowel preceding it, as in "rope", "dense" and "cheese".

Silent U: When it appears between the letters G and E, I or Y, as in the words "guess", "plague", "guide" and "guy", the letter U is silent.

2.1.3 Long Vowel Sounds

Long-A sound /ai/, sounds like the letter name A

Rule 1: In words like "Jake" and "late", the vowel letter A is followed by a consonant, which is then followed by a silent E. The letter E is silent, while the letter A has a long-A sound. The simple rule is that in the patterns A_E or VCe, the vowel letter A must have the long-A sound.

The silent E causes the "A" to be pronounced in the same way as its name. Typically, this follows the CVCe or VCe patterns, as in "lake" or "ate".

Rule 2: The letter team "-AY" can also produce the long-A sound, as in the words "way" or "okay".

Rule 3: The vowel team (digraph) "AI" can also produce the long-A sound, as in the words "paid", "wait" and "claim".

Rule 4: When the standalone "A" occurs in a syllable that ends in "A", such as in the words "ba-by", "A-pril" or "a-corn", the standalone "A" can produce the long-A sound.

Rule 5: Only a few vowel teams end in "-EA", which represents the long-A sound found in words like "great", "steak" and "break".

Rule 6: When the letter team "-EY" is used at the root's end, it denotes the long-A sound found in words like "obey" and "prey".

When "-EY" occurs within a syllable, it becomes "EI", which also represents the long-A sound found in words like "their", "eight" and "veil".

Long-E sound /ee/, sounds like the letter name E

Rule 1: The vowel team (digraph) "EE" stands for the long-E sound found in words like "meet", "queen" and "bee".

Rule 2: The vowel team (digraph) "EA" stands for the long-E sound found in words like "mean" and "cream". The majority of the long-E sound, as in the highest frequency is represented by the digraphs "EE" or "EA".

Rule 3: When found in the form "E_E" -that is, when in the VCe or CVCe patterns-the "silent E" causes the first "E" to be pronounced as a long-E sound, as in the words "here", "eve" and "mere".

Rule 4: Occasionally, the vowel team (digraph) "-IE" produces the long-E sound, as in the words "believe" and "chief".

Rule 5: The long-E sound can be produced using a single letter E in the spelling patterns "she", "he", "me" or "be". Indeed, "-E" is a long consonant in syllables that end in the letter-E, as in the words "she", "me", "be" or "fe-ver".

Rule 6: When a word ends in the letter-Y and this word has more than three letters, this letter-Y produces a long-E sound, as in the words "majesty" and "puppy".

Rule 7: When the vowel team (digraph) "-EY" is used as a suffix in a word, it sounds like the letter-Y in "puppy", as in the words "turkey", "honey" and "valley".

Long-I sound /igh/, sounds like the letter name I

Rule 1: When in the form "I_E" -that is, when in the CVCe or VCe patterns-the "silent E" causes the I to be pronounced as a long-I sound, as in the words "bike" and "hike".

Rule 2: When the final letter in the syllable is I/-Y, the long-I sound can also be made with a single I/-Y, as in the words "idea", "hi", "I", "my", "sky" and "ty-rant". Usually, in three-letter words in the form "__y", the letter Y stands for the long-I sound, such as in "fly", "fry", "cry", "spy", "why", "shy", "try" and "dry".

Rule 3: When the vowel team (digraph) "-IE" appears at the end of the root, it is stressed and produces a long-I sound, as in "pie", "tie" and "die". This is uncommon, however and this sound often appears in three-letter words in the form "_ie".

Rule 4: The spelling pattern-IGH produces the long-I sound found in words like "fight", "sigh", "might" and "right".

Long-O sound /oa/, sounds like the letter name O

Rule 1: When in the form "O_E" -that is, when in the VCe or CVCe patterns- the "silent E" causes the "O" to be pronounced as a long-O sound, as in the words "code" and "home".

Rule 2: The vowel team (digraph) "OA" makes the long-O sound, as in words like "toad", "goat" and "boat".

Rule 3: When the letter O is the final letter in the syllable, as in the words "o-ver", "o-kay" and "go", a single "O" can also produce the long-O sound.

Rule 4: The vowel team "OW" is another way to represent the long-O sound, as in the words "low", "mow" and "bowtie".

Rule 5: The vowel team "-OE" represents the long-O sound found in words like "toe" and "doe".

Long-U sound /yoo/, sounds like the letter name U

Rule 1: When in the form "U_E" -that is, when in the VCe or CVCe patterns- the "silent E" causes the letter U to be pronounced as a long-U, as in the words "mule" and "cube".

Rule 2: When the letter U is the final letter in the syllable, as in the words "Hu-go" and "fu-el", a single U can also represent the long-U sound.

Rule 3: When the letter U is the final letter in the syllable and follows the letters L or R, the long-U sound becomes /oo/, as in the words "flu" and "rumour".

2.1.4 Short Vowel Sounds

Short vowel sounds generally occur in the initial and medial positions of words or closed syllables, but they infrequently occur in the final positions.

Short-A Sound /a/, as in "cat"

Rule: When used within a closed syllable, such as in the words "tap", "rap", "cat" and "that", the vowel letter A represents the short-A sound /a/.

Short-E Sound /e/, as in "bed"

Rule 1: When the vowel letter E occurs within a closed syllable, as in the words "pet", "fled" and "felt", this vowel letter represents the short-E sound.

Rule 2: When the vowel letter E is in the initial position and followed by a consonant in the same syllable, as in "egg" "end", "ef-fort", "es-timate" and "ex-tra", this vowel letter represents the short-E sound.

Rule 3: In brief, the digraph "-EA" stands for the short-E sound, which includes the words "head", "meant", "health" and "pleasure" .

Short-I Sound /i/, as in "fit"

Rule 1: When the vowel letters I/-Y occur within a closed syllable, as in the words "bit", "symbol", "pig" and "dim-ple", this vowel letter represents the short-I sound.

Rule 2: When the vowel letter I is in the initial position and followed by a consonant in the same syllable, as in "it" and "ig-loo", this vowel letter represents the short-I sound.

Short-O sound /o/, as in "fox"

Rule 1: When the vowel letter O occurs within a closed syllable, as in the words "dot", "soft", "pop" and "cost", this vowel letter represents the short-O sound.

Rule 2: When the vowel letter O is in the initial position and followed by a consonant in the same syllable, as in "off", "of-fice" and "oc-topus", this vowel letter represents the short-O sound.

Short-U sound /u/, as in "duck"

Rule 1: When the vowel letter U occurs within a closed syllable, as in the words "dust", "hush" and "but", this vowel letter is short.

Rule 2: When the vowel letter U is in the initial position and followed by a consonant in the same syllable, as in "up", "ut-most" and "ugly", this vowel letter represents the short-U sound.

2.1.5 Other Vowel Sounds

As mentioned previously, the category of "**other vowel sounds**" includes diphthongs, variant vowel sounds, r-controlled vowel sounds and the schwa. Accordingly, the generalisation of those sub-categories will be demonstrated. Vowel diphthongs are introduced first.

Vowel Diphthongs. The term "vowel diphthong" refers to the speech sound created when two vowels in a vowel team work together to make a smooth transition between vowel sounds, such as /oi/ in the word "boy" and /ou/ in the words "house" and "cow" (Bear et al., 2015; Blevins, 2017). The following is a list of diphthongs represented by digraphs:

Diphthong /ou/, as in "house"

The most frequently used spellings for the /ou/ sound are the vowel pairs "OU" and "OW", as in "house" and "cow".

Rule 1: "OU" is a vowel team for the unique English vowel sound /ou/, which is heard in the word "shout". Typically, the letter team "OU" rather than the letter team "OW" is used in the word.

Rule 2: "OW" is used at the end of the root, as in "how" and "allow".

Rule 3: "OW" is used in front of a final L, D or N, as in "owl", "crowd" and "frown". When preceded by other consonants, "OW" is substituted for "OU", as in "couch".

However, the eye has no way of knowing which sound is represented by a given "OW". Readers must be prepared to employ whatever sound makes the most sense in the given context.

Diphthong /oi/, as in "toy"

The most frequently used spellings for the diphthong /oi/ are "OY" and "OI", as in the words "toy" and "oil".

Rule 1: The vowel team "OI" represents the diphthong /oi/ sound, as in the word "point". It is used within the root instead of "OY". However, only in the word "tortoise" is the sound /oi/ severely muffled.

Rule 2: The letter team "OY" is used at the end of the root, such as in "boy", "toy" and "enjoy". If it is within the root, "OY" is replaced by "OI", as in the words "boil", "coil" and "spoil".

Variant Vowel Sounds. The category of variant vowel sounds includes the short /oo/ sound, the long /oo/ sound and the broad-O sound /or/, which are represented by "AU", "AW" and "AL (L)".

Short /oo/ sound, as in "good"

The short /oo/ sound refers to the short sound of the letter team "OO". The most common spellings are as follows:

Rule 1: The letter team "OO" represents the short /oo/ sound found in the words "book", "cook", "foot", "took" and "shook".

Rule 2: The spelling pattern-OUL can represent the short /oo/ sound in words like "could" and "would".

Rule 3: The letter U represents the short /oo/ sound in words that include the syllables "bull", "pull", "full" or "bush".

Long /oo/ sound, as in "moo"

The long /oo/ sound is a reference to the long sound of the letter team "OO". The following spellings are the most frequently used:

Rule 1: The letter team "OO" represents the long /oo/ sound, as in "moon", "boom" and "zoo".

Rule 2: When used at the end of a root, the spelling pattern-UE can represent the long /oo/ sound when the /y/ component of the long /yoo/ sound is lost, as in "glue" and "true".

Rule 3: When the /y/ part of the long /yoo/ sound is lost, such as in "rule", "flute" or "dude", the letter-U can represent the long/oo/ sound when in VCe or CVCe patterns (*AmE*).

Rule 4: In other words, when the long-U sound /yoo/ is pronounced without the /y/ component, only the /oo/ component is pronounced, as in "ruby" and "truth".

Rule 5: The letter team "-EW" was initially reserved for the long-U sound /yoo/, as in the word "few". However, in some spellings, the sound "-EW" is influenced by L and R and the /y/ component of the long /yoo/ sound is lost; thus, "-EW" represents the long /oo/ sound in words like "flew", "grew", "brew" and "strew".

Rule 6: In some words, the letter team "-OU" represents the long /oo/ sound, such as "soup", "cougar", "through", "coup" and "tourism".

Broad-O sound /or/, as in "law", "haul" and "tall"

The sound /or/ refers to the broad-O sound in this context. "OR" (which is illustrated in the R-controlled vowel section), "AL (L)", "AU" and "AW" are the most frequently used spellings for the broad-O sound.

Rule 1: The broad-O sound can be represented by the vowel team "AU", as in "sauce". It is used within the root instead of "AW".

Rule 2: The broad-O sound can be represented by the vowel team "AW", as in jaw. It is used at the end of the root, such as in "law", "saw", "straw" and "drawback".

Rule 3: Before the final L, K or N, "AW" is used instead of "AU", such as in "crawl", "pawn" and "hawk". Usually, before other consonants, "AW" becomes "AU", as in "pause", "autumn" and "audio".

R-Controlled Vowels. This category discusses vowels that are r-controlled or r-influenced. In such vowels, the letter R appears at the end of the word or is followed by a different consonant. Typically, the letter R alters the sound of the preceding vowel letters in those words.

/air/ sound, as in "hair"

The most frequently used spellings for the /air/ sound are AIR for chair, ARE for bare and EAR for wear.

Rule 1: /air/ is represented by the spelling pattern AIR, as in the words "air", "fair", "hair" and "stair".

Rule 2: /air/ is represented by the spelling pattern-ARE, as in the words "are", "care" and "glare".

Rule 3: /air/ is represented by the spelling pattern-EAR, as in "bear", "pear" and "swear".

/ar/ sound, as in "hard"

The sound /ar/ is an r-controlled vowel. The letter team "AR" is the most frequently used for the /ar/ sound.

Rule: The /ar/ sound is represented by the letter team "AR". Usually, the R is either at the end of the word, as in "far" or followed by a different consonant, as in "hard". Originally, the letter A in the middle of the syllable would represent a short /a/ sound, but it has been influenced by the following R, which changes the short /a/ sound into the broad-A sound /ar/.

/or/ sound, as in "porch"

The sound /or/ is also classified as a broad-O sound, as discussed previously. It is represented by the variant vowels "AW", "AU" and "AL (L)".

The sound /or/ is represented by the letter team "OR" in the r-controlled vowel category.

Rule 1: Generally, the /or/ sound is represented by the letters "OR". Typically, the letter R appears at the end of a word, as in "for" or is followed by another consonant, as in "torn".

Rule 2: The sound OAR is also used in words like "board", "coarse" and "oar".

/ur/ sound, as in "bird", "fur" and "her"

The sound /ur/ is also a vowel sound controlled by the letter R. The most frequently used spellings for the /ur/ sound are IR for bird, UR for fur and ER for her. The spelling pattern EAR can also be used to represent the /ur/ sound.

Rule 1: The letter team "-IR" can be used to represent the sound /ur/. Originally, the letter I in the middle of a syllable produced a short sound, but this has been changed by the letter R at the end of a word or the R preceding another consonant, as in "fir", "bird" or "dirty".

Rule 2: The letter team "-UR" is also used to represent the sound /ur/, as in "fur" and "turn". Normally, the letter U in the middle of the syllable represents the short-U sound /u/, but it is changed by the letter R at the end of a word, as in "blur"; or by the letter R followed by another consonant, as in "burn"; or by the R being doubled within the word, as in "hurry".

Rule 3: As in "her", the sound /ur/ is represented by the letter team "-ER". Typically, the letter E in the middle of the syllable represents the short-E sound /e/, but this is changed by the letter R at the end of a word, as in "refer" or by the letter R followed by another consonant, as in "herd". Indeed, -ER is also a very common suffix.

Rule 4: In the word "learn", the sound /ur/ is represented by the spelling pattern

EAR. When EA is followed by the letter R and another consonant, the R converts the short-E sound into the r-controlled vowel sound /ur/.

Schwa /uh/. Schwa is an English vowel sound that frequently occurs in an unstressed syllable. Within a word, a syllable that receives little emphasis may have an indistinct vowel sound, as in the first syllable of "about", the second syllable of "definition" or the final syllables of "doctor" or "table" (Bear et al., 2020).

According to some linguists, this is a variant of a particular sound caused by a decrease in the stress on that sound within a word. Additionally, it is referred to as a murmur or neutral sound. In phonics, it is challenging to teach the rules for identifying this sound in words (Blevins, 2017).

The schwa sound is the /uh/ sound found in the word "alarm". According to some linguists, it is not a sound but a phonetic variant or allophone (Blevins, 2017).

The vowel sound /uh/ can be spelt with any of the following vowels: A, E, I, O or U, as in the words "alone", "happen", "direct", "gallop" and "circus".

Numerous multisyllabic words that begin with an unaccented syllable contain this sound. The following is a list of words containing the schwa sound:

Tab. 2.1

about *	again *	along	appear	awake
above **	ago *	American *	applause	aware **
account **	agree **	among **	ashore	away **
adult **	ahead	aside	afloat	annoy
asleep **	awoke *	alarm	another **	avoid **
afraid **	alone **	apart	await	

* means the word is on the vocabulary list at National Curriculum level 2; ** means on the list at level 3.

2.2 Consonant Sounds

2.2.1 Hard and Soft Consonants

The terms "hard and soft consonants" refer exclusively to the letters C and G. The terms "hard" and "soft" should be strictly reserved for these two letters (Bishop, 1986).

When the letter C is soft, it represents the /s/ sound, as in the word "cent".

When the letter C is hard, it represents the /k/ sound, as in the word "crisis".

When the letter G is soft, it represents the /j/ sound, as in the word "gymnast".

When the letter G is hard, it represents the sound /g/, as in the word "goat".

Rule 1: Soft C rule: When the letter C appears immediately before the letters I, E or Y, it is soft, as in the word "cent".

Rule 2: Hard C rule: When the letter C does not immediately precede the letters I, E or Y, it is hard. Alternatively, when it appears immediately before the letters A, O or U and other consonants, the letter C represents the sound /k/, as in the word "cracker".

Rule 3: Soft G rule: When the letter G appears immediately before the letters I, E and Y, it is soft, as in the word "gym".

Rule 4: Hard G rule: When the letter G does not immediately precede the letters I, E or Y, it is hard. Alternatively, when it appears immediately before the letters A, O or U and other consonants, the letter G represents the sound /g/, as in the word "gold".

2.2.2 Voiced, Unvoiced Consonants and Nasal Consonants

Consonant sounds are produced by closing the mouth and restricting or completely interrupting the voice, in contrast to vowel sounds produced by opening the mouth and allowing the voice to freely emerge (Bishop, 1986).

Consonant sounds vary in the degree to which the voice is used to pronounce them. As a result, they are classified as voiced, unvoiced and nasal consonants (Bishop, 1986)

These three classifications are generalized as below:

Tab. 2.2

Categories	Definition	Consonant Sounds
Unvoiced Consonants	When the voice is not used in pronouncing a consonant sound, only the breath is used (Bishop, 1986).	/p/
		/t/
		/k/
		/f/
		/s/
		/ch/
		/sh/
		/th/ (thing)
		/h/

续表

Categories	Definition	Consonant Sounds
Voiced Consonants	When the voice is used to pronounce a consonant sound, the sound is voiced.	/b/
		/d/
		/g/
		/v/
		/z/
		/j/
		/zh/
		/w/
		/th/ (this)
		/r/
		/l/
		/y/
Nasal Consonants	When a consonant sound is nasalised, the mouth is closed and the voice transmits the sound through the nose.	/m/
		/n/
		/ng/

Note: *According to Blevins* (2017), *unvoiced consonants are also called voiceless consonants. In this guide, the two terms are used interchangeably.*

2.2.2.1 Rules for Voiced Consonants: Their Consonant Sounds

B /b/, as in "bat"

P /p/ is its voiceless or unvoiced counterpart (Blevins, 2017).

Rule 1: The most frequently used spelling for the /b/ sound is the letter B, as in "bat", "bag" and "cab". It is a very reliable sound that has no other associated sound.

Rule 2: When the consonant letter B follows the letter M, as in the words "climb" and "lamb", the consonant letter B is silent. In other words, in the word team MB, the letter B is silent.

Rule 3: When the consonant letter B appears before the letter T, as in "doubt" or "debt", the letter B is silent. In other words, in the word team BT, the letter B is silent.

Rule 4: When the letter B is doubled in a word, as in "lobby" or "rubber", one letter B is silent.

D /d/, as in "dog"

T /t/ is its voiceless or unvoiced counterpart.

Rule 1: The letter D is most frequently used to represent the /d/ sound, as in "dog", "dive" and "duck". It is quite reliable for this sound.

Rule 2: The letter D can also represent the /t/ sound, as in the words "liked" or "hoped". In other words, when the consonant immediately before the suffix-ED in a word is a unvoiced consonant, the suffix-ED represents the unvoiced consonant phoneme /t/.

Rule 3: The letter D is occasionally used to represent the /j/ sound, as in the words "graduate", "soldier", "badge", "schedule" and "education". In those instances, the unstressed I and /y/ components of the unstressed long-U /yoo/ sound convert the /d/ sound into a /j/ sound (Bishop, 1986).

Rule 4: When the letter D is doubled in a word, as in "daddy" or "ladder", one letter D is silent.

G /g/, as in "gate"

The K /k/ sound is its voiceless counterpart.

Rule 1: The most frequently used spelling for the /g/ sound is the letter G, as in "gate", "goat" and "bag". This is also known as a "hard consonant sound". The letter G with the sound /g/ is referred to as a "hard consonant". It is not very reliable for this sound because it can represent a variety of other sounds.

Rule 2: When the letter G appears directly before the letters I, E or Y, it is frequently referred to as a "soft G". For instance, it denotes the /j/ sound in words like "gentle", "gem", "gym", "magic", "agent", "age" and "page".

Rule 3: When the letter G does not immediately precede the letters I, E, Y; or when it immediately precedes the letters A, O or U and other consonants; the letter G represents the sound /g/, as in the words "game", "goat", "gust" and "groom".

Rule 4: There are several notable exceptions or irregulars to the above mentioned Rule 3: "girl", "get", "gill" and "gift".

Rule 5: When it immediately precedes the letter H, as in the consonant team "GH", the letter G is silent, as in the words "light", "night", "might", "tight", "eight" and "sleigh".

Rule 6: When it immediately precedes the letter N, as in the consonant team

"GN", the letter G is silent, as in the words "sign", "reign", "design" and "gnat".

Rule 7: When the consonant digraph "GH" contains the letter G, the digraph represents the /f/ sound found in the words "tough", "rough"; "enough", "cough", "slough" and "roughen".

V /v/, as in "vase"

The F /f/ sound is its voiceless or unvoiced counterpart.

Rule: The letter V is most frequently used to represent the /v/ sound, as in "vase", "vegetable" and "viva". The letter V is reliable for the sound /v/ since it is not assigned to any other sound.

Z /z/, as in "zoo"

S /s/ is its voiceless or unvoiced counterpart.

Rule 1: The letter Z is most frequently used to represent the /z/ sound, as in "zebra", "zoom" and "zipper".

Rule 2: When the letter S is between vowels, as in "easy", "raisin", "nose" and "music", the /z/ sound can be represented by this letter.

J /j/, as in "jet"

CH /ch/sound is its voiceless counterpart.

Rule 1: The letter J is most frequently used to represent the /j/ sound, as in "jam", "January" and "jump". This letter is highly reliable because it almost always refers to the /j/ sound. Conceivably, when the letter G appears before the letters I, E and Y, it denotes the /j/ sound.

Rule 2: Rarely does the letter J appear in the final position of a word. When the /j/ sound is in the final position, it is represented by-DGE, as in "dodge" or by-GE, as in "huge".

W /w/, as in "wagon"

The /w/ sound is also known as a voiced semivowel.

Rule 1: The letter W is most frequently used to represent the /w/ sound, as in "warm", "wasp" and "water". It is an unreliable consonant letter because it doubles as a vowel in the vowel diphthong "OW", as in the word "throw".

Rule 2: When the letter Q immediately follows the letter U, the /w/ sound can also be represented by the letter U. That is, in the letter team "QU", the letter Q represents the /k/ sound and the letter U represents the /w/ sound, as in the word "quack". The letter Q never stands alone; it always goes with the letter U.

Rule 3: When the letter W is part of the letter team "WR", it is silent, as in the words "write", "wrap" and "wrack".

Rule 4: The letter W is a member of the consonant team "WH", which includes only initial consonants. The sound of the letter W varies by region. Some pronounce it like /w/, while others pronounce it as an unvoiced /w/.

Rule 5: When the letter W functions as a consonant and precedes the letter A within a syllable, it converts the short-A sound to the short-O sound, as in "want" and "wash".

Rule 6: When the letter W functions as a consonant and precedes the letter O in a syllable, it converts the short-O sound to the short-U sound, as in the words "wonder" and "won".

TH /th/, as in "this" (voiced)

Rule 1: The digraph "TH" is most frequently used to represent the voiced /th/, as in the words "the" or "that". In English, voiced /th/ sounds are more frequent.

Rule 2: The digraph "TH" occasionally stands for the sound /t/ as in the word Thomas and thyme.

R /r/, as in "rock"

In most American dialects, the R /r/ sound is a voiced, resonant consonant.

Rule 1: The letter R is most frequently used to represent the /r/ sound, as in "rock", "reap" and "ring". It is highly reliable and not associated with any other sound.

Rule 2: The letter R is influential enough to convert all short vowel sounds within a syllable to r-controlled vowel sounds when it comes at the end of a word or before a different consonant, as in "far", "fork", "bird" and "hurt".

Rule 3: When the letter R is between two vowel sounds, this means that when the next sound after the letter R in the word is a vowel sound, the sound of the letter R is moved to the next syllable. This leaves the preceding vowel unchanged, as in the words "car-ry", "hur-ry", "ber-ry" and "bor-row". In these words, when the R is doubled, the first R is silent and the second R goes with the vowel sound.

Rule 4: "RH" is a letter combination of Latin origin for the sound /r/, which means that the letter H is silent, as in "rhino" and "rhyme".

Rule 5: "WR" is a native English letter team for the sound /r/, which means the letter W is silent, as in "write", "wrist" and "wrap".

L /l/, as in "leaf"

The L /l/ is a voiced consonant.

Rule 1: The /l/ sound is often represented by consonant letter L in a word such as in the words "look", "live" and "sleep".

Rule 2: When the letter L is doubled in a word or just at the end of a word or syllable, such as "bell", "hell" and "hall", it is generally silent or muffled.

Rule 3: When found in the same syllable, the letter L is silent before F, M, K or D, as in the words "calf", "calm" and "could".

Y /y/, as in "yo-yo"

The /y/ sound is also known as a semivowel.

Rule 1: The /y/ sound is represented by the letter Y, as in the words "yellow", "beyond" and "yes". The letter Y is not a reliable indicator of the /y/ sound. Only about 3% of the time does this letter stand for the consonant /y/ sound in the initial position of a word or syllable.

Rule 2: When the letter Y is not in the initial position of a word or a syllable, it nearly always represents a vowel sound (97% of the time). The basic three vowel sounds are the long-I sound /igh/, the long-E sound /ee/ and the short-I sound /i/.

Rule 3: The letter Y stands for the short-I sound /i/ when it is within the syllable, as in the words "gym" and "sym-bol".

Rule 4: The letter Y stands for the long-I sound /igh/ when it is the very last letter in the root of the word or of the syllable, as in "by", "cry", "fly" and "de-ny".

Rule 5: In the spelling pattern Y_E, the letter Y represents the long-I sound /igh/, as in "type", "style" and "a-na-lyse".

Rule 6: The vowel team "YE" stands for the long-I sound /igh/, as in the words "bye" and "rye".

Rule 7: The letter Y stands for the long-E sound /ee/ when it is in a suffix and is the very last letter in a word which has more than three letters, as in the words "candy", "hap-py" and "his-to-ry".

Note: According to Bishop (1986), some linguists and dictionaries classify the long-E sound of Y as a short-I sound because the two sounds in unstressed syllables are nearly invisible to novice readers. However, Bishop (1986) believed that it would be far easier for the layman reader to decode unfamiliar words by using the long-E sound for the letter Y.

/zh/ sound, as in "treasure"

The /zh/ sound is never represented by the letter combination "ZH" because it does not occur in English words. Generally, the /zh/ sound is described by the suffixes-S, -SI and-GE.

Rule 1: As in "leisure", "pleasure" and "treasure", the /zh/ sound is represented by the letter-S. That is, if the letter S follows a vowel letter or the letter R precedes it, it represents the /zh/ sound found in words like "leisure" and "version".

Rule 2: The /zh/ sound is represented by the spelling-SI in words like "confusion", "decision" and "illusion". Generally, Bishop (1986) asserts, this group of words derives from Latin.

Rule 3: The /zh/ sound can also be represented by the suffix-GE, as in "beige", "collage", "garage" and "montage". This group of words is almost entirely composed of words of French origin (Bishop, 1986).

2.2.2.2 Rules for the Unvoiced (Voiceless) Consonants

P /p/, as in "pig"

B /b/ is its voiced counterpart.

Rule 1: The letter P is most frequently used to represent the /p/ sound, as in "pen", "play" and "pin". It is highly reliable and not associated with any other sound.

Rule 2: When the letter P is immediately followed by the letters N, S or T, as in "pneumonia", "psychology" and "pterosaur", the letter P is usually silent.

Rule 3: When the letter P is doubled in words such as "supper", "happy" and "floppy", one letter P is silent.

Rule 4: The letter P is also a component of the digraph "PH", which stands for the /f/ sound, as in "phone".

T /t/, as in "tin"

D /d/ is its voiced counterpart.

Rule 1: The letter T is most frequently used to represent the /t/ sound, as in "top" and "cat". It is quite reliable.

Rule 2: The letter T is usually omitted from words borrowed from French, such as "bouquet", "debut" and "ballet".

Rule 3: When the letter T is doubled in a word, such as in "little", one letter T is silent.

Rule 4: In the spelling pattern "-TCH", as in the word "watch", T is a silent letter and the sound for-TCH is /ch/.

Rule 5: When the letter T is between the letter S and the suffixes-le or-en, it is silent, as in the words "hasten", "often", "nestle", "castle" and "hustle".

Rule 6: The letter T is also included in the digraph "TH", as in the words "this" or "thing".

Rule 7: The consonant cluster "TR" contains the letter T, as in "tree".

Rule 8: When the letter T immediately precedes an unstressed long-U sound, it represents the /ch/ sound because the /y/ component of the long-U sound /yoo/ distorts the /t/ sound into the /ch/ sound, as in "nature", "picture" and "actual".

Rule 9: The letter T represents the /sh/ sound immediately before a suffix containing an unstressed I followed by another vowel. The unstressed I transforms the /t/ sound into a /sh/ sound, as in "nation", "motion", "partial" and "patient".

K /k/, as in "kin"

G /g/ is its voiced counterpart.

Rule 1: Occasionally, the /k/ sound is represented by the letter K, as in "kid" and "kind". It is highly reliable because no other sound has been assigned to it.

Rule 2: In most cases, the /k/ sound is represented by the digraph "CK", as in the word "sock".

Rule 3: When the letter K is immediately followed by the letter N, as in the words "know", "knock" and "knot", the letter K is usually silent. In other words, in the letter team KN, K is silent.

Rule 4: The letter Q is frequently used to represent the sound /k/, but Q cannot stand alone. It should be immediately followed by the letter U, as in the words "queen", "quilt" and "quack".

Rule 5: The /k/ sound is sometimes represented by the letter C when this letter is directly before the letters A, O or U and other consonants, as in the words "cat", "cut", "cold" and "cluster".

F /f/, as in "fin"

V/v/ is its voiced counterpart.

Rule 1: The letter F is most frequently used to represent the /f/ sound, as in "find", "beef" and "fan". It is relatively reliable because no other sound has been assigned to it.

Rule 2: The consonant team "PH" can represent the /f/ sound, as in the words "phone" and "pharmacy".

Rule 3: When in the final position, the digraph "-GH" may stand for the /f/ sound when preceded by the vowel teams "AU" or "OU", as in the words "laugh" and "enough". In other words, GH stands for the /f/ sound in the spelling patterns -AUGH and-OUGH.

Rule 4: At the end of a word, the /f/ sound can be represented by the letter team "-FF". Usually, "-FF" occurs immediately after the short vowel sound and one F is silent in this doubling, as in "cliff" and "off".

Rule 5: The letter F also represents the /v/ sound, as in the word "of".

S /s/, as in "sink"

Z/z/ is its voiced counterpart.

Rule 1: As in the words "sing", "sun" and "loss", the /s/ sound is most frequently represented by the letter S. It is quite unreliable since it has been assigned to other sounds.

Rule 2: The /s/ sound can be represented by the suffix-SS immediately following a short vowel sound in the root, but one S is silent. Examples include "hiss", "bliss" and "kiss".

Rule 3: In English, the /s/ sound is represented by the suffix -SS, as in -LESS, -NESS, -RESS and-ESS, as in the words "hopeless", "sadness", "actress" and "princess". When the letter S is doubled in those suffixes, one S is silent.

Rule 4: The sound /s/ can be represented by the letter C when it is directly before the letters I, E and Y as in "city", "cent" and "cyber".

Rule 5: When the consonant cluster "SC" immediately precedes the letters I, E and Y, the letter C represents the soft C sound /s/, which means that the "SC" cluster represents the /s/ sound found in words like "scene" and "science".

Rule 6: When the consonant cluster "SC" precedes the letters A, O and U and other consonants, the letter C has the hard sound /k/. Therefore, the "SC" cluster stands for the consonant blend /sk/, as in the words "scatter", "scoop" and "script".

CH /ch/, as in "cheese"

The /ch/ sound is an unvoiced consonant. It is a mixture of the /t/ and /sh/ sounds. The J /j/ sound is its voiced counterpart.

Rule 1: As in "cheese" or "lunch", the /ch/ sound is frequently represented by the digraph "CH". This is not very reliable because it can also stand for the /k/ sound in Greek-derived words such as "character" and "chemical".

Rule 2: The digraph "CH" represents the /k/ sound in Greek and these Greek roots can be combined to form consonant clusters such as "CHR-", "CHL-" and "SCH-", as in "Christ", "chloride" and "school".

Rule 3: The /ch/ sound is also represented by the root suffix-TCH, as in the words "ditch", "pitch" and "hatch".

SH /sh/, as in "shot"

The /zh/ sound is its voiced counterpart.

Rule 1: The digraph "SH" is frequently used to represent the /sh/ sound, as in the words "shark", "ship" and "fish". This digraph is a very reliable transcription of the sound /sh/.

Rule 2: The /sh/ sound is occasionally represented by alternative spellings, such as the S in "sure" and "sugar".

Rule 3: The sound /sh/ is represented by "-TI", as in "nation", "option", "diction" and "function". These words are of Latin origin.

Rule 4: In words derived from French, the /sh/ sound is represented by the digraph "CH", as in "Chicago", "chef", "chiffon" and "chic". By sight, it is difficult to tell the difference between the /sh/ and /ch/ sounds in "CH".

Rule 5: As in "special", "glacier", "racial" and "official", the /sh/ sound is represented by "-CI". These are all Latin-derived words and the unstressed I in the word converts the soft C sound /s/ to a /sh/ sound.

Rule 6: As in the word "passion", the /sh/ sound is represented by "-SSI-". These are all Latin-derived words and the unstressed I in the word converts the SS sound /s/ to a /sh/ sound, as in "session", "profession", "confession" and "procession".

WH /hw/, as in "wheel"

The WH /hw/ sound is dwindling and being primarily replaced by the /w/ sound.

Rule 1: The digraph "WH" is used to represent the /hw/ sound. The digraph "WH" occurs only at the beginning of a word or syllable.

Rule 2: The digraph "WH" can also be used to represent the /h/ sound, as in "who", "whose" and "whole".

TH /th/, as in "thumb"

Rule: The digraph "TH" is most frequently used to represent the /th/ sound, such as in "thin", "thing" and "bath". This digraph is relatively reliable because it only represents the unvoiced /th/ sound found in the words "thick", "thirsty" and "thread", as well as the voiced /th/ sound found in the words "the", "their" and "there". In general, the probability that the letter team TH represents the unvoiced consonant phoneme /th/ is lower than the probability that it stands for the voiced consonant phoneme /th/.

H /h/, as in "hut"

The sound of the letter H is nothing more than a breath.

Rule 1: The letter H is the most frequently used spelling for the /h/ sound, as in "hat", "hey" and "hike". When the letter H appears at the beginning of a word, it is relatively reliable.

Rule 2: The letter H is silent in a group of words borrowed from French or Latin, such as "hour", "honour", "vehicle" and "exhaust".

Rule 3: The letter H is silent in "RH" as in "rhyme", "rhinoceros" and "myrrh" which are of Latin origin.

Rule 4: The sound /h/ is represented by "WH" as in the words "who", "whole", "whom" and "whose".

2. 2. 2. 3　Rules For the Nasal Consonants

M /m/, as in "moon"

Rule 1: The letter M is most frequently used to represent the /m/ sound, as in "mat", "mop" and "ham". When the letter M appears at the beginning of a word, it is highly reliable.

Rule 2: "MB" and "MN" are the two digraphs for the consonant /m/, as in the words "lamb", "comb" and "column".

Rule 3: When the letter M is doubled in words such as "hammer", "common" and "summer", one letter M is silent.

N /n/, as in "net"

Rule 1: The letter N is the most frequently used spelling for the /n/ sound, as in "name", "nod" and "can". The letter N is highly reliable because it is the only letter associated with this sound.

Rule 2: "KN", "PN", "ND" and "GN" are all digraphs for the sound /n/, as in the words "knife", "pneumonia", "handsome" and "sign".

Rule 3: When the letter N is doubled, as in the words "funny", "sunny", "kennel" and "dinner", one letter N is silent.

NG /ng/, as in "ring"

Rule 1: "-NG" is a special consonant letter team for the final consonant sound /ng/. It is never used at the start of a word or syllable.

Rule 2: It frequently comes after a vowel sound, as in "flying", "strong" and "length".

2. 2. 3　Consonant Clusters

A consonant cluster is the written form of a consonant blend. A consonant blend refers to the sound unit of two or three letters at the beginning or end of words that are blended. Every sound in the blends is kept and pronounced, if only briefly (Bear et al., 2020). Not all consonant clusters are in the initial position; some may be in the final position.

Tab. 2. 3

Cluster	Blend	Examples
CL	/kl/	As in cliff, close and clement

续表

Cluster	Blend	Examples
DR	/dr/	As in dress, drive and dream
FL	/fl/	As in flower, flee and fly
SN	/sn/	As in snap, snore and snail
SP	/sp/	As in spring, splash and wasp
ST	/st/	As in stamp, sting and best
TR	/tr/	As in tree, trip and travel
GR	/gr/	As in green, grape and ground
GL	/gl/	As in glad, glue and glee
SK	/sk/	As in ski, skunk and frisk
BR	/br/	As in broom, bride and bright
BL	/bl/	As in blood, bloom and blame
CR	/kr/	As in crab, creepy and climb
SC	/sk/	As in scooter, scope and scan
SM	/sm/	As in smile, smell and smoke
FR	/fr/	As in frog, fry and free
SL	/sl/	As in slim, slide and sleep
PR	/pr/	As in prince, price and present
PL	/pl/	As in plus, please and play
SW	/sw/	As in swing, swim and sweet
TW	/tw/	As in twin, two and twist
QU	/kw/	As in queen, quill and quiet
SCR	/skr/	As in scream, script and scramble
SPL	/spl/	As in splash, splendid and split
SPR	/spr/	As in spring, spread and sprawl
STR	/str/	As in street, stripe and string
CHR	/kr/	As in Christmas, chrome and Christ
THR	/thr/	As in throw, thrive and three
SHR	/shr/	As in shrug, shrink and shred
PHR	/fr/	As in phrase

2.2.4 Consonant Digraphs

Consonant digraph refers to a consonant team or pair that represents a single consonant sound.

Tab. 2. 4

Digraph	Sound	Examples
TH	/th/	As in this
TH	/th/ voiceless	As in thing
WH	/w/ or /hw/	As in what
CH	/ch/	As in cherry
CH	/k/	As in Christ
PH	/f/	As in photo
SH	/sh/	As in shoe
-GH	/gh/	As in laugh
GH	/g/	As in ghost
NG	/ng/	As in ring

2. 2. 5 Silent Consonants

Most letters in the English alphabet are silent in words occasionally. However, people say these words without consciously knowing the silent consonant letters. Usually, consonants are silent because the sound of a particular word has changed over time but the spelling has remained constant. Silent consonants also occur in words borrowed from other languages. Some silent consonants come from letter interactions, while others derive from obsolete forms of pronunciation (Bishop, 1986). In the following table, silent consonants are listed by their different categories.

Tab. 2. 5

Categories	Silent Consonant	Rules	Examples
1. Letter Interactions		When a native English suffix beginning with a vowel is added to roots that contain a short vowel followed by a single consonant letter, the consonant letter is doubled to keep the initial vowel short, while the additional consonant is silent.	rub-rub**b**ed, hop-hop**p**ed big-big**g**er fun-fun**n**y fat-fat**t**est top-top**p**ing
	Silent L	When LL or L follows a single A or O, the short A becomes an "AW" sound, as in "bald" and "ball", while the short O becomes a long O sound, as in "cold" and "roll". L is not silent at this point. However, if the final letter is K or M, the L becomes silent, as in "talk" or "calm".	calm talk folk

续表

Categories	Silent Consonant	Rules	Examples
1. Letter Interactions	Silent T	When a word ends in "-st" before the suffix "-le".	hust-le cast-le nest-le
		When a word ends in "-st" or "-ft" before the suffix "-en".	soft-en fast-en hast-en
2. Obsolete consonant sounds	KN-	K is always silent before N at the beginning of a root word.	know knock knee
	WR-	W is always silent before R at the beginning of a root word.	write wrist wrench
	GN	G is silent before the letter N; this may be either at the beginning or the end of a word.	sign gnaw
	-MB	When the letter B is after the letter M in a word, the letter B is silent.	lamb climb crumb
	-MN	When the letter N is after the letter M, the letter N is silent.	environment condemn autumn
	-GH	In other words, when the vowel preceding "GH" is long, "GH" is silent in spoken language. When short vowels precede "GH", "GH" is pronounced as a /f/ sound.	eight right fight night though
3. Individual Silent Consonant	Silent H	"H" is silent in root words borrowed from French.	hour, exhibition, oh, honour, heir, hourly, dishonesty, herbal, heiress
		"H" is sometimes silent after the prefix ex-	exhibit exhibition
		"H" is silent after "G" at the beginning of a syllable.	ghetto, spaghetti, ghost, ghastly

续表

Categories	Silent Consonant	Rules	Examples
3. Individual Silent Consonant	Silent P	"P" is always silent at the beginning of a word if the consonant after "P" cannot be blended with "P".	pneumonia
4. Scholarly Insertion	Silent B		debt
	Silent C		muscle
	Silent S		island

2.2.6 Summary of Special Consonant Letters

2.2.6.1 The Letter Q

The letter Q could be deleted from the English alphabet and replaced by the letter K. The letter Q always stands for the /k/ sound but the letter U always follows it.

The cluster "QU" stands for the /kw/ sound, as in "queen", "quiet" and "quail". This is a Latin style of spelling this blend.

As in the words "antique", "mosquito" and "bouquet", the digraph "QU" represents the /k/ sound, whereas the letter U is silent.

2.2.6.2 The letter X

The letter X is frequently used to represent three distinct sounds:

–X is a single letter for the consonant blend /ks/, as in "fox", "box", "ox" and "wax".

–X is a single letter for the consonant blend /gz/, as in "exact", when the letter X is the last letter of an unstressed syllable and directly followed by a vowel or a silent H.

–X is a single letter for the consonant sound /z/ when found at the beginning of the word, as in "xylophone".

2.3 Phonograms (Word Families)

2.3.1 Definitions

A **phonogram** is a term that refers to word families or word patterns. It has been used to teach spellings since the 1600s (Bear et al., 2020; Blevins, 2017). Linguistically, the phonogram is the rime. The term "rime" is generally used in combination with the term "onset"; these refer to the two parts of a syllable.

A **rime** is a unit in a syllable that contains the vowel and everything following it, including consonants, whereas an **onset** is a consonant, consonant blend or digraph that precedes the rime in the syllable. For instance, in the word "tag", the rime unit is "ag" and the onset is the consonant "t".

2.3.2 Benefits of Knowing Phonograms

Learners can use phonograms-such as "-at" in fat, sat, pat and rat-in early independent writing and in reading connected text (decodable readers).

Since these word families or word chunks appear in many primary-level stories, it is critical to master them to develop reading fluency. As learners encounter more multisyllabic words, they understand that the words may contain different components such as phonograms, suffixes, prefixes and smaller words. This insight may significantly aid them in quickly and efficiently decoding words (Blevins, 2017).

In comparison, phonograms are consistent and generalisable. According to research, of the 286 phonograms that appear in primary-level texts, 272 (95%) are pronounced identically in every word (Durrell, 1963, as cited by Blevins, 2017). Likewise, those 272 reliable phonograms appear in 1437 words (Blevins, 2017).

As a result, researchers and educators have noted that the utility of phonograms enables the generation of a large number of words using a relatively small number of phonograms. According to Wylie and Durrell (1970, as cited by Blevins, 2017), the following 37 phonograms can be used to generate nearly 500 primary school words.

Tab. 2.6

-ack as in lack	-ank as in frank	-eat as in beat	-ill as in bill
-ock as in block	-ump as in lump	-ail as in tail	-ap as in nap
-ell as in bell	-in as in bin	-oke as in broke	-unk as in trunk
-ain as in train	-ash as in lash	-est as in nest	-ine as in dine
-op as in hop	-ake as in cake	-at as in bat	-ice as in dice
-ing as in sing	-or as in for	-ale as in gale	-ate as in fate
-ick as in lick	-ink as in blink	-ore as in bore	-ame as in blame
-aw as in law	-ide as in hide	-ip as in hip	-uck as in duck
-an as in fan	-ay as in hay	-ight as in night	-ir as in tapir
-ug as in jug			

2.3.3 Disadvantages of Phonogram Instruction

Phonograms are typically introduced through analogy phonics instruction, which will be discussed in detail in the following sections. They can help considerably with early reading and spelling. However, Blevins (2017) suggested that phonograms should not be the sole focus as they are extremely limited in enabling word analysis, forcing readers to rely heavily on analogy to identify words. They will then be less adept at thoroughly analysing words.

Interestingly, while young learners are instructed to memorise word chunks visually, little emphasis is placed on the actual letter-sound relationships, which may obstruct students' development of phonemic awareness and phonics ability. It is not recommended to begin with phonograms when teaching beginners and fundamental letter-sound relationships should be taught first (Blevins, 2017). This means that synthetic phonics instruction should be preferred over analogy-based phonics instruction.

The following alphabetical list contains phonograms adapted from Blevins (2017) and Fry et al. (1993).

(1) Short-A sound /a/ phonograms.

Tab. 2. 7

-**ab** as in cab	-**ack** as in lack	-**act** as in fact	-**ad** as in mad	-**aft** as in raft
-**ag** as in bag	-**am** as in ham	-**amp** as in camp	-**an** as in fan	-**ance** as in dance
-**anch** as in ranch	-**and** as in land	-**ang** as in fang	-**ank** as in bank	-**ant** as in pant
-**ap** as in map	-**ash** as in cash	-**ask** as in mask	-**asm** as in spasm	-**asp** as in gasp
-**ast** as in cast	-**at** as in mat	-**atch** as in match	-**ath** as in math	-**ax** as in tax

(2) Short-E sound /e/ phonograms.

Tab. 2. 8

-**ead** as in head	-**ealth** as in health	-**eath** as in death	-**eck** as in deck	-**ed** as in bed
-**edge** as in hedge	-**eft** as in left	-**eg** as in beg	-**eld** as in held	-**elf** as in self
-**ell** as in bell	-**elp** as in help	-**elt** as in belt	-**em** as in them	-**en** as in den
-**ence** as in hence	-**ench** as in bench	-**end** as in bend	-**ength** as in length	-**ense** as in dense
-**ent** as in dent	-**ep** as in step	-**ept** as in kept	-**esh** as in mesh	-**ess** as in less
-**est** as in nest	-**et** as in bet	-**etch** as in fetch	-**ext** as in next	

(3) Short-I sound /i/ phonograms.

Tab. 2. 9

-ib as in bib	**-ick** as in lick	**-id** as in bid	**-iff** as in cliff	**-ift** as in lift
-ig as in big	**-ilk** as in milk	**-ill** as in bill	**-ilt** as in tilt	**-im** as in him
-imp as in limp	**-in** as in fin	**-ince** as in mince	**-inch** as in finch	**-ince** as in mince
-ing as in sing	**-ing** as in hinge	**-ink** as in mint	**-ip** as in hip	**-is** as in his
-ish as in fish	**-ive** as in five	**-ix** as in fix	**-isk** as in risk	**-isp** as in crisp
-iss as in hiss	**-ist** as in list	**-it** as in fit	**-itch** as in pitch	**-ive** as in five
-ix as in fix				

(4) Short-O sound /o/ phonograms.

Tab. 2. 10

-ob as in mob	**-ock** as in mock	**-od** as in nod	**-oft** as in loft	**-og** as in hog	**-omp** as in stomp
-ond as in bond	**-op** as in hop	**-ot** as in lot	**-otch** as in blotch	**-ough** as in cough	**-ox** as in fox

(5) Short-U sound /u/ phonograms.

Tab. 2. 11

-ome as in come	**-on** as in son	**-ough** as in rough	**-ove** as in dove
-ub as in hub	**-uch** as in much	**-uck** as in duck	**-ud** as in mud
-uff as in buff	**-ug** as in bug	**-ulk** as in bulk	**-udge** as in judge
-ull as in dull	**-um** as in drum	**-umb** as in thumb	**-ump** as in lump
-un as in bun	**-unch** as in bunch	**-ung** as in lung	**-unk** as in junk
-unt as in blunt	**-up** as in pup	**-us** as in bus	**-ush** as in rush
-utt as in butt	**-utch** as in hutch	**-ut** as in but	**-ust** as in dust

(6) Long-A sound /ai/ phonograms.

Tab. 2. 12

-ace as in face	**-ade** as in made	**-age** as in cage	**-aid** as in laid
-ail as in sail	**-ain** as in main	**-aint** as in faint	**-aise** as in raise

续表

-ait as in wait	**-ake** as in bake	**-ale** as in male	**-ame** as in name
-ane as in lane	**-ange** as in range	**-ape** as in cape	**-ase** as in base
-aste as in taste	**-ate** as in late	**-ave** as in cave	**-ay** as in day
-aze as in maze	**-eak** as in break	**-eigh** as in neigh	**-ey** as in hey

(7) Long-E sound /ee/ phonograms.

Tab. 2. 13

-e as in be	**-ea** as in pea	**-each** as in peach	**-ead** as in lead	**-eak** as in beak
-eal as in heal	**-eam** as in beam	**-ean** as in mean	**-eap** as in heap	**-ear** as in dear
-ease as in lease	**-east** as in beast	**-eat** as in feat	**-eath** as in heath	**-eave** as in leave
-ee as in bee	**-eech** as in beech	**-eed** as in feed	**-eek** as in leek	**-eel** as in feel
-eem as in deem	**-een** as in been	**-eep** as in beep	**-eer** as in deer	**-eet** as in feet
-eeze as in breeze	**-iece** as in niece	**-ief** as in brief	**-ield** as in field	

(8) Long-I sound /igh/ phonograms.

Tab. 2. 14

-ibe as in tribe	**-ice** as in dice	**-ide** as in hide	**-ie** as in pie
-ied as in cried	**-ier** as in drier	**-ies** as in ties	**-ife** as in wife
-igh as in high	**-ight** as in fight	**-ike** as in bike	**-ild** as in mild
-ile as in mile	**-ime** as in dime	**-ind** as in find	**-ine** as in fine
-ipe as in wipe	**-ire** as in fire	**-ise** as in rise	**-ite** as in bite
-ive as in five	**-uy** as in buy	**-y** as in by	**-ye** as in bye

(9) Long-O sound /oa/ phonograms.

Tab. 2. 15

-o as in go	**-oach** as in coach	**-oad** as in road	**-oak** as in soak
-oal as in foal	**-oam** as in foam	**-oan** as in loan	**-oast** as in toast
-oat as in goat	**-obe** as in robe	**-ode** as in code	**-oe** as in foe
-oke as in coke	**-old** as in fold	**-ole** as in dole	**-oll** as in doll

续表

-**olt** as in bolt	-**ome** as in home	-**one** as in bone	-**ope** as in cope
-**ose** as in rose	-**ost** as in host	-**ote** as in note	-**ove** as in stove
-**ow** as in row	-**own** as in known		

(10) Long-U sound /yoo/ phonograms.

Tab. 2. 16

-**ew** as in few	-**ube** as in tube	-**ue** as in cue	-**uke** as in puke
-**une** as in tune	-**ute** as in mute		

Note: In British English, words like "dude", "tube", "due", "dune", "tune", "mute" and "duke" belong to the long-U sound group. In American English, they are classified as belonging to the long-U sound group, however, the letter U is pronounced as long-/oo/ sound as in the word goose.

(11) Diphthong /oi/ phonograms.

Tab. 2. 17

-**oil** as in boil	-**oin** as in coin	-**oint** as in point
-**oise** as in noise	-**oist** as in moist	-**oy** as in boy

(12) Diphthong /ou/ phonograms.

Tab. 2. 18

-**ouch** as in pouch	-**oud** as in loud	-**ounce** as in ounce
-**ount** as in count	-**ound** as in found	-**our** as in our
-**out** as in about	-**outh** as in mouth	-**ouse** as in mouse
-**own** as in down	-**owl** as in howl	-**ow** as in bow

(13) Variant Vowel long /oo/ phonograms.

Tab. 2. 19

-**ew** as in flew	-**o** as in do	-**oo** as in boo	-**ood** as in mood
-**oof** as in hoof	-**ool** as in pool	-**oom** as in room	-**oon** as in noon
-**oop** as in loop	-**oose** as in loose	-**oot** as hoot	-**ooth** as in booth

续表

-**ooze** as in snooze	-**oup** as in soup	-**ube** as in lube	-**uce** as in spruce
-**ude** as in rude	-**ue** as in cue	-**uke** as in luke	-**ule** as in mule
-**ume** as in fume	-**une** as in dune	-**ure** as in cure	-**uth** as in truth
-**ute** as in cute			

Note: In British English, words like "dude", "tube", "due", "dune", "tune", "mute" and "duke" belong to the long-U sound group; in American English, they are classified as belonging to the long /oo/ sound group. Based on phonic decoding rules, those words are classified as belonging to the long-U sound group.

(14) Variant Vowel short /oo/ phonograms.

Tab. 2. 20

-**ood** as in good	-**ook** as in look	-**oot** as in foot
-**ush** as in bush	-**ull** as in bull	-**ould** as in could

(15) Variant Vowel sound /or/ (broad-O sound) phonograms.

Tab. 2. 21

-**all** as in ball	-**alk** as in talk	-**alt** as in salt	-**aught** as in taught	-**aunch** as in launch
-**aunt** as in haunt	-**ault** as in fault	-**aw** as in law	-**awl** as in crawl	-**awn** as in fawn
-**ong** as in long	-**oss** as in boss	-**ost** as in cost	-**oth** as in sloth	-**ought** as in ought

(16) R-controlled vowel sound /air/ phonograms.

Tab. 2. 22

-**air** as in fair	-**are** as in fare	-**ear** as in pear

(17) R-controlled vowel sound /ur/ phonograms.

Tab. 2. 23

-**earn** as in learn	-**erb** as in herb	-**erge** as in merge	-**erk** as in clerk
-**erm** as in term	-**ern** as in fern	-**erve** as in nerve	-**ir** as in fir
-**ird** as in bird	-**irk** as in smirk	-**irst** as in first	-**irt** as in dirt
-**irth** as in birth	-**ur** as in fur	-**urb** as in curb	-**urge** as in urge
-**urse** as in curse	-**url** as in curl	-**urn** as in burn	-**urk** as in lurk
-**urt** as in hurt			

(18) R-controlled vowel sound /ar/ phonograms.

Tab. 2. 24

-**ar** as in far	-**ard** as in hard	-**arge** as in large	-**ark** as in bark
-**arm** as in farm	-**arn** as in barn	-**arp** as in sharp	-**art** as in dart

(19) R-controlled vowel sound /or/ phonograms.

Tab. 2. 25

-**oar** as in boar	-**oor** as in door	-**orch** as in porch	-**ord** as in ford	-**ore** as in core
-**ork** as in fork	-**orm** as in norm	-**orn** as in corn	-**ort** as in fort	-**our** as in four

Section 3 Phonics Instruction Approaches

This section aims to prepare trainees to use different approaches to phonics instruction.

Main Goals	This section aims to help trainees to master: 1. the differences between the three main types of phonics instruction. 2. the scope and sequence of phonics instruction in the SSP model.
Specific Objectives	In this section, trainees should be able to master: 1. the necessities for phonics instruction. 2. three types of instruction approach: Synthetic phonics instruction, analytic instruction and analogy instruction. 3. the key characteristics of effective synthetic phonics instruction. 4. the prerequisites of phonics instruction. 5. why and how to instruct alphabet recognition. 6. the benefits of decodable text. 7. differences among sight words, high-frequency words and irregulars. 8. approaches to tackle irregulars.

3.1 Necessities of Phonics Instruction

This instructional guide discusses how to teach phonics via systematic and explicit phonics instruction approaches. Although, as Bald (2007) notes, phonics alone is not sufficient and English spelling does not precisely correspond to speech sounds, phonics provides language learners with the most direct path to becoming proficient readers and writers.

According to the International Literacy Association (ILA, 2019), English is an alphabetic language with 26 letters representing 44 sounds. While only around 84% of English words are phonetically regular, teaching the fundamental letter-sound combinations is highly beneficial and necessary for learners because once they grasp the "code-breaking" rules (Blevins, 2017), the majority of spoken words become accessible in print. This ability to decode rules is critical for developing into a fluent reader. When beginners acquire automatic word recognition ability, they devote more mental energy to comprehending the meaning of the text and develop an appreciation of reading and literature.

Therefore, this instructional guide concentrates on the primary goal of early reading at word level that relies on systematic and explicit phonics to achieve reading fluency (automatic word recognition).

As the preceding section explains, phonics refers to letter-sound relationships, a necessary component of the reading and writing practice for primary language learners. It is regarded as beneficial to all learners, including EFL learners in China, as well as being harmful to none and critical for some (Papp, 2020).

For instance, phonics is critical for learners who struggle to read; or who have had very little exposure to English before entering primary school; or who have had very little exposure to English books; or who have had very few opportunities to develop their oral languages (Blevins, 2017; Carroll et al., 2011; DEST, 2005; ILA, 2019; Papp, 2020). This applies to the majority of Chinese EFL learners. As a result, phonics instruction can assist EFL learners to develop an understanding of the correspondences between letters and sounds.

Thus, the focus of this instructional guide is on systematic and explicit synthetic phonics, which are both discussed and illustrated.

3.2 Introduction to Phonics Instruction

Phonics or the set of English decoding rules is not a method of instruction or education in and of itself. It is not the same as the term "**phonics instruction**", which refers to the activities in which phonics is taught (ILA, 2018). There are numerous approaches to teaching phonics (Blevins, 2017; ILA, 2019). Three types of phonics instruction are most frequently used: The synthetic phonics instruction approach, the analytic phonics instruction approach and the analogy phonics instruction approach. The two main approaches used at primary level are synthetic phonics and analytic phonics instruction (Blevins, 2017; Papp, 2020). Analogy phonics instruction focuses on word families and can be combined with either of the other two approaches.

For many years in English-speaking countries, the main source of contention has been between the synthetic and analytic phonics instruction approaches (Sprague, 2014; Parker, 2019). Now, experts or authorities agree that while phonics can be taught in various ways, the explicit and systematic phonics instruction approach is recommended (ILA, 2019; Papp, 2020). According to the ILA (2019), "explicit" means that letter-sound relationships should be introduced explicitly, while the term "systematic" refers to instruction that should progress from simple to more complex skills. Additionally, being systematic implies that instruction should incorporate a review and repetition cycle to ensure mastery and progress from known to unknown, which facilitates learning. The explicit and systematic instruction approach is considered more direct, timely and effective than the "discover" model (ILA, 2019). In such a context, the term "discover model" refers to analytic the phonics instruction approach while the term "systematic and explicit model" refers to the synthetic phonics instruction approach.

3.3 The Synthetic Phonics Instruction Approach

3.3.1 Definition

Synthetic phonics (SP), as the name implies, is primarily concerned with synthesising letter sounds to pronounce unfamiliar words (Johnson & Watson, 2007). SP refers to a phonics instructional approach that begins with individual sounds and ends with blending sounds to form words (Bear et al., 2020). This approach is considered explicit and systematic, with concrete examples for students to build upon as they understand the printed code and how words are spelt (ILA, 2018).

3.3.2 Illustration of the Synthetic Phonics Instruction Approach

The synthetic phonics instruction approach requires learners to combine individual letter sounds to form words. For instance, if learners are taught that the letter T has the sound /t/ and the digraph "EA" is pronounced as a long-E sound, they will be able to vocalise the word "T-EA" /tea/.

The majority of synthetic phonics programs begin by teaching learners the letter-sound correspondences for consonants, short vowels, consonant digraphs like "sh", "th" or "wh", as well as clusters such as "bl" and "st". More complex pattern layers are then introduced, such as long vowels, r-controlled vowels, digraphs and variant vowels. However, this is not a rigid pattern and can be modified to meet the needs of individual learners as long as it is explicit and systematic (ILA, 2018, 2019).

3.3.3 Characteristics of the Synthetic Phonics Instruction Approach

(1) It is a component-to-whole or bottom-up approach that utilises letter sounds.

Letter-sound correspondences are taught in a logical order.

(2) The instructional period is brief and well-paced, typically a little more than a term.

(3) With practice, learners are instructed to blend sounds to form words.

(4) Letter sounds are quickly mastered and learners can immediately sound and blend.

(5) Learners acquire the ability to spell concurrently with the acquisition of the ability to read.

(6) Teaching can be accomplished using visually appealing resources, games, activities, stories or chants.

(7) Teaching provides opportunities for language development on a holistic and comprehensive level.

(8) It is a comprehensive solution that benefits all learners, particularly struggling readers with limited exposure to English, because it does not require an already-established sight vocabulary repertoire.

(9) It concurrently develops learners' phonemic awareness and their ability to decode words (Bald, 2007; Blevins, 2017; Carroll et al., 2011; ILA, 2019; Johnson & Watson, 2007).

3.3.4 Teaching Sequence of the Synthetic Phonics Instruction Approach

(1) Learners are taught the letter names.

(2) Each letter's associated sound is taught and reviewed.

(3) Some generalisations or rules may be discussed and explained.

(4) The concept of sound blending to create words is taught.

(5) Opportunities are provided for blending unfamiliar words in context.

3.3.5 Model of Synthetic Phonics Instruction for Reference

(1) On the blackboard, write the letter "S".

(2) Explain to learners that the letter "S" stands for the /s/ sound in the word "sit" (do not write out /s/).

(3) On the blackboard, write the word "sit" and ask a volunteer to circle the letter "s".

(4) Slowly blend the word "sit", with the teacher's finger running beneath each letter.

(5) Instruct learners to think of additional words that begin with the letter "S" and write these on the blackboard.

(6) Instruct volunteers to circle the letter "S" in each word.

(7) Continue by providing a list of simple decodable words based on the previously taught sound-spelling relationship for the /s/ sound and have learners blend these sounds into words.

3.4 The Analytic Phonics Instruction Approach

3.4.1 Definition

The analytic phonics instruction approach is also referred to as indirect or implicit phonics and, occasionally the "discover approach". With this whole-to-part approach, students begin with whole words and are asked to deduce the letter-sound relationship, which is the focus of this teaching section.

3.4.2 Illustration of the Analytic Phonics Instruction Approach

The analytic phonics instruction approach gained popularity among those who believed that if learners discover these principles on their own, they should internalise them. This approach, however, depends on the student's ability to segment words orally, which requires a high level of phonemic awareness and a large, already-established vocabulary. This approach is inappropriate for struggling readers or those with limited exposure to English, such as EFL learners (Blevins, 2017; Parker, 2019). Additionally, learners should receive separate instruction in phonemic awareness to prepare them for this particular instruction approach.

The analytic phonics instruction approach has been used in place of the synthetic phonics instruction approach during the initial reading stage. However, it has been deemed ineffective because covering the entire alphabetic code in this manner is too time-consuming due to the sight word memorisation required and the "discovery model of instruction". Parker (2019) argued that completing phonics instruction using this approach may take five to six years.

3.4.3 Characteristics of the Analytic Phonics Instruction Approach

(1) Letter-sound correspondences are not taught sequentially.

(2) Patterns or letter-sound relationships are based on analysis of the entire word.

(3) The teaching period is significantly longer than systematic synthetic phonics instruction approach, typically five to six years (Parker, 2019).

(4) Learners are not instructed to practise blending sounds to form words.

(5) It necessitates a large collection of already-established sight words as a start-

ing point for analysis.

(6) It requires strong phonemic awareness on the part of learners to distinguish sounds from words orally, rather than assisting in their development.

3.4.4 Teaching Sequence of the Analytic Phonics Instruction Approach

(1) The following list of words share a common phonic element. On the blackboard, words such as "pen", "pity" and "pat" may be written.

(2) Learners are instructed to examine the words to determine what they have in common, with the emphasis on finding a similar sound.

(3) Once a typical sound is identified, the spelling associated with the sound may be discussed and explained.

(4) Learners are asked to articulate generalisations, such as by saying, "The letter P represents the /p/ sound".

3.5 The Analogy Phonics Instruction Approach

3.5.1 Definition

The analogy phonics instruction approach enables learners to identify new words by utilising segments of previously learned written words. Those already-identified word segments are frequently referred to as word families, phonograms or word chunks (Blevins, 2017; DEST, 2005).

3.5.2 Illustration of the Analogy Phonics Instruction Approach

As the definition indicates, this instruction approach is concerned with phonograms. Learners use this approach to locate recognisable word chunks within a word to assist them in determining the word sound. It is frequently used in conjunction with synthetic phonics instruction to address the irregularities in the English language. For instance, if learners are familiar with the sound of "-ould", they may be able to sound out "would" and "should" if they are also familiar with the letter W and the diphthong "SH".

The analogy phonics instruction approach can assist learners in developing an understanding of more complex phonics concepts, such as the pattern layer of the orthography. According to the ILA (2018), the first layer is the alphabetic layer, which involves acquiring elemental letter-sound correspondences via synthetic phonics instruction. The second layer is the pattern layer, which can be used with analogy phonics instruction. In short, learners are encouraged to first learn letter-sound relationships through synthetic phonics and then use these analogies to learn word patterns, which can help supplement early reading instruction.

Additionally, Blevins (2017) suggested that the analogy phonics instruction approach is inappropriate for phonics beginners. If beginners are taught to memorise word families visually, little emphasis is placed on letter-sound relationships, which may impair the development of phonemic awareness and individual decoding rules in phonics. This instruction approach has several advantages for word analysis but should be used with caution. In China, the analogy phonics instruction approach is included in several popular primary school English textbooks.

3.5.3 Teaching Sequence of the Analogy Phonics Instruction Approach

(1) The target phonogram is written on the blackboard, for example, "-ight".

(2) Following that, the phonogram's sound is taught and discussed.

(3) Several similar words that contain the suffix "-ight" are highlighted for reading.

(4) Learners are encouraged to consider additional words that end in "-ight".

3.6 Key Characteristics of the Effective Synthetic Phonics Instruction Approach

Apart from effective phonics instruction being explicit and systematic, the ILA (2019) states that it must possess-as a minimum-the following seven key characteristics:

3.6.1 Readiness Skills

Before learning the phonics decoding rules, the learners should at least have been taught alphabet recognition and possess fundamental phonemic awareness.

3.6.2 Scope and Sequence

A substantial scope and sequence of phonics decoding rules will progress from simple to complex while taking advantage of prior knowledge. This sequence encourages the formation of as many words as possible early on and focuses on teaching high-utility skills. There is no one-size-fits-all scope or sequence as long as the instructions strive to connect concepts and to progress through a series of sub-skills in a stair-step fashion to maximise the learner's chance of success. In general, the scope and sequence of the course can be tailored to the learners' needs.

3.6.3 Blending

As previously stated, the explicit and systematic phonics instruction (synthetic) approach develops phonemic awareness and phonics decoding rules concurrently. This is dependent on blending. Blending is the primary strategy for teaching learners to sound out words and it must be modelled and practised frequently. It is simply the association of letter sounds in order to read a word. It is the focus of early phonics instruction but plays a role in the learner's transition from monosyllabic to multisyllabic word reading.

3.6.4 Dictation

To help learners transfer their developing phonics skills to writing effectively, dictation is critical. Dictation can help learners improve their spelling and their comprehension of common English spelling patterns, as well as assist learners in applying these phonics skills in writing. Alternatively, learners are given increasing opportunities to practise their developing abilities to express themselves in writing.

3.6.5 Word Awareness

Word building and sorting are critical activities for increasing learners' word awareness. For instance, learners are given a set of letters and asked to create a series of words in specific sequences. Also, they are provided with a list of words containing various phonemes. And required to sort those words based on different phonemes. These activities help them develop their ability to work flexibly with letter sounds and thoroughly analyse words for their component sounds and spellings. Conjointly, this is beneficial as a transition from monosyllabic to polysyllabic words.

3.6.6 Reading Connected Text

The purpose of phonics instruction is to help learners develop their ability to read connected text independently. At the beginner level of reading instruction, decodable or controlled text helps learners develop a sense of comfort with and control over their reading growth. This should be a critical learning tool in early phonics instruction. These types of phonics-based texts must be reread to develop fluency and discussed to improve comprehension.

3.6.7 High-Frequency Words

The most frequently occurring sight words in English are called high-frequency words. Certain sight words are irregular, meaning they do not follow certain English spelling rules. Other sight words or words with a high frequency of occurrence are regular and must be recognised quickly. Additional time should be allocated to learning sight words.

3.7 Scope and Sequence of the SSP Instruction Approach

Both the scope and sequence of the systematic synthetic phonics instruction approach are dynamic and can be tailored to meet the needs of individuals. Nonetheless, this is a point of contention in this domain. According to some scholars, long vowel sounds should be taught first because they are easier to distinguish auditorily than short vowel sounds. Additionally, long vowel sounds "speak their names". Other scholars believe that long vowel sounds are complex and should be taught only after learners grasp how the phonics system works. That is, they advocate the initial use of short vowel sounds, especially for CVC patterns of short vowels. Blevins (2017) recommended the following sequence:

(1) Teach short vowel sounds first because efficiency and ease of learning are critical and the simplicity of CVC words benefits struggling readers.

(2) Combine consonants and short vowels so that words can be generated as early as possible.

(3) As early as possible, ensure that the majority of consonants taught are continuous consonants.

(4) Select a sequence that enables the maximum number of words to be generated.

(5) Progress from simple to more complex sound spellings as follows:

(A) Short Vowels and consonants in combination.

(B) Digraphs (ch, sh, th, wh).

(C) Blends (r-blends, s-blends, l-blends).

(D) Final e (a_e, e_e, i_e, o_e, u_e).

(E) Long vowels (multiple spellings).

(F) Variant vowels (oo, au, aw) and diphthongs (ou, ow, oi, oy).

(G) Silent letters, inflectional endings (-ed, -s, -ing).

3.8 Alphabet Recognition Requirements

Since English is an alphabetic language, it is necessary to understand the alphabet principle. This refers to a collection of letters that represent a series of sounds. Learners must be able to recognise letters in various contexts and forms, such as lower and upper case.

The second requirement for reading is that learners must be able to rapidly identify the printed forms of letters in and out of sequence, as well as the sound most frequently associated with each letter.

According to previous research, learners who can accurately and quickly recognise letters find it easier to learn about letter-sound relationships than those who struggle with alphabet recognition because the former group can devote more "mental energy" to letter-sound relationships. Additionally, speed can assist young readers in developing automaticity and fluency. Thus, both accuracy and speed reflect the extent to which students have mastered letter identities (Blevins, 2017; ILA 2019).

3.9 Guidelines for Alphabet Instruction

(1) Begin by teaching letter names to learners. Once students know these names, teachers will be able to use familiar labels to assist students in grasping the alphabetic principle.

(2) Introduce learners to the shapes and sounds of letters.

(3) Tailor letter lessons to the learners' specific needs.

(4) Assist learners in recognising the distinctions and similarities between letters.

(5) When introducing sound-spelling relationships, include keywords and illustrations.

(6) Adapt the pace of instruction to the learners' needs.

(7) Include multi-sensory activities.

(8) Alphabet books are critical.

3.10 Benefits of Alphabet Books

Alphabet picture books present the letters of the alphabet in order. Numerous alphabet books centre on a theme that will pique students' interest. Alphabet books can be used to reinforce alphabet recognition while assisting in the development of vocabulary. Such books are an excellent choice for EFL language beginners who lack vocabulary accumulation and they offer the following advantages (Blevins, 2017):

(1) They aid in the oral language development of beginner readers.

(2) They assist beginners in memorising letter sequences.

(3) They assist novices in associating sounds and letters.

(4) They can assist beginners in developing their vocabulary and general knowledge. During elementary school, students gain a significant amount of knowledge about the world. These books are highly beneficial to students with a limited understanding of the world.

(5) They can be used to help EFL learners improve their vocabulary.

(6) Conceivably, they appeal to at-risk readers who are intimidated by dense text.

3.11 Tips for Teaching with Alphabet Books

(1) Read the books aloud without pausing to allow learners to enjoy the language or illustrations.

(2) Reread the book and discuss points of interest, such as identifying objects in the illustrations that begin with the sound represented by the letter on that page. Maintain a lighthearted and playful tone throughout the discussion.

(3) Create letter charts using words and images from an alphabetic book and have learners match the words and images to the appropriate letter/sound.

(4) Instruct learners to create their alphabetic books based on the patterns taught in class (Blevins, 2017).

3.12 Sight Words, High-Frequency Words and Irregulars

For fluent reading, sight words are necessary. These include words with a high frequency of occurrence and many are considered irregular because they deviate from the commonly taught sound-spelling relationship. According to research, learners do not acquire irregular words as readily or as quickly as they do regular words. As a result, learners must be explicitly taught irregular sight words.

3.13 "Irregulars" in the English language

Some sources indicate that around 84% of words in the English language follow regular spelling patterns (ILA, 2019). Meanwhile, others estimate that between 50 and 85% of words in English follow regular spelling patterns, depending on the method of calculation used (Bald, 2007). Based on this estimation, of the remaining 16% of the words, only 3% are highly unpredictable (Bryson, 1990, as cited by Blevins, 2017). These irregulars, as they are called, can be taught or explained through word families (Bald, 2007) or acquired through decodable text reading with the teacher's guidance and explanation. Thus, after instruction in letter-sound relationships, phonograms may be introduced and explained to help learners address these irregulars.

For instance, while "ough" is the most irregular sound pattern in English, the group "ough" can be taught in groups as phonograms (word families) as follows:

- "ought": fought, brought, sought, wrought.
- "ough": tough, rough, enough.
- "ough": though, dough, although.

3.14 Suggested Teaching Steps for High-Frequency Words

(1) State the word aloud and incorporate it into a sentence.

(2) While reading the sentence, write it on the blackboard and highlight the high-frequency word.

(3) Discuss the word and any of its unique characteristics.

(4) Instruct learners to spell the word aloud while the teacher points to each letter.

(5) As learners write the word on paper, have them spell it out.

3.15 The Most Frequent Word List

This chart summarises the 150 most frequently occurring words in printed English, as determined by the American Heritage Word Frequency Book, cited in Blevins (2017).

Tab. 3.1

the **	could **	they *	use *	of *
no *	at *	may *	and *	make *
be *	water *	a *	than *	this *
go *	to *	first *	from *	good *
in *	been **	I *	new *	is *
long *	have *	write *	you *	little *
or *	our *	that *	very *	by *
used *	it *	after **	one **	me **
he *	words *	had *	man *	for *
called **	not *	too *	was *	just *
will *	any *	on *	where **	each *
day *	are *	most *	about *	same *
but *	know *	how *	right *	what *
get *	up *	look *	all *	through *
out *	think *	where *	back *	them *
such *	when *	much *	then *	here *
we *	before *	she *	take *	there *
also **	many **	why *	can **	around *

续表

some *	things *	an *	another *	so *
help *	your *	came **	these *	put *
which *	come **	would *	years *	their *
work **	other *	different *	said **	three *
its *	away *	if *	word *	who *
again *	do *	must *	now *	off *
into *	because *	people *	went **	has **
does **	my *	old *	more *	part *
made *	number *	her *	even *	over *
two *	place *	did **	like *	well *
down *	him *	as **	only *	see *
with *	way *	time *	his *	find *

* means on the vocabulary list at National Curriculum level 2 and ** means on the list at level 3.

3.16 Definition of Decodable Text

Decodable text is also referred to as a decodable reader, a phonics reader, accountable text, connected text, phonics-based text (Bear et al., 2020), controlled text (Blevins, 2017; ILA, 2019). It is a straightforward book organised around repeated phonics features throughout the text.

3.17 Characteristics of Decodable Text

Decodable readers are likely to be progressive in the reading presentation they offer in the following areas:

(1) Subtitles.

(2) One sentence per page, followed by two sentences per page.

(3) One-syllable compound words, followed by two-syllable compound words.

(4) Proper nouns, nouns and plurals.

(5) Pronouns, particularly personal pronouns.

(6) Present and past tense verbs.

(7) Adjectival and adverbial phrases.

(8) Speech bubbles indicating the beginning of direct speech.

(9) Commas, prepositions, conjunctions, questions and exclamation marks are all examples of punctuation.

3.18 Benefits of Decodable Text

(1) This type of book allows beginner readers to put into practice their newly acquired knowledge of words and see numerous words that function in similar ways (Bear et al., 2020).

(2) As Johnson and Watson (2007) suggested, phonics sessions should be integrated into text reading activities, which provide opportunities for students to apply and develop the phonics skills they have been learning.

(3) A series of decodable texts corresponding to each set of taught letter sounds can be used to assist learners in reading captions and sentences containing regular and irregular words composed of the taught letter sounds.

(4) As Carroll et al. (2011) stated, reading decodable text can serve as a means of reinforcing and practising decoding rules in context, as well as boosting confidence.

(5) Reading connected texts is critical for developing a stronger foundation in early reading, especially when confronted with less controlled graded readers.

(6) Decodable text contains words with a high frequency of occurrence, including some irregular sight words. Thus, the text enables learners to convert some frequently occurring irregular words into sight words.

3.19 Summary of Synthetic Phonics Instruction Procedures

3.19.1 Instruction on Alphabet Recognition

3.19.2 Instruction on Individual Letter-Sound Relationships (Decoding Rules)

(1) Consonants–single consonant.

(2) Consonant digraphs.

(3) Consonant blends.

(4) Silent letters.

(5) Short vowels.

(6) Long vowels.

(7) Other vowel sounds.

–diphthongs.

–variant vowel sounds.

-r-controlled vowel sounds.

-schwa (optional).

3.19.3 Decodable Readers and High-Frequency Words (Optional)

3.19.4 Phonograms and Irregulars (Optional)

Section 4 Guidelines for and Sample Lessons in the SSP Model

This section aims to reinforce trainees' phonics instruction knowledge and skills in the SSP model.

Main Goals	This section mainly aims at helping trainees to master: 1. the guidelines of phonics instruction in teaching alphabet, decoding rules and sight words. 2. the teaching process of the SSP model: Alphabet, decoding rules and sight words.
Specific Objectives	In this section, trainees will be able to demonstrate: 1. the process of instructing alphabet recognition. 2. the process of instructing single consonant sounds in the SSP model. 3. the process of instructing consonant digraphs in the SSP model. 4. the process of instructing consonant clusters in the SSP model. 5. the process of instructing silent consonant letters in the SSP model. 6. the process of instructing short vowel sounds in the SSP model. 7. the process of instructing long vowel sounds in the SSP model. 8. the process of instructing other vowel sounds in the SSP model. 9. the ways of instructing phonograms, sight words and irregulars. 10. to understand the dos and don'ts of class teaching.

4.1 Alphabet Recognition Instruction with Alphabet Books

4.1.1 Teaching Goals

(1) To assist learners in memorising letter sequences.

(2) To assist learners in associating a letter with a sound.

(3) To assist learners in developing their phonemic awareness.

(4) To aid in the oral language development of learners.

(5) To assist learners in developing their vocabulary and word knowledge.

4.1.2 Guidelines

(1) Select the appropriate letter sequence to instruct. Letter sequence as in the alphabet song is recommended.

(2) Determine whether to teach upper or lower case letters or both, based on the students' cognitive abilities.

(3) Begin by teaching letter names, followed by shapes and sounds.

(4) Assist learners in distinguishing between similar letters such as b and d.

4.1.3 Sample Lesson

(1) Pre-reading.

-On the blackboard, write the target letter in both upper and lower case.

-If any similar letters exist, compare them to the target letter.

-Assess learners' familiarity with the letter sound and their ability to name words that begin with this sound. For instance, F stands for fun; F stands for flamingo. Of course, they can name things from the book using pictures.

-Introduce the story's characters and their names. Have learners speculate why the author chose these animals and names.

-Display the book's cover and illustrations to elicit predictions from learners.

(2) While reading.

-Read the story aloud the first time to acquaint learners with the language and plot.

-Reread the story and instruct learners to search for and identify the target letter. Allow learners to indicate when they hear the initial letter of a word.

-On the subsequent reading, instruct students to seek items that begin with the target letter and attempt to match these items to the words on the page.

(3) After reading.

-Instruct learners to locate all the items in the book that begin with the target letter and enjoy the letter chant, if one exists.

-Create a list of words that begin with the target letter and sound. Play a quick game to reinforce the sound.

4.2 Single Consonant Instruction in the SSP Model

4.2.1 Teaching Goals

(1) To familiarise learners with the most frequently used spellings for each consonant sound.

(2) To familiarise learners with the common letter sounds associated with each letter.

4.2.2 Guidelines

(1) Instruct learners to memorise only the most frequently used spellings for each consonant sound.

(2) In lessons, prioritise simple CVC words over consonant clusters and digraphs.

(3) Having taught the letter K, the letters C and G can be taught in pairs.

(4) The letter Q can be taught independently of the letter K.

4.2.3 Sample Lesson

Single Consonant Sounds

(1) Phonics Principle: The letter S stands for the /s/ sound.

(2) Step 1: Review. Reread the story or passage which contains previously taught letter sound relationships. Instruct learners to practise oral blending to develop phonemic awareness.

(3) Step 2: Letter-Sound Relationship Introduction.

-Explain to learners that the letter "S" represents the /s/ sound in the word "sock".

-On the blackboard, write "sock" with a picture.

-Then, as the teacher runs his or her finger beneath each letter, blend the word "sock".

-Ask a volunteer to highlight the letter "S".

-Draw attention to this letter by asking students to state the letter's sound /s/.

-Continue by having learners create a word list that includes letter S and the /s/ sound.

-Write the words more clearly on the blackboard with illustrations for EFL learners.

(4) Step 3: Word Blending.

-On the blackboard, write simple words beginning with the target letter S.

-Write simple words that learners have already been taught.

-Write one or two sentences containing those words and some other high-frequency words.

For example: Sat, sad, sock.

Mat, mad, rock.

Sam is sad.

I sat on the rock.

-Instruct learners to construct as many words as possible using the letters a, o, I, s, t and m.

(5) Step 4: Word Recognition and Sound Discrimination.

On the blackboard, write a list of simple words with the target letter S and sound /s/. Have learners identify which one is the word the teacher is currently reading.

(6) Step 5: Decodable Text (Optional for EFL Learners).

Provide decodable reading practice for learners based on the target letter-sound relationship and previously acquired words. This step is optional, depending on their educational progress and abilities.

(7) Step 6: Dictation (Optional for EFL learners).

Dictate simple vocabulary words from the day's lesson and record the answers on the blackboard. This is intended to assist learners in segmenting words and associating the words with the spelling. For EFL learners, the corresponding pictures can be displayed to help them connect the spelling to the meaning. This step is optional, depending on their educational progress and abilities.

4.3 Consonant Digraphs Instruction in the SSP Model

4.3.1 Teaching Goals

(1) To familiarise learners with consonant digraph sounds.

(2) To assist learners in rapidly identifying "letter pairs" within words.

4.3.2 Guidelines

(1) Two consonants that appear together in a word and represent only one sound are called consonant digraphs: SH, CH, TH, WH, PH, GH and NG.

(2) After learners have mastered all the single consonants, teach them the consonant digraphs.

4.3.3 Sample Lesson

Consonant Digraphs

(1) Phonics Principle. The digraph "SH" is a common spelling for the /sh/ sound, as in "shoot".

(2) Step 1: Review. Reread the story or passage which contains previously taught letter-sound relationships. Have learners practise oral blending to develop phonemic awareness.

(3) Step 2: Letter-Sound Relationship Introduction.

-Explain to learners that the combination of the letters "S" and "H" stands for the /sh/ sound, as in "ship".

-On the blackboard, write "ship" and draw a picture.

-Then, with the teacher's finger running beneath each letter, blend the word "ship".

-Have a volunteer highlight the letters "SH".

-Refer to the letter team "SH" by having learners state the sound of the letters "SH".

-Continue having learners generate a list of words that contain the /sh/ sound and the digraph SH.

-Add the words to the blackboard, preferably with illustrations for EFL learners.

(4) Step 3: Word Blending.

-On the blackboard, write simple words beginning with the target letter.

-Write simple words that learners have already been taught.

-Write one or two sentences containing those words and some other high-frequency words.

For example: Sock, shock, sop, shop.

Fish, dish, hush, rush.

The ship is big.

I wish I had a red dish.

-Instruct learners to construct as many words as possible using the letters a, o, I, sh, m, f and p.

(5) Step 4: Word Recognition and Sound Discrimination.

On the blackboard, write a list of simple words with the target digraph SH and sound /sh/. Have learners identify which one is the word the teacher is currently reading. For instance: ship, fish, dish, wish or rush.

(6) Step 5: Decodable Text (Optional for EFL Learners).

Provide decodable reading practice for learners based on the target letter-sound relationship and previously acquired vocabulary. This step is optional, depending on their educational progress and abilities.

(7) Step 6: Dictation (Optional for EFL Learners).

Dictate simple vocabulary words from the day's lesson and record the answers on the blackboard. This is intended to assist learners in segmenting words and associating them with spelling. For EFL learners, the corresponding pictures can be displayed to help them connect the spelling to the meaning. This step is optional, depending on their educational progress and abilities.

4.4 Consonant Clusters Instruction in the SSP Model

4.4.1 Teaching Goals

(1) To familiarise learners with consonant cluster sounds.

(2) To assist learners in identifying "consonant clusters" within words.

4.4.2 Guidelines

(1) A consonant cluster consists of two or three consonants that occur together in a word and retain their sounds when blended. A consonant blend refers to the sounds represented by each cluster. Thus, the term "cluster" denotes the written form, whereas the term "blend" denotes the spoken form.

(2) Clusters are highly reliable. When the two letters are used together in a word, they almost always represent the blended sounds of each consonant.

(3) The lone significant exception is "SC", which could stand for the /sk/ sound, as in "scare" or the letter C could be silent, as in "science".

(4) Consonant clusters are classified into three major categories and three minor categories as follows:

Tab. 4.1

r-blend clusters	br, cr, dr, fr, gr, pr, tr
l-blend clusters	bl, cl, fl, gl, pl
s-blend clusters	sc, sk, sl, sm, sn, sp, st, sw
other blends clusters	tw, qu
three-letter consonant clusters	str, spt, thr
	chr, phr, shr (digraph+consonant)
four-letter consonant cluster	ngth, as in "strength" (digraph+digraph)

(5) After the single consonant and digraph, teach the consonant cluster.

(6) Categorical instruction rather than individual instruction is recommended.

(7) This whole section could be optional for EFL learners, depending on time constraints, their knowledge and abilities, as well as their phonemic awareness because the letters retain their sound. Learners with good phonemic awareness can sound out the letters.

4.4.3 Sample Lesson

Consonant Clusters

(1) Phonics Principle: S-blend cluster.

(2) Step 1: Review: Reread the story or passage which contains previously taught letter-sound relationships. Instruct learners to practise oral blending to develop phonemic awareness.

(3) Step 2: Letter-Sound Relationship Introduction.

-On the blackboard, write the words "snake", "stone" and "spot".

-In each word, underline the clusters "sn", "st" and "sp".

-Remind learners that the sounds are /sn/, /st/ and /sp/ (no need to write out the sound with slashes).

-Loudly blend each word as the teacher runs his or her finger beneath each letter.

-Ask a volunteer to highlight the letters "sp", "st" and "sn".

-Point to each cluster and invite learners to state chorally the sounds represented by the clusters.

-Continue to have learners create a word list that includes the target sounds.

-Add these words to the blackboard, preferably with illustrations for EFL learners.

(4) Step 3: Word Blending.

-On the blackboard, write simple words beginning with the target letter.

-Write simple previously learned words which learners can compare with the words containing the target letter.

-Write one or two sentences containing those words and some high-frequency words.

For example: Sock, shock, sop, shop.

Spot, stop, spit, snap.

I spot a sock/shop.

-Encourage learners to construct as many words as possible using the letters a, o, e, s, m, t, p and sh.

(5) Step 4: Word Recognition and Sound Discrimination.

On the blackboard, write a list of simple words with the target letter and sound. Have learners identify which one is the word the teacher is currently reading. Stop, stick, spit, spot and snap are just a few examples.

(6) Step 5: Decodable Text (Optional for EFL Learners).

Provide decodable reading practice for learners based on the target letter sound, its relationship and previously learned words. This step is optional, depending on their educational progress and abilities.

(7) Step 6: Dictation (Optional for EFL Learners).

Dictate simple vocabulary words from the day's lesson and record the answers on the blackboard. This is intended to assist learners in segmenting words and associating them with spelling. The corresponding pictures can be displayed to help EFL learners connect the spelling to the meaning. This step is optional, depending on their educational progress and abilities.

Adapted from Blevins (2017)

4.5 Silent Consonant Letters Instruction in the SSP Model (Optional When Needed)

The majority of consonant letters in the alphabet are occasionally silent in words. In general, consonants are silent because the pronunciation of a word has changed over time while the spelling has remained constant. Furthermore, silent consonants appear in words borrowed from other languages. Readers are occasionally unaware of such consonants when reading those words.

4.5.1 Teaching Goals

(1) To teach learners that words contain silent consonant letters.

(2) To assist learners in comprehending the rules governing the identification of silent consonants in words.

4.5.2 Guidelines

(1) The 15 most frequent silent consonant letter spellings among 170000 frequent words (Burmeister, 1971; Blevins, 2017) are listed in the table below. The letter in bold is silent.

Tab. 4.2

tch /ch/ as in ha**t**ch	**d**g /j/ as in lo**d**ge	**w**r /r/ as in **w**rite
kn /n/ as in **k**now	**g**n/n/ as in si**g**n	m**b**/m/ as in lam**b**
ps/s/ as in **p**sychology	**l**k /k/ as in ta**l**k	**l**m /m/ as in ca**l**m
r**h** /r/ as in r**h**ino	**d**j/j/ as in a**d**just	w**h**/h/ as in w**h**o
bt /t/ as in de**b**t	g**h**/g/ as in g**h**ost	m**n**/m/ as in hym**n**

(2) When necessary, but only after consonants, consonant clusters and consonant

digraphs, teach the silent consonant letters. Typically, silent letters are taught to intermediate and advanced learners when they encounter them in reading.

4.5.3 Sample Lesson

Silent Consonant Letters

(1) Phonics Principle. Silent letter spelling for "WR", as in "write".

(2) Step 1: Review. Reread the story or passage which contains previously taught letter-sound relationships. Have learners practise oral blending to develop phonemic awareness.

(3) Step 2: Letter-Sound Relationship Introduction.

-Explain to students that sometimes a letter does not represent a sound in a word; this is called a silent letter.

-On the blackboard, write "write" and emphasise that when the letters W and R work together, the letter W becomes silent.

-Then, as the teacher runs his or her finger beneath each letter, blend the word "write".

-Instruct a volunteer to highlight the letters "WR" and indicate which letter is silent.

-Ask learners to state the sound of the letters "WR" by pointing to the letters "WR".

-Continue to have students generate words beginning with the letters "WR" and ask them to look for these letter pairs in books or classrooms.

-Put on the blackboard a list of words that begin with "WR", preferably with illustrations for EFL learners.

(4) Step 3: Word Blending.

-On the blackboard, write simple words beginning with the target letter.

-Write simple words that have been previously learned so they can be compared to words beginning with the target letter.

-Create one or two sentences that include those words and some other frequently used words.

For example: Rap, wrap, wing, wring.

Wreck, wrong, wrist, wrinkle.

I wrap the wings.

-Instruct learners to construct as many words as possible using the letters wr, a, e, i s, t, p and ck.

(5) Step 4: Word Recognition and Sound Discrimination.

On the blackboard, write a list of simple words with the target letter and sound. Have learners identify which one is the word the teacher is currently reading. For example, "write", "wrist", "wreck" and "wrap" .

(6) Step 5: Decodable Text (Optional for EFL Learners) .

Provide decodable reading practice for students based on the target letter-sound relationship and previously acquired words. This step is optional, depending on their educational progress and abilities.

(7) Step 6: Dictation (Optional for EFL Learners) .

Dictate simple vocabulary words from the day's lesson and record the answers on the blackboard. This is intended to assist learners in segmenting words and associating them with spelling. For EFL learners, the corresponding pictures can be displayed to help students connect the spelling to the meaning. This step is optional, depending on their educational progress and abilities.

Adapted from Blevins (2017)

4.6 Short Vowel Sounds Instruction in the SSP Model

4.6.1 Teaching Goals

To assist learners to recognise the letter - sound relationship of a particular short vowel

4.6.2 Guidelines

Teach short vowel sounds using words with simple CVC structures like "cat", "sun" and "big" .

CVC Words for Instruction

Tab. 4.3

Short-A sound /a/	Short-E sound /e/	Short-I sound /i/	Short-O sound /o/	Short-U sound /u/
bad *	bed *	bib	box **	bud
bag **	bet	big **	cob	bug
cat **	fed	bit *	cot	bun
cab	get **	did **	dog **	bus **
can **	hen	dig *	fog	but **
cap **	jet	dip	fox	cub

续表

Short-A sound /a/	Short-E sound /e/	Short-I sound /i/	Short-O sound /o/	Short-U sound /u/
cat **	led	fix *	got **	cup *
dad **	leg **	fit *	hog	cut *
fan	let **	hid *	hop	dug **
fat *	men **	him **	hot **	fun *
gas	met	hip	job *	gun *
had **	net	hit *	jog	hug
has **	pen **	kid **	lot *	hut
hat	pet *	kit	mom **	jug
jam	red **	lid	mop	mud
lab *	set	lip	not **	mug
mad *	ten **	lit **	pod	nut
man **	vet	pig **	pop	pup
map **	web	pin	pot	rub
mat	wet *	pit	rod	rug
pad	yes **	rib	son **	run **
pal	yet *	rid	top *	sub
pan		rip		sum
pat		sit **		sun
rag		six **		tub
ram		tip		tug
ran **		wig		
rap		win *		
rat		zip		
sad **				
sat				
tag				
tan				
tap				
van				
wag				

* means on the vocabulary list at National Curriculum level 2 and ** means on the list at level 3

4.6.3 Sample Lesson

Short Vowel Sounds

(1) Phonics Principle. The letter A can stand for the short-A sound /a/, as in "cat".

(2) Step 1: Review. Reread the story or passage which contains previously taught letter-sound relationships Have learners practise oral blending to develop phonemic awareness.

(3) Step 2: Letter-Sound Relationship Introduction.

-Explore with learners the possibility of the letter A standing for the short-A sound /a/, as in "cat".

-Write "cat" on the blackboard and display a cat image.

-Then, with the teacher's finger running beneath each letter, blend the word "cat".

-Ask a volunteer to highlight the letter "A".

-Ask learners to state the sound associated with the letter "A".

-Continue to have learners generate words that contain the letter short-A.

-Put the list of short-A words on the blackboard, preferably with illustrations for EFL learners.

(4) Step 3: Word Blending.

-On the blackboard, write simple words beginning with the target letter.

-Write simple words that have been previously learned so they can be compared to words beginning with the target letter/.

-Create one or two sentences that include those words and some other frequently used words.

For example: At, sat, mat, cat.

Am, mad, lap, sad.

The cat sat on the mat.

I am mad.

-Encourage learners to create as many words as possible using the letters a, s, t, m, c, d and p.

(5) Step 4: Word Recognition and Sound Discrimination.

On the blackboard, write a list of simple words with the target letter and sound. Have learners identify which one is the word the teacher is currently reading. Consider "ham", "lamb", "fab" and "nap".

(6) Step 5: Decodable Text (Optional for EFL Learners).

Provide decodable reading practice for learners based on the target letter sound, its relationship and previously learned words. This step is optional, depending on their educational progress and abilities.

(7) Step 6: Dictation (Optional for EFL Learners).

Dictate simple vocabulary words from the day's lesson and record the answers on the blackboard. This is intended to assist learners in segmenting words and associating them with spelling. For EFL learners, the corresponding pictures can be displayed to help students connect the spelling to the meaning. This step is optional, depending on their educational progress and abilities.

Blevins (2017)

4.7 Long Vowel Sounds Instruction in the SSP Model

4.7.1 Teaching Goals

To assist students in recognising the letter-sound correspondences for specific long vowel sounds

4.7.2 Guidelines

(1) Introduce long vowel sounds through simple, one-syllable words. The CVCe structure (consonant-vowel-consonant-e) is recommended to begin the instruction as this pattern is beneficial and reliable for long vowels. Since the final "e" is silent in this structure, it is also referred to as a silent-e. In some books, it is referred to as the e-marker, which serves as a diacritical mark to alert the reader that the preceding vowel was almost certainly a long vowel sound.

(2) Contrasts between the CVC and CVCe patterns can be used in the instruction to demonstrate how a single letter can make a major difference to the vowel sound of a word.

The following reference list contains the CVC and CVCe pattern contrasts:

Tab. 4.4

Word list of CVC and CVCe pattern contrasts

bit-bite	past-paste	can-cane	us-use
cod-code	rag-rage	cub-cube	fat-fate
dim-dime	rip-ripe	fad-fade	not-note

续表

Word list of CVC and CVCe pattern contrasts			
fin-fine	scrap-scrape	glob-globe	fin-fine
grad-grade	slid-slide	hat-hate	pal/pale
hop-hope	spin-spine	kit-kite	shin-shine
man-mane	twin-twine	mat-mate	pan-pane
mad-made	wag-wage	rob-robe	hid-hide
tap-tape	not-note	rod-rode	slop-slope
van-vane			

These lists of VCe words can be used for instruction:

Long-A sound in VCe patterns:

Tab. 4. 5

VCe Words List: Long-A sound /ai/ A_E pattern				
ace	age *	bake	base	blade
blame	blaze	brace	brake	brave **
cage	cake *	came **	cane	cape
case	cave	chase	crane	crate
date *	daze	drape	face *	fade
fake	fame	flake	flame	game *
gate **	gave **	gaze	glaze	grace
grade	grape *	grate	grave	haste
hate **	haze	jade	lace	lake *
lame	lane	late *	made **	make *
male	mane	mate	name *	pace
page **	pale **	pane	paste	pave
place *	plane *	plate **	quake	race **
rage	rake	rate	rave	safe *
sake	sale **	same **	save **	scale
scrape	shade	shake **	shame **	shape **
shave	skate	slate	snake **	space *
spade	stage	stake	stale	state **

续表

VCe Words List: Long-A sound /ai/ A_E pattern				
take *	tale	tame	tape **	taste **
trace	trade **	vane	vase	wade
wage	wake *	wave **	waste **	whale **
* means on the vocabulary list at National Curriculum level 2 and ** means on the list at level 3.				
EXCEPTIONS: Advantage, are, average, breakage, cabbage, climate, courage, delicate, furnace, have, manage, message, palace, passage, private, purchase, senate, separate, surface, village				

Long-I sound in VCe patterns:

Tab. 4.6

Long-I sound /igh/ I_E pattern			
bike *	bite	bride	chime
crime	dice	dime	dine
dive	drive *	file	fine *
five *	glide	hide **	hike **
hive	kite *	lice	life **
like *	lime	pine	pipe
price **	pride **	rice *	ride **
ripe	rise **	shine	side **
slice	slide	slime	smile **
spice	spike	spine	stride
strike	stripe	swine	tide
tile	time *	twice	twine
vine	while **	white *	wide **
wife **	wipe	wise **	write *
* means on the vocabulary list at National Curriculum level 2 and ** means on the list at level 3.			
EXCEPTIONS: Active, aggressive, automobile, determine, engine, expressive, favourite, figurine, give, justice, live, machine, magazine, massive, native, notice, office, opposite, police, practice, promise, representative, routine, service			

Long-O sound in VCe patterns:

Tab. 4. 7

Long-O sound /oa/O_E pattern				
bone	broke **	choke	chose	code
cone	dome	drove **	globe	hole **
home *	hope **	hose	joke **	lone
mole	nose *	note **	poke	pole
role **	rode **	rope **	rose **	slope
smoke **	spoke **	stole **	stone **	stove
stroke	those **	tone	vote	whole **
woke **	zone			
* means on the vocabulary list at National Curriculum level 2 and ** means on the list at level 3.				
EXCEPTIONS: Above, become, come, done, glove, gone, improve, lose, love, lovely, move, movement, none, purpose, remove, shove, some, something, welcome, whose				

Long-U sound in VCe patterns:

Tab. 4. 8

Long-U sound /yoo/ U_E pattern					
cube	cute *	cure	fuse	mule	use *
* means on the vocabulary list at National Curriculum level 2 and ** means on the list at level 3.					
EXCEPTIONS: Assure, conclude, crude, flute, include, June, measure, pleasure, prune, rude, rule, sure, treasure					

Apart from the VCe pattern and the "silent-E" marker, many vowel spellings are formed by vowel digraphs. Vowel digraphs, such as "AI", "AY" and "EE", are also called vowel pairs or vowel teams. Numerous vowel teams consist of long vowel sounds.

Tab. 4. 9

Vowel digraphs of long-A sound /ai/			
Vowel digraph	Sounds	Example	Predictability
AI	Long-A sound /ai/	rain	74%
EI		rein	40%
-AY		say	96%
-EY		convey	20%

续表

Vowel digraphs of long-A sound /ai/			
Vowel digraph	Sounds	Example	Predictability
EA	Long-E sound /ee/	seat	51%
EE		bee	86%
-EY		key	58%
-IE		chief	51%
OA	Long-O sound /oa/	boat	94%
OW		snow	50%
EW	Long-U sound /yoo/	few	95%

4.7.3 Sample Lesson

Long Vowel Sounds

(1) Phonics Principle. The letter team "EA" and "EE" can stand for the long-E sound /ee/, as in "bee".

(2) Step 1: Review. Reread the story or passage which contains previously taught letter-sound relationships. Have learners practise oral blending to develop phonemic awareness.

(3) Step 2: Letter-Sound Relationship Introduction.

-Explore with learners the possibility that the letters "EA" and "EE" stand for the long-E sound /ee/, as in "bee".

-Write "bee", "seat" and "field" on the blackboard and demonstrate with pictures.

-Then, as the teacher runs his or her finger under each letter, blend the words.

-Ask a volunteer to highlight the letters "EA" and "EE".

-Ask learners to state the sound for the letters "EE" and "EA".

-Continue to have learners generate words containing the letters "EE" and "EA" and that begin with the long-E sound.

-Put a list of long-E sounding words on the blackboard, preferably with pictures for EFL learners.

(4) Step 3: Word Blending.

-Write simple words on the blackboard using the target letters.

-Write simple words that learners have already been taught.

-Write one or two sentences containing those words and some other high-frequency words.

For example: Bet, beat, fed, feed.

Leaf, need, flea, bee.

The bee is on the leaf.

-Instruct learners to construct as many words as possible using the letters ee, ea, s, d, t, p, k and l.

(5) Step 4: Word Recognition and Sound Discrimination.

On the blackboard, write a list of simple words with the target letter and sounds. Have students identify which one is the word the teacher is currently reading. "Clean", "flee", "bee", "mean", "bean" and "seat" are all examples.

(6) Step 5: Decodable Text (Optional for EFL Learners).

Provide decodable reading practice for learners based on the target letter-sound relationship and previously acquired words. This step is optional, depending on their educational progress and abilities.

(7) Step 6: Dictation (Optional for EFL Learners).

Dictate simple vocabulary words from the day's lesson and record the answers on the blackboard. This is intended to assist learners in segmenting words and associating them with spelling. For EFL learners, the corresponding pictures can be displayed to help learners connect the spelling to the meaning. This step is optional, depending on their educational progress and abilities.

Adapted from Blevins (2017)

4.8 Other Vowel Sounds Instruction in the SSP Model

4.8.1 Teaching Goals

(1) To familiarise learners with the letter-sound correspondences of diphthongs.

(2) To familiarise learners with the letter-sound correspondences of variant vowels.

(3) To familiarise learners with the letter-sound correspondences of r-controlled vowels.

(4) To familiarise learners with the schwa (optional).

4.8.2 Guidelines

(1) Diphthongs.

Diphthongs are vowel sounds produced by the mouth gliding (Blevins, 2017; Bear et al., 2020).

-The diphthong /oi/ is denoted by the letters OY or OI, as in "boy" or "oil".

-The diphthong /ou/ is denoted by the letters OU or OW, as in "blouse" or "cow".

(2) Variant Vowel Sounds.

Certain vowel digraphs represent sounds that are not commonly classified as long or short vowel sounds; these are referred to as variant vowel sounds:

Tab. 4. 10

Variant vowel sound	Corresponding digraph	Examples	Percentage
/ou/	OU	house	35
	OW	how	48
Long /oo/	UI	fruit	53
	OO	food	59
Short /oo/	OO	look	36
/or/ (broad-O sound)	AW	hawk	100
	AU	haul	94

(*Adapted from Blevins*, 2017)

Note: *i*) *The broad-O sound /or/ is also classified as an r-controlled vowel sound in the preceding table. ii*) *The digraph "OO" is assigned both a long and a short /oo/ sound, with the long /oo/ sound being more frequent in words. While there is no way to determine which /oo/ sound corresponds to the given "OO" visually, readers may attempt both versions to determine which makes the most sense in the context; this may be determined by the reader's accumulation of listening vocabulary* (*Bishop*, 1986; *Blevins*, 2017).

(3) R-Controlled Vowel Sounds.

Bear et al. (2020) referred to r-controlled vowels as r-influenced vowels. In r-controlled words, the letter R affects the way the preceding vowel is pronounced. More specifically, when the letter R appears at the end of a word or just before a different consonant letter, the letter R converts the preceding short vowel sound into an r-controlled vowel sound, such as in "far", "bird", "fork" and "burn" (Bishop, 1986). The following table lists r-controlled vowels:

Tab. 4. 11

R-controlled vowel sound	Common spelling patterns	Examples
/ur/	-ER	her, fern, herb, perfect
	-IR	bird, first, girl, stir
	UR	urn, purse, burn, curl
	EAR	earn, learn, pearl, search

续表

R-controlled vowel sound	Common spelling patterns	Examples
/ar/	AR	far, barn, harsh, arm
/or/	OR	fork, horn, for, horse
	OAR	board, coarse, oar, soar
/air/	AIR	hair, fair, pair, stair
	-ARE	care, aware, share, scare
	-EAR	bear, pear, tear, wear

(4) Schwa.

According to some linguists, the schwa is not a distinct sound but a variant of an unstressed sound in a word. Therefore, it is referred to as a murmuring or neutral sound. It is complicated to teach. While the schwa can typically be learned through daily reading and listening, it is optional for EFL learners, depending on their teachers and the teaching schedule.

4.8.3 Sample Lesson

Diphthong /oi/

(1) Phonics Principle. The letter teams "OY" and "OI" can stand for the sound /oi/, as in "boy" and "boil".

(2) Step 1: Review. Reread the story or passage which contains previously taught letter-sound relationships. Have learners practise oral blending to develop phonemic awareness.

(3) Step 2: Letter-Sound Relationship Introduction.

-Explain to learners that the letters OY and OI can stand for /oi/ as in boil.

-Put the words "boy" and "boil" on the blackboard and display matching images.

-Then, with the teacher's finger running beneath each letter, blend the words "boy" and "boil".

-Assign a volunteer to highlight the letters "OY" and "OI".

-Ask learners to state the sound for the letters "OY" and "OI".

-Continue to have students generate words that contain the diphthong /oi/.

-Put the list of words containing the diphthong /oi/ on the blackboard, preferably with illustrations for EFL learners.

(4) Step 3: Word Blending.

-On the blackboard, write simple words beginning with the target sounds.

–Write simple words that learners have already been taught to compare.

–Write one or two sentences containing those words and some other high–frequency words.

For example: Boy, point, boil, toy.

Joy, oyster, join, noise.

The boy enjoys the toy.

–Encourage learners to construct as many words as possible using oi, oy, b, l, n, c and j.

(5) Step 4: Word Recognition and Sound Discrimination.

On the blackboard, write a list of simple words with the target letters and sound. Have learners identify which one is the word the teacher is currently reading. Consider joy, boy, noise and soil.

(6) Step 5: Decodable Text (Optional for EFL Learners).

Provide decodable reading practice for learners based on the target letter sound, its relationship and previously learned words. This step is optional, depending on their educational progress and abilities. Typically, at this point, decodable readers can be distributed to EFL learners to boost their confidence and reinforce decoding rules. Certain high–frequency irregular words are remembered as sight words due to reading decodable readers, while others can be acquired through phonograms.

(7) Step 6: Dictation (Optional for EFL Learners).

Dictate simple vocabulary words from the day's lesson and record the answers on the blackboard. This is intended to assist learners in segmenting words and associating them with spelling. For EFL learners, the corresponding pictures can be displayed to help them connect the spelling to the meaning. This step is optional, depending on their educational progress and abilities.

Adapted from Blevins (2017)

4.9 Instruction of Phonograms, Sight Words and Irregulars

Given the sample instructions represented above, learners have theoretically been equipped with phonics decoding rules up to this point. If possible, EFL learners should be provided with decodable readers to boost their confidence in phonics reading and decoding rules. Some of the more frequently occurring irregular words are learned as sight words, while others are learned as phonograms. High–frequency phonograms can be introduced to students at this time, if possible during reading sessions, because the letter–

sound relationships are already being established in their minds as they read. As Blevins (2017) pointed out, phonograms are inappropriate for beginner students. Alternatively, students may prefer to read via analogy rather than letter-sound correspondence. After mastering letter-sound relationships, readers can eventually recognise words by sight (to build their sight word vocabulary) and recognise common spelling patterns (phonograms) in unfamiliar words, which is critical for developing reading fluency. As mentioned previously, 84% of regular words can be decoded during this process, while some irregulars can be acquired through sight words or phonograms.

Overall, therefore:

(1) Phonograms, particularly those with a high frequency, can be instructed when necessary.

(2) Sight words can be acquired or accumulated through the use of decodable or graded readers.

(3) Both phonograms and sight words can be used to teach irregular words.

The National Curriculum for English Compulsory Education requires only fundamental letter-sound relationships. Therefore, the preceding section includes content on phonics decoding rules and phonics instruction, which are the primary objectives of the instructional guide. Tables containing sight words, phonograms and other resources are included as appendices.

4.10 Discussion on Rules and Generalisations

Through systematic and explicit synthetic phonics instruction, learners' attention shifts from individual letters to letter-sound relationships, including blending and segmenting sounds in different words or word patterns. With sufficient opportunities for practice and experimentation, phonics decoding rules or generalisations are gradually categorised and internalised in their minds. While these rules or generalisations are beneficial for students to practise and apply to specific spelling patterns, they should not be over-emphasised or taken as absolute. In that regard, Blevins (2017) established the following teaching guidelines to follow when instructing students on rules or generalisations:

(1) Avoid emphasising rules in phonics instruction, which is merely a tool to assist learners in focusing on specific spelling patterns to decode and recognise various unfamiliar words.

(2) Teach only the most valuable rules to learners and avoid using technical lan-

guage in instruction.

(3) Emphasise the application of rules rather than their verbalisation; once learners understand how to apply a rule, there is no reason to spend time on it.

(4) Teach learners the rules at the optimal time for comprehension and application.

(5) Avoid presenting rules as absolutes. Ensure learners understand critical exceptions to these generalisations.

The following table contains a list of generalisations. It was updated by Blevins (2017), who discovered that fewer than half of the rules worked up to 75% of the time. As a result, some adaptations have been made in this guide. Only decoding rules that account for over 95% of utility are listed. Furthermore, the generalisations are ordered by utility rate:

Tab. 4.12

Category	Generalisation	Example	Utility
Consonant Generalisations	1. When the letter C is before O or A, it has a /k/ sound.	cat	100%
	2. When-CK is at the final position of a word, it has a /k/ sound.	cock	100%
	3. In the spelling pattern-ight, the letter team "GH" is silent.	right	100%
	4. In the letter team "KN", K is silent.	knock	100%
	5. In the letter team "WR", W is silent.	write	100%
	6. When one consonant letter is doubled in a word, one letter is silent.	berry	99%
	7. When the letter C is before I or E, it has an /s/ sound.	cent	96%
Vowel Generalisations	8. The letter team "EE" represents the long-E sound /ee/.	bee	98%

4.11 Phonics Lesson Don'ts

Blevins (2017) proposed several "don'ts" for teachers to consider, based on extensive observations of phonics classes. The corresponding guidelines were adapted for the EFL context in this guide:

(1) Avoid instruction that fails to communicate directly to learners what they should perceive and how the teacher wants them to respond.

(2) Avoid correcting learners' errors immediately. Provide feedback following the provision of self-monitoring and self-correction opportunities.

(3) Avoid addressing exceptions to rules that learners are learning in a defective

manner.

(4) Avoid using imprecise or technique-specific terminology in instruction. For instance:

(A) Instead of asking, "What sounds do you see at the end of the word cat?", please say "hear" instead of see.

(B) Instead of saying, "The letter T makes a /t/ sound", please say "The letter T stands for the T sound".

(C) Instead of saying, "The letters OI are a diphthong", please say "The vowel pair / vowel team/ letter team / digraph stands for the /oi/ sound".

4.12 Phonics Lesson Dos

Blevins (2017) compiled a list of recommendations for teachers, based on systematic and explicit phonics instruction. These suggestions were tailored to the EFL context in this guide.

(1) Maintain a logical sequence.

(2) Be explicit in instructing students on letter-sound correspondences.

(3) Consistently provide weekly or daily lessons.

(4) Maintain the focus of each lesson.

(5) Begin a lesson by utilising what students already know.

(6) Incorporate a review into each lesson via, for example, blending exercises or repeated reading.

(7) Tailor the scope and sequence of instruction to the learners' needs and receptive abilities.

(8) Integrate dictation or other spelling activities into phonics instruction.

Appendices　Word List for Instruction Reference

Part Ⅰ　Consonant Sounds List

The following tables contain two types of word lists:

(1) For instruction, the basic vocabularies required by the National Curriculum for English Compulsory Education are listed alphabetically by letter sound.

(2) Word list adapted from Blevins' (2017) "phonics instruction list". The adaptations are based on Hepplewhite (2020) and National English Curriculum for Compulsory Education (2011).

Blevins (2017) and Hepplewhite (2020) suggested the following uses for the word list:

(1) To compile a list of words for the blending exercise.

(2) To construct sentences or connected text to practice reading.

(3) To create sorting games based on words.

(4) To compile a list of words for use in dictation and spelling.

/b/ as in bat

Words begin with /b/ sound in National Curriculum					
baby *	back *	bad *	bag *	ball *	banana *
basketball *	be *	bear *	beautiful *	bed *	before *
begin *	beside *	between *	big *	bike *	bicycle *
bird *	birthday *	black *	blackboard *	blue *	boat *
body *	book *	box *	boy *	bread *	breakfast *
bring *	brother *	brown *	bus *	busy *	but *
by *	background	balloon **	bamboo **	banana *	bank **

续表

Words begin with /b/ sound in National Curriculum					
basic **	basket **	bathroom **	beach *	bean **	beat **
because *	become **	bedroom **	beef **	believe **	bell **
below **	beast	better **	bill **	birth **	biscuit **
bit **	bully **	burn **	blind **	block **	blood **
blouse **	blow **	board **	bored	boring **	born **
boss **	borrow **	both **	bottle **	bottom **	bowl **
brain **	brave **	break **	bridge **	bright **	Britain **
British **	brush **	build **	building **	burn **	business **
/b/ represented by B in initial position					
back *	bad *	badge	bag *	bait	bake
ball *	balloon **	ban	band **	bank **	bar
barn	base *	basket **	bass	bat **	batch
bath **	bathe	beach *	bead	beak	beam
bean	bear *	beast	bed **	bee *	beef **
been **	beet	beg	bell **	belt **	bench
bend	bent	best **	bet	bib	bid
big *	bike *	bill **	bin **	bind	birch
bird *	bit **	bite	boar	boast	boat *
bog	boil **	bold	bone	book *	boom
boost	boot	bop	born **	boss **	botch
both **	bottle **	bound	bow	bowl **	box *
boy *	buck	bud	budge	bug	bull
bum	bump	bun	bunch	bunk	bunt
burn *	burst	bus *	but *	butterfly	button
buzz	by *				
/b/ represented by B in final position					
bib	cab	cob	club **	crab	crab
crib	cub	grab	job *	knob	lab **
rib	rob	rub	scrub	sob	sub

* means vocabulary list on national curriculum level 2 and ** means on level 3.

/d/ as in dog

Words begin with /d/ sound in National Curriculum

dad	dance *	day *	dear *	desk *	difficult *
dinner *	dirty *	do *	doctor *	door *	down *
duck *	daily **	danger **	dangerous **	dark **	date **
daughter **	dead **	deaf **	deal **	dear *	December **
decide **	decision	deep **	degree **	delicious **	depend **
describe **	desk *	develop **	development	dialogue **	diary **
dictionary **	die **	difference **	different **	difficult *	difficulty
dig **	dining **	discover **	direct *	direction *	director *
discovery *	discuss **	discussion	divide **	dish **	dollar **
double **	doubt **	dream **	drive **	drop **	dry **
dumpling **	during **				

/d/ represented by D in initial position

dad	debt	dig **	disk	door *	dune
damp	deck	deep **	deer	den	dent
desk *	dew	did **	die **	dig **	dill
dim	dime	dine	ding	dip	dirt
dirty *	dish **	disk	dive	do *	dock
doe	dog *	doll *	dollar	dome	done *
door *	dose **	dot	down *	doze	duck *
due	dug	dull	dump	dune	dunk
dusk	dust	dye			

/d/ represented by D in final position

bad *	bead	bed *	bid	bird *	braid
bread *	bud	cloud **	cod	creed	did **
fad	fed	feed **	food *	freed	glad **
good *	greed	hand *	hid **	hood	kid *
lad	laid *	lead **	led **	lid	load
loud **	mad **	mood	mud	need **	nod *
pad	paid **	plead	plod	pod	pond
raid	read *	red *	rid	road **	rod
sad *	said **	seed	sled	slid	sod

续表

/d/ represented by D in final position					
speed *	spud	stead	steed	stood **	toad
wed	weed	wood **	word *		
* means vocabulary list on national curriculum level 2 and ** means on level 3.					

/f/ as in fan

Words begin with /f/ sound in National Curriculum					
face *	family *	fan *	far *	farm *	farmer *
farm *	fast *	father *	favorite *	feel *	film *
find *	fine *	fish *	floor *	flower *	fly *
food *	foot *	feet **	football *	for *	friend *
from **	fruit *	**ph**oto *	fact **	factory **	fail **
fair **	fall **	famous *	fantastic **	fat **	fear **
February **	feed **	feeling **	festival *	fever *	few *
field *	fifteen *	fifth *	fifty *	fight *	fill *
finally *	finger *	finish *	fire *	first *	fisherman *
fit *	five *	fix *	flag *	follow **	foot *
feet *	force **	foreign **	forest **	forget **	fork **
form **	forty **	four *	fourteen **	fourth **	France **
free *	fresh **	Friday **	fridge **	friendly **	from *
front *	fruit *	full ***	fun *	funny **	future **
/f/ represented by F in initial position					
fad	fade	fail **	faint	fair **	fake
fall **	false	fame	fan *	far *	farm *
fast *	fate	feast	feather	fed **	feed **
feel *	fell	fence	few **	fib	fig
fight *	file	film *	fine *	fire *	first **
fish *	fist	fit **	five **	foam	foe
foil	fold	folk	fond	fool	foot *
football *	for *	force	fork **	form **	fort
four **	fowl	fox **	fun **	fur	fuse
fuzz					

续表

/f/ represented by F in final position					
beef	brief	chef	chief	deaf **	elf
goof	grief	hoof	if **	knife **	leaf **
loaf	off *	proof	reef	roof	scarf
shelf	spoof	wolf			
/f/ represented by-ff in medial/ final position					
cliff	coffee	cuff	huff	puff	fluffy
/f/ represented by PH in initial position					
phone *	phoneme	phonics	photo *	photograph *	phrase
physics **	physical				
/f/ represented by PH in final position					
cough **	enough **	laugh **	rough	tough	photograph *
* means vocabulary list on national curriculum level 2 and ** means on level 3.					

/g/ as in gate

Words begin with /g/ sound in National Curriculum					
game *	girl *	get *	give *	go *	good *
goodbye *	grandpa *	grandfather *	grandma *	grandmother *	grass *
great *	green *	garden *	gate **	glad **	glass *
glove **	glue **	go *	gold **	government **	grade **
grammar **	granddaughter	grandparent	grandson	grape *	grey **
ground **	group **	grow **	guard **	guess **	guest **
guide **	guitar **	gun **			
/g/ represented by G in initial position					
gain	game *	gap	gasp	gate *	gave **
gear	geese	get *	gift *	gill	girl *
give *	go *	goal **	goat	goes **	gold **
golf	gone **	good *	goof	goose	guitar **
gum	gun **	gush	gust		
/g/ represented by G in the final position					
bag *	big *	bog	bug	chug	clog
dig **	dog *	drag	drug	dug **	fig

续表

/g/ represented by G in the final position					
flag *	fog **	frog	hog	hug **	jig
jug	keg	lag	leg *	log	lug
meg	mug	nag	peg	pig *	plug
rag	rig	rug	sag	shag	shrug
smug	snag	snug	tag	tug	twig
wag	wig	zag	zig		
* means vocabulary list on national curriculum level 2 and ** means on level 3.					

/h/ as in hat

Words begin with /h/ sound in National Curriculum					
hair *	half *	hand *	happy *	have *	he *
head *	healthy *	hear *	heavy *	hello *	help *
her *	here *	hi *	high **	him *	his *
holiday *	home *	horse *	hospital *	hot *	hour *
house *	how *	hungry *	habit **	hall **	hamburger **
handbag	handsome **	hang **	happen **	hard *	hardly **
harmful	hat **	hate **	headache	heart **	heat **
helpful *	hen **	hero **	hers **	herself **	hide **
high **	hill *	himself **	history **	hit **	hobby **
hold **	hole **	home **	hometown *	homework **	honest **
hope **	horse **	hospital *	hotel **	however **	huge **
human *	humorous *	hundred *	hungry *	hurry *	hurt *
husband **					
/h/ represented by H in initial position					
hair *	half *	hall **	halt	ham	hammer
hand *	hang **	hard *	hare	has *	hat **
hate **	have *	hay	he *	head *	heal
hear **	heard *	heart *	heat	heel	help *
hen **	her *	here *	high **	hill *	him *
hip	his *	hit *	hive	hoe	hog
hold **	hole **	home *	hood	hoof	hook

续表

/h/ represented by H in initial position					
hop	hope **	horn	horse *	hose	hot *
house *	how *	hum	hung **	hunt **	hurl
hurt *	husk	hut			
* means vocabulary list on national curriculum level 2 and ** means on level 3.					

/j/ as in jump

Words begin with /j/ sound in National Curriculum					
juice **	jump **	jacket *	January **	Japan **	Japanese **
job *	join **	joke **	journey **	July **	June **
just *					
/j/ represented by J in initial position					
jab	jacket **	jade	jail	jam	jar
jaw	jay	jeans	jeep	jerk	jet
jig	job *	jog	join	joke *	jolt
joy **	jug	juice *	July *	jump **	jump rope
June **	junk	jury	just **		
/j/ represented by-DGE in final position					
badge	bridge **	budge	dodge	edge	fidget
fudge	gadget	grudge	ledge	lodge	nudge
ridge	smudge	wedge			
/j/ represented by GE, -GE and G					
garage	gee	gem	general **	generous	genius
geography *	George	geranium	germ	giant	ginger
gingerbread	giraffe *	gym **	gypsy	age *	change **
collage	courage **	damage	danger **	engineer **	forge
fringe	hinge	huge **	large **	magic **	manage **
message **	orange *	package	page **	passage **	pigeon
rage	stage **	singe	strange **	stranger	urgent
village **	wage				
* means vocabulary list on national curriculum level 2 and ** means on level 3.					

/k/ as in kite

Words begin with /k/ in National Curriculum

kid *	kind *	kitchen *	kite *	cake *	call *
can *	candy *	cap *	car *	card *	cat *
class *	clean *	clever *	clock *	close *	clothes *
close *	cloud **	coat *	cold *	color *	come *
computer *	cook *	cool *	cousin *	cow *	crayon
cry *	keep *	key *	keyboard *	kick *	kill *
kilo *	kilometer *	king *	kiss *		

/k/ represented by K in initial position

kale	keen	keep *	kelp	kettle	kept **
key **	kid *	kill **	kilt	kind *	king **
kiss **	kit	kite *	kitten		

/k/ represented by K in medial/final position

bank **	beak	bike *	bleak	book *	break **
cook *	desk *	fork **	hook	leak	look *
milk *	oak	pink *	peek	seek	shook **
sick **	silk **	sock *	speak *	think *	took **
weak **	week *				

/k/ represented by-CK in medial / final position

back *	black *	block **	brick	buck	bucket
checkers	chick	chicken *	click **	clock *	crack
deck	dock	duck *	jack	kick **	lack
lick	lock **	locket	luck **	muck	neck **
nickel	pack **	packet **	pick **	pocket **	quack
quick **	rack	racket	rock *	rocket	sack
shack	shock	sick *	slack	slick	snack
sock *	socket	speck	stack	stick **	stock
stockings	stuck **	suck	tack	tick	ticket **
track	trick	truck **	thick **	wick	wreck

/k/ represented by C in initial position

cap *	cake *	call *	came **	camp **	can *
Canada **	cap **	cape	car *	card *	care **

续表

/k/ represented by C in initial position					
clock *	candy *	cartoon **	come *	cat *	color *
coal *	coast **	coat *	cook *	cool *	cover **
coin **	copy *	crayon **	corn *	cost *	cot
cough *	could **	count **	corner **	cover **	cow *
cup *	cry *	crazy	cross **	cut *	cute *
* means vocabulary list on national curriculum level 2 and ** means on level 3.					

/l/ as in leaf

Words begin with /l/ sound in National Curriculum					
lake *	late *	left *	leg *	library *	light *
like *	listen *	little *	live *	long *	look *
love *	luck **	lab *	lady **	land **	language **
large **	last *	later **	laugh **	law **	lay **
lazy **	lead **	leader *	leaf **	learn *	least **
leave **	lemon **	lend	less **	letter *	level **
lie **	life **	lift **	line **	lion *	list **
litter **	lively **	local **	lock **	London **	lonely **
lose **	lot *	loud **	lovely **	low **	luck **
lucky	lab **				
/l/ represented by L in the initial position					
lab **	lace	lack	lad	ladder	lag
laid	lake *	lamp	land **	lane	lap
lash	last *	latch	late *	leaf *	leak
lean	leap	least **	leaves **	left **	leg *
lemon *	lend	less *	lest	let *	lick
lie **	life **	lift **	light *	like *	limp
line **	link	lion *	lip	list **	lit **
live *	loaf	loan	local **	log	lose **
long *	look *	loose	lot *	love *	luck **
lug	lump	lunch *	lunchbox		

续表

/l/ sound in the final position					
bail	boil **	bowl **	cancel **	coal	coil
cool *	fail **	feel *	foil	girl *	hotel **
heal	heel	jail	mail	meal **	nail
national	oil **	pupil	pencil *	pool **	pretzel
rail *	sail	school **	seal	special *	soil
steal *	steel	tail *	tool **	towel	veal
veil	wheel **				
/l/ represented by-LL in final position					
ball *	bill **	call *	dill	doll *	dull
fall **	fill **	ill *	hall **	hill *	kill **
mill	pill **	sell *	small *	still **	tell *
tall *	wall *	well *	will *	yell	
* means vocabulary list on national curriculum level 2 and ** means on level 3.					

/m/ as in mop

Words begin with /m/ sound in National Curriculum					
make *	man *	men **	many *	map *	math *
me *	meet *	milk *	minute *	Miss *	monkey *
month *	moon *	morning *	mother *	mouth *	Mr. *
Mrs. *	much *	music *	my *	machine **	mad **
magazine **	magic **	main **	manage **	manager	March **
mark **	market **	marry **	match **	matter **	may *
maybe **	meal **	mean **	meaning **	meat *	meeting **
member **	mention **	menu **	mess **	message **	method **
meter **	middle *	might **	mile **	milk *	mind **
mine **	miss **	missing *	mistake **	mix **	mobile **
model **	modern **	Monday **	money *	more **	most **
mum **	mountain **	mouse *	mouth *	move *	movie
museum	musician	must *	myself **		
/m/ represented by M in the initial position					
mad **	made **	maid	main **	make *	man *

续表

/m/ represented by M in the initial position					
mane	many *	map *	marble	march *	marry *
mask	mat	match **	may *	meal **	mean **
meat *	men **	mend	menu **	mess **	met **
mice	mild	mile **	milk **	mill	mind **
mine **	mirror *	miss **	mist	missing	mitten
mix **	moan	moat	monkey *	moon *	mop
more **	most **	motorcycle	mouse *	mouth *	move *
much *	music *	mud	mug	my **	must *
/m/ represented by M in final position					
beam	bottom **	broom	clam **	dream **	drum
film **	farm *	firm	form **	from **	gram
gum	ham	him *	hum	jam	mum *
mom **	plum	ram	roam	room *	Sam
gem	scream	gloom	seam	seem	slam
storm **	swim *	steam	sum	team **	them *
term **	whom **	worm	warm *	yam	yum
zoom					
* means vocabulary list on national curriculum level 2 and ** means on level 3.					

/n/ as in nest

Words begin with /n/ sound in National Curriculum					
name *	near *	new *	next *	nice *	night *
no *	noodle *	nose *	not *	now *	nurse *
national	natural	nature **	nearly **	necessary **	neck **
need **	neither **	nervous **	never *	news **	newspaper **
nine **	nineteen **	ninety **	ninth **	nobody *	nod
noise **	noisy *	none **	noon **	nor **	north **
northern	nose *	not *	notebook **	nothing **	notice **
November **	number **				
/n/ represented by N in initial position					
name *	neck **	next *	nine **	not *	nature **

续表

/n/ represented by N in initial position					
need **	nice *	no *	note **	nail	noodle *
nest	net	new *	newspaper **	next *	nice *
nine **	night *	nib	nip	ninth **	ninety **
no *	nod **	noise **	noon **	north **	nose *
not *	note **	now *	number **	nurse *	nut
/n/ represented by N in final position					
an *	balloon **	born **	bean **	been **	bin **
brain **	burn **	button	can *	cartoon **	clean *
cousin *	coin	corn **	den	down *	drain
fan *	fin	flown	fun **	gain	garden *
green *	grin	hen **	horn	in *	Jean
join **	lesson *	lemon **	lion *	learn *	man **
mean **	men *	noon **	moon *	pain **	pan
pen *	pain **	plan **	queen **	rain *	ran **
* means vocabulary list on national curriculum level 2 and ** means on level 3.					

/p/ as in pig

Words begin with /p/ sound in National Curriculum					
panda *	parent *	park *	party *	pen *	pencil *
people *	photo *	picture *	pig *	place *	plane *
planet **	plant *	play *	playground *	please *	police *
potato *	pupil	put *	pacific	page **	pain *
paint **	pair *	palace **	pale **	pancake **	panda *
paper *	pardon **	part **	pass **	passage **	passenger **
passport **	past **	patient **	pay **	peace **	pear **
perfect **	perhaps **	period **	person **	personal **	pet *
phone *	photograph *	physics **	pick **	picnic **	pie **
piece **	pilot **	pink *	pioneer **	pity **	plan **
plane **	planet **	player	playground *	pleasure **	plenty **
pocket **	poem **	point **	policeman **	policewoman **	polite **
pollute **	pollution	possible **	post **	postcard **	postman **

续表

Words begin with /p/ sound in National Curriculum					
pound **	practise **	praise **	prepare **	present **	president **
pretty **	price **	pride **	primary *	print **	private **
prize **	probably **	problem **	produce **	product **	program **
progress **	project **	promise **	pronounce **	pronunciation	proper **
protect **	proud **	provide **	publish **	purple **	purpose **
push **	playground				
/p/ in initial position					
pack **	pad	page **	pail	pain **	paint **
pal	pale **	pan	pant	pass **	past **
patch	paw	pay **	pea	peace **	peak
pear **	pedal	peel	peg	pen *	pencil *
penny	pet *	pickle	pie *	pig *	pike
pill	pillow	pin	pine	pint	pipe
pit	pod	point **	poke	pole	pond
pop	pork	port	post **	potato *	pour **
puddle	puff	pull **	pumpkin	punish **	puppet
purse	push **	put *	pull **	puzzle	
/p/ represented by P in final position					
cap *	camp **	cheap **	chop	clip	crop
cup *	deep **	dip	develop **	drop **	flap
flip	flop	help *	hip	hop	jump *
keep *	lamp **	lap	leap	lip	map *
mop	nap	peep	pep	pop	pup
rap	rip	sap	sheep *	sip	skip
sleep *	slip	soup *	soap	stamp **	step **
stop *	sweep *	tap *	tip	top *	trap
trip **	up *	weep	whip	wrap	whip
zip					
* means vocabulary list on national curriculum level 2 and ** means on level 3.					

/r/ as in rap

Words begin with /r/ sound in National Curriculum

rain *	read *	red *	rice *	right *	river *
room *	ruler *	run *	rabbit *	race **	radio **
railway **	rainy	raise **	rapid **	reach **	ready **
real *	realize **	really **	reason **	receive **	recently
record **	refuse **	regret **	relationship **	relative **	relax **
remain **	remember **	repair **	research **	rest **	restaurant **
result **	return **	review **	rich **	ride **	ring **
rise **	risk **	river **	road **	robot *	rock **
role **	rope **	rose **	round **	row **	rubbish **
rule **	rush **	Russia **	Russian **		

/r/ represented by R in the initial position

rabbit *	ramp	rack	radio **	rag	rail
rain *	raise **	rake	ram	ramp	ranch
range	rank	rap	rat	rate	rattle
rave	raw	ray	real *	red *	rent
rib	rich **	ride **	rig	right *	rim
ring **	rink	rip	ripe	rise	road **
roast	rob	robe	rock **	rocket **	rod
roll	roof	room *	root	rope **	rose **
rot	round **	row **	rub	rude	rug
run *	rush **				

/r/ in final position

bear *	car *	chair *	dear *	door *	finger **
four **	guitar **	hammer	her *	jar	later **
letter *	pear **	spider	zipper		

/r/ represented by WR

wrap	wreck	wriggle	wrinkle	wrist	write *
wrote **	wreath	wrench	wrong *	writer	

* means vocabulary list on national curriculum level 2 and ** means on level 3.

/s/ as in sun

Words begin with /s/ sound in National Curriculum					
sad *	say *	school *	schoolbag *	science *	season *
see *	sing *	sister *	sit *	skirt *	slow *
small *	snow *	sock *	some *	sometimes *	song *
sorry *	soup *	speak *	sport *	spring *	stand *
star *	stop *	story *	street *	strong *	study *
subject *	summer *	sun *	sunny *	supermarket *	sweater *
swim **	sing *	slow *	small *	song *	sorry *
soup *	speak	sport *	spring *	stand *	star *
stop *	story *	storm **	street *	strong *	study *
safe *	salad **	sale **	salt **	same **	sand **
sandwich *	satisfy *	Saturday **	save **	say *	scarf **
scientist **	scissors **	score **	screen **	sea *	search **
season *	seat **	second **	secret **	secretary	seldom **
sell *	send **	sense **	sentence **	safety **	separate **
September **	serious **	serve **	service **	set **	seven **
seventeen *	seventh **	seventy **	several **	sick **	side **
sign **	silence	silent **	silk **	silly **	silver **
similar **	simple **	since *	sing *	single **	sir **
situation **	six **	sixteen **	sixth **	size **	skate **
skill **	skirt **	sky **	sleep *	sleepy	slow *
small *	smart **	smell **	smile **	smoke **	smooth **
snake **	so *	social **	sock *	sofa **	soft **
solve **	sometimes *	somewhere **	son **	song *	soon **
sorry *	sound **	soup *	south **	southern	space *
spare **	speak *	speaker *	special **	speech **	speed **
spell **	spend **	spirit **	spoon **	sport **	spread **
spring *	square **	stamp **	stand *	standard **	star **
start **	state **	station *	stay **	steal **	step **
stick **	still **	stomach **	stomachache	stone **	stop *
store **	straight **	strange **	strawberry **	student *	strict **
stupid	succeed **	success **	successful	such **	sudden **
suggest **	suggestion	support *	suppose *	surface *	sweet **
Sunday **	survey **				

续表

/s/ represented by S in the initial position					
safe*	sad*	sage	said**	sail	sake
sale**	salt**	same**	sand**	sandwich**	sang**
sap	sat**	safety**	save**	saw**	sax
say*	sea*	seal	see*	seed	seek
seem*	seen**	sew	sick**	side**	sieve
sigh	sight	sign**	silk***	sill	since**
sing*	sink	sip	sir**	sit*	six**
size**	so*	soak	soap	soar	sock*
sod	soft**	soil**	some*	son**	song*
soon**	soot	sore**	sort	soul	sound**
soup*	sour	south**	sow	sub	such*
sue	suit	sum	sun*	surf	
/s/ represented by S in the final position					
bus*	circus	gas**	octopus	this*	plus
us*	yes*				
/s/ represented by-SS in the final position					
boss**	class**	kiss**	less**	loss**	mess**
moss	pass**	toss			
other spellings					
/s/ represented by C in initial position					
ceiling	celery	cell	cellar	cement	cent**
center**	cereal	cigar	cinch	cinder	circle**
circus	citizen**	city*	cycle	cylinder	celebrate**
central**	century**	certain**	certainly		
/s/ represented by-CE in final position					
ace	advice**	Alice	bounce	brace	Bruce
chance**	choice**	dance*	France**	face*	fence
force**	glance	grace	ice*	lace	mice
nice*	notice**	office**	ounce	pace	peace**
palace**	place*	piece**	practice**	race**	rice*
since**	slice	space*	spruce	twice**	voice**

* means vocabulary list on national curriculum level 2 and ** means on level 3.

/t/ as in top

Words begin with /t/ sound in National Curriculum					
table **	take **	talk **	tall **	taxi **	tea **
teacher **	tell **	tiger **	time **	tired **	to **
today **	toilet **	tomato **	tomorrow **	too **	toy **
turn **	TV **	tennis *	tenth *	term *	terrible *
test *	text *	ticket *	tidy *	tie *	tiger *
time *	tiny *	to *	today *	together *	toilet *
tomato *	tomorrow *	ton *	tonight *	too *	tool *
tooth *	toothache *	top *	total *	touch *	tour *
tourist *	towards *	tower *	town *	toy *	twelfth *
twelve *	twentieth *	twice *	two *		

/t/ represented by T in the initial position					
table **	tail **	tape *	task *	tail *	take **
talk **	tall **	tame	taxi *	tea *	teen
telephone **	tell **	ten **	team *	tick	tide
tie *	ticket *	time **	tin	tip	tie *
to **	toad	toe	told *	tomato **	ton
tone	tool	toothbrush	top *	torn *	toss
tote	touch *	tough	tour *	tow	towel
town *	toy *	tub	tube	tuck	tug
tune	turn **	turtle			

/t/ represented by T in the final position					
bat	beat *	beast *	bit *	boat *	but **
cat **	carrot *	cheat	cent *	coast *	coat *
cost *	cut *	dot	eat *	fat *	feet *
fit *	fast *	first *	foot *	get **	goat
got *	great *	hat **	heat *	hit *	hot **
hurt *	jacket *	jet	let **	lot *	mat
meat *	meet *	met *	most *	neat	next *
net	not **	nut	paint *	pat	pet *
past *	pilot *	point *	pot	put *	quit
rat	rabbit *	rest *	right *	sat *	seat *

续表

/t/ represented by T in the final position					
set *	shut *	sit **	shout *	spot	sweet
test *	treat *	wait *	want *	wallet *	west *
wet *	what **	wheat	yet *	unit *	visit *

* means vocabulary list on national curriculum level 2 and ** means on level 3.

/v/ as in vase

Words begin with /v/ sound in National Curriculum					
vegetable *	very *	visit *	vacation **	valuable *	value **
victory **	video **	village **	violin **	visit *	visitor
voice **	volleyball **				
/v/ represented by V in the initial position					
valentine	van	vase	violin **	vain	van
veal	vein	vet	vent	verse	very *
vest	view	vine	visit *	voice **	vote
/v/ represented by-VE in the final position-					
active **	arrive **	brave **	cave	cove	dive
dove	drive *	drove **	five **	gave **	give *
glove	grave	grove	have *	hive	leave
live *	love *	move *	nerve	pave	prove
rave	save **	serve **	shave	sleeve	stove
wave **	weave	wove			

* means vocabulary list on national curriculum level 2 and ** means on level 3.

/w/ as in wagon

Words begin with /w/ sound in National Curriculum					
wait *	walk *	want *	warm *	wash *	watch *
water *	way *	we *	wear *	weather *	week *
welcome *	well *	white *	window *	windy *	winter *
with *	woman *	women *	wonderful *	word *	worker *
worry *	write *	wrong *	wake *	wall *	wallet **
war **	warn **	waste **	weak **	wealth **	website **

续表

Words begin with /w/ sound in National Curriculum					
Wednesday **	weekday **	weekend **	weigh **	weight **	welcome *
west **	western	wet **	wheel **	whether **	while **
white *	wide **	wife **	wild **	will *	win *
wind **	wing **	winner **	wise **	within **	wolf **
wish *	without **	wonder **	wood **	world *	worse **
worst **	worth **	would **	wound **	writer	
/w/ represented by W in the initial position					
wad	wade	wag	wage	wagon	waist
wait *	wake *	walk *	wall *	wand	want *
war *	ware	warm *	warn *	wash *	wasp
waste **	watch *	water *	wave **	wax	way *
we *	weak **	wealth **	wear *	weave	wet **
weak **	week **	weep	weigh **	weird	weed
well *	went **	west **	wet **	wick	wide **
wife **	wig	wild **	will *	wilt	win *
wind **	window *	wing **	wink	wipe	wire
wise **	wish *	wit	with *	woke **	wolf **
won **	wood **	wool	word *	work *	world *
worm	worry **	worst *	would **		
* means vocabulary list on national curriculum level 2 and ** means on level 3.					

/y/ as in yo-yo

Words begin with /y/ sound in National Curriculum					
year *	yellow *	yes *	yesterday *	you *	young *
your **	yard *	yet **	yours *	yourself **	
/y/ represented by Y in the initial position					
yacht	yak	yam	yank	yard	yarn
yawn	year *	yeast	yellow *	yes *	yield
yoke	you *	young	your **	yowl	yo-yo
yuck					
* means vocabulary list on national curriculum level 2 and ** means on level 3.					

/z/ as in zoo

Words begin with /z/ sound in National Curriculum					
zoo *	zero **				
/z/ represented by Z in the initial position					
zag	zap	zeal	zebra	zero **	zest
zinc	zing	zip	zipper	zone	zonk
zoo *	zoom				
/z/ represented by-ZZ in the mid and final position					
blizzard	buzzard	buzz	fizz	fuzz	
/z/ represented by-ZE in the mid and final position					
dozen	frozen	breeze	daze	doze	freeze
sneeze	wheeze	prize **	quiz	size **	sneeze
snooze	squeeze	whiz			
other spellings for /z/					
amuse	as **	because *	birds *	boys *	cars *
cheese **	chose **	close *	daisy	dogs **	easy *
excuse **	fuse	girls **	has *	hose	is **
noise *	nose **	pause	please **	raise *	rose *
shoes *	suppose **	tease	these *	those *	was **
wise **					
* means vocabulary list on national curriculum level 2 and ** means on level 3.					

/ch/ as in cheese

Words begin with /ch/ sound in National Curriculum					
chair *	chicken *	child *	China *	children *	Chinese *
chalk **	change **	cheap **	check **	cheer **	chess **
chocolate **	choice **	choose **	chopsticks **		
/ch/ represented by CH in the initial position					
chain	chair *	chalk **	change **	chap	chapter
charge	charm	chart	chase	chat	cheap **
cheat	check *	checker	checkup	cheer *	cheerful
cheese **	cheeseburger	cherry	chess **	chest	chestnut
chew	chick	chicken *	child *	children *	chilly

续表

/ch/ represented by CH in the initial position					
chime	chimney	chin	chip	chipmunk	chirp
chocolate *	choose **	chop	chose **	chow	chuckle
chum	chunk	churn			
/ch/ represented by CH in final position					
beach *	bench	branch	bunch	church	clinch
couch	crunch	each **	hunch	inch	lunch *
much *	munch	peach	perch	pinch	punch
quench	ranch	reach **	rich **	sandwich **	search **
such *	teach	touch *	trench		
/ch/ represented by-TCH in final position					
batch	catch *	clutch	crutch	ditch	fetch
hitch	hutch	itch	latch	match **	notch
patch	pitch	scratch	sketch	snatch	stitch
stretch	switch	watch *	witch		
* means vocabulary list on national curriculum level 2 and ** means on level 3.					

/sh/ as in shark

Words begin with /sh/ sound in National Curriculum					
she *	sheep *	ship **	shirt *	shoe **	shop *
short *	shorts **	shut **	shy **	shake **	shall **
shame **	shape **	shine **	should *	shoulder **	shout **
show *	shower **				
/sh/ sound in the initial position					
shack	shade	shadow	shake	shall **	shallow
shame **	shampoo	shape **	share *	shark **	shave
shake **	she *	shear	sheep *	sheet	shelf **
shell	shield	shift	shin	shine **	ship *
shirt *	shock **	shoe *	shoelace	shoot	shop *
shore	short *	shorts *	shot	should *	shoulder **
shout **	shove	shovel	show *	shower **	shuck
shut **	shy **				

续表

/sh/ represented by SH in the final position					
ash	blush	brush**	bush	cash**	clash
crash	crush	dash	dish	fish*	flash
fresh**	gash	gush	lash	leash	mash
mesh	mush	push**	rash	rush**	smash
splash	trash	wash*	wish*		
/sh/ represented by-TI in final position					
action**	addition	attention**	fraction	nation**	station**
vacation**	patient**				
/sh/ represented by-CI in final position					
social**	delicious**	musician	precious	suspicion	vicious
* means vocabulary list on national curriculum level 2 and ** means on level 3.					

/zh/ as in treasure

/zh/ sound in the medial position					
Asia	decision	casual	exposure	measure	occasion
pleasure**	television*	treasure	usual**	vision	
* mean vocabulary list on national curriculum level 2 and ** means on level 3.					

Voiced /th/ as in th

Words begin with voiced /th/ sound in National Curriculum					
those*	that**	the**	their**	them**	then**
there**	these**	they**	this**	than*	though*
voiced /th/ sound in the initial position					
than*	the**	them**	there**	they**	those**
thus	that**	their**	then**	these**	this**
though*					
voiced /th/ sound in the final/middle position					
bathe	gather	smooth*	together*	whether*	weather*
* means vocabulary list on national curriculum level 2 and ** means on level 3.					

Voiceless /th/ as in thumb

Words begin with voiceless /th/ sound in National Curriculum					
thin *	think *	thank *	theatre **	thick **	thing **
thirsty **	thirteen **	third **	thought **	thousand **	three **
through **	throw **	Thursday **			
voiceless /th/ sound in the initial position					
thank *	Thanksgiving	theatre **	theme	thermometer	thick **
thermos	thief	thimble	thin *	thing **	think *
third **	thirsty **	thirteen **	thirty **	thread	through **
thorn	thought **	thousand **	three **	thump	thunder **
throw **	thumb	thief			
voiceless /th/ sound in the final position					
bath **	birth **	booth	both **	broth	cloth
death **	fifth **	fourth **	growth	length	math *
month *	moth	mouth *	north *	oath	path
sixth **	south **	teeth **	worth **	tooth *	
* means vocabulary list on national curriculum level 2 and ** means on level 3.					

/hw/ as in wheel

Words begin with /hw/ sound in National Curriculum					
what *	when *	where *	why *	whose *	who *
/hw/ sound in the initial position					
whale	what *	whatever **	wheat	whom **	why *
wheel **	wheelbarrow	wheelchair	when *	whenever **	where *
wherever **	which *	whisker	whisper	whistle	while *
* means vocabulary list on national curriculum level 2 and ** means on level 3.					

/ng/ as in ring

Words with /ng/ sound in National Curriculum					
angry *	bring *	evening *	interesting *	morning *	spring *
strong *	thank **	think *	wrong *		
/ng/ sound in the medial/ final position					
angry *	hang **	finger **	hung **	hunger	king **

续表

/ng/ sound in the medial/ final position					
long *	longer **	rang **	ring **	rung **	sang **
sing *	song *	thing **	wing **	strong *	strength
young *	bank **	drink *	drunk **	honk	ink
thank *	pink *	link	sank	sunk	junk
tank	wink	rank			
* means vocabulary list on national curriculum level 2 and ** means on level 3.					

Part Ⅱ Vowel Sounds List

Blevins (2017) suggests the following methods for utilizing the word list in this section:

1) To compile a list of words for the blending exercise.
2) To construct sentences or connected text to practice reading.
3) To create sorting games based on words.
4) To compile a list of words for use in dictation and spelling.

Long-A sound /ai/ as in cake

base	blade	brace	brake	brave **	cage
cake *	came **	case **	cave	chase	date **
face *	fade	flake	flame	game *	gate **
gave **	grace	grade **	grape *	lake *	late *
made **	make *	maze	male	name *	page **
place *	plate **	race **	rake	sale **	same **
save **	shame **	shake **	shape **	skate **	space *
state **	take *	tale	tape **	trace	trade **
vase (*AmE*)	wade	wake *	wave **	whale **	aid
aim	bait	braid	braille	brain **	chain
claim	drain	fail **	faint	faith	frail
grain	jail	laid **	maid	mail	main **
nail	paid **	paint **	pain **	praise **	raid
rain *	rainy	raise **	sail	Spain **	stain
strain	tail *	trail	train *	vain	waist

续表

wait *	bay	birthday *	clay	day *	gay
gray	hay	jay	lay **	may *	maybe **
pay **	play *	player	pray	ray	say *
spray	stay **	sway	today *	tray	way *

* means on the vocabulary list of national curriculum level 2 and ** means level 3.

Long-E sound /ee/ as in feet

be *	me *	we *	bee	beech	beef **
beep	beet	cheer **	cheep	cheese **	creep
deed	deep **	deer	fee	feed **	feel **
feet *	flee	free *	greed	green *	greet **
heed	jeep	keep *	knee **	meet *	need **
peek	peel	peep	queen **	reef	screech
screen **	see *	seed	seek	seem **	seen **
seep	sheep *	sheet	sleep *	sleet	speech **
speed **	steel	steep	street *	sweep *	sweet **
teen	teeth **	three **	tree *	weed	week *
weep	wheel **	beach *	bead	beak	beam
bean **	beat **	bleach	bleak	cheap **	cheat **
clean *	cream	deal **	dear *	dream **	each **
east **	eat **	feast	flea	gleam	heal
heap	heat **	jeans **	lead **	leaf **	leak
lean	leap	leash	least **	meal **	mean **
meat *	near *	pea	peach	peak	peace **
plead	reach **	read *	real **	scream	sea *
season *	seam	seat *	sneak	speak **	steal
steam	stream	tea *	teach **	team **	treat **
weak **	wheat	yeast	zeal	any *	baby *
beauty	bunny	candy *	carry **	chilly	city *
county	daddy	daisy	dirty *	dizzy	dusty
duty	easy *	eighty *	family *	forty *	fifty *
funny **	fuzzy	gravy	happy **	jelly	kitty

续表

lady **	lately	lobby	lucky	many *	mommy
muddy	navy	ninety *	only **	party *	penny
plenty **	pony	pretty **	puppy	quickly	sandy
seventy *	shiny	silly	sixty *	sleepy	slowly
smoothly	sticky	story *	strawberry *	sunny *	thirty **
thirsty **	tidy *	tricky	ugly **	windy *	belief
believe **	chief	brief	field **	fierce	grief
niece	thief	pierce	relief	shield	yield

* means on the vocabulary list of national curriculum level 2 and ** means level 3.

Long-I sound /igh/ as in bike

bike *	bite	bride	chime	chive	dime
dine	dive	drive	fine **	fire *	five **
grime	hike	hive	ice *	kite *	life **
like *	lime	line **	live *	mice	mile **
mine **	nice *	nine **	pike	pine	pipe
price **	rice *	ride **	ripe	rise **	shine **
side	spice	spike	splice	stride	strive
tide	time *	tire	twice	twine	whine
white *	wide **	wife	wise *	by *	cry *
dry **	fly *	fry	my *	pry	shy **
sky **	sly	spy	try *	why *	bind
blind **	child *	climb **	find *	grind	hind
kind *	mild	mind **	rind	wild *	wind **
die **	lie **	pie **	tie **	tight	thigh
bright **	fight *	flight	fright	high **	knight
light *	might **	night *	right *	sign **	sight

* means on the vocabulary list of national curriculum level 2 and ** means level 3.

Long-O sound /oa/ as in boat

bold	bolt	cold *	fold	go *	gold **
hold **	jolt	mold	no *	old *	poll

续表

pro	roll	scold	scroll	so *	sold **
stroll	told **	toll	troll	volt	alone **
broke **	choke	chose **	close *	clothes *	code
dome	doze	drove **	froze **	globe	hole
home *	hope *	hose	joke **	nose *	note **
phone *	poke	pole	pose	robe	rode **
rope **	rose **	slope	smoke *	spoke **	stone **
stove	stroke	those *	tone	vote **	wrote **
yoke	zone	boat *	cloak	coal	coast **
coat *	croak	float	foam	goal **	goat
groan	Joan	load	moan	moat	oak
oat	road **	roam	roast	soak	soap
throat **	toad	toast	below **	blow **	bow
bowl **	crow	flow	flown **	glow	grow **
grown **	know *	known **	low **	mow	pillow
row **	shadow	show *	shown **	slow *	tow
snow *	sparrow	swallow	throw **	thrown **	willow
window *	yellow *	doe	foe	toe	

* means on the vocabulary list of national curriculum level 2 and ** means level 3.

Long-U sound /yoo/ as in cube

cube	cute *	fume	fuse	huge **	mule
muse	mute	puke	use *	bugle	community
future **	human **	humid	humor **	January **	menu
museum *	music *	pupil	regular	uniform **	union
unit **	united	university **	usually	usual ** ya	few *
view	review	argue	continue *	cue	fuel
rescue	value	beautiful *	beauty		

* means on the vocabulary list of national curriculum level 2 and ** means level 3.

Short-A /a/ as in cat

act **	add *	am **	as **	at *	back *
bad *	bag *	ban	bank **	basket **	bat **

续表

batch	bath **	black *	blast	bamboo **	branch
brand	brass	cab	camp *	can *	cap *
cast	cat *	catch *	champ	clan	clap
clash	class * (*AmE*)	crack	craft	cramp	crash
dad	damp	dash	drag	fact **	fad
fan *	fast * (*AmE*)	fat **	flag **	flap	flash
flat **	gap	gas **	gasp	glad **	glass * (*AmE*)
grab	grand	grant	graph (*AmE*)	grass * (*AmE*)	had **
ham	hand *	has **	hat **	hatch	jack
jam	jazz	lack	lad	lag	lamp **
land **	lap	lash	last * (*AmE*)	latch	mad **
man *	map *	mash	mask (*AmE*)	mass	mast (*AmE*)
mat	match *	math **	nag	nap	pack **
pad	pal	pam	pant	pants	pass **
past **	pat	patch	path	plan **	plant *
quack	rack	rag	ram	ramp	ran **
rant	rap	rash	rat	sack	sad *
sag	sand **	sap	sat **	scratch	slab
slack	slam	slant	snap	span	splash
snack	stamp **	stand *	strand	tab	tack
tag	tan	tap	task * (*AmE*)	than **	that *
track	trap	van	vat	wag	yam

* means on the vocabulary list of national curriculum level 2 and ** means level 3.

Short-E sound /e/ as in bed

bed *	beg	bell **	belt **	bench	bend
bent	best **	bet	bled	blend	bless
cell	cent	check **	chess *	chest	crest
deck	den	desk *	dress *	egg *	elf
elm	end **	fed	fell *	fled	fresh **
gem	get *	help *	hem	hen **	jet
kept **	led **	left *	leg *	lend **	less **

续表

letter *	lemon *	let *	men *	mend	mesh
mess **	met **	neck **	nest	net	peck
peg	pen *	pest	pet *	press	red *
rest **	sell *	send *	sent **	set **	seven **
shelf **	shell	sled	slept **	smell **	spell **
spend **	spent **	west **	bless	end **	less **
press **	stem	wet **	when *	wreck	yell
yes *	yet **				
other spellings					
ahead	bread *	breakfast *	dead **	feather	head *
health **	heaven	heavy *	instead **	lead *	leather
meant **	read *	ready **	spread **	sweater *	thread
wealth **	wealthy	weather *	dense	fence	hedge
ledge	pledge	sense **	tense	wedge	

* means on the vocabulary list of national curriculum level 2 and ** means level 3.

Short-I /i/ as in fish

bib	bid	big *	bill	bit	blimp
blink	brick	chick	chill	chin	click
clip	crib	crisp	did **	dig *	dill
dim	dip	dish **	disk	drink *	drip
fib	fig	fill **	fin	fish *	fist
fit *	fix **	flick	flip	gift *	gig
gill	glint	hid	hill *	him *	hip
his *	hiss	hit **	in *	ink	inn
is **	it *	kick **	kin	kiss **	lick
lid	lift *	link	lip	list *	milk *
mill	miss **	mitt	mix **	nip	pick **
pig *	pill **	pin	pink *	pit	rib
rich **	rid	rig	rim	rip	shift
ship *	sill	sink	sip	sit *	six **
skin	skip	skill **	slick	slid	slim **

续表

slip	splint	sprint	stick	stink	swim *
thin *	think *	this *	tick	trim	trip **
twig	which **	whip	wick	wig	will **
win *	wink	wish *	wit	zip	

* means on the vocabulary list of national curriculum level 2 and ** means level 3.

Short-O sound /o/ as in lock

blob	block **	blot	bop	box *	chop
clock *	cob	cod	cot	crop	dock
doll *	dot	drop **	flock	flop	fog
fox **	frog	gob	got **	hog	hop
hot *	job *	jog **	knob	knock **	knot
lock **	log	lot *	mom *	mop	nod **
not *	on *	ox	plod	plop	plot
pod	pond	pop	pot	prop	rob
rock **	rod	rot	shock **	shot	shop *
slop	slot	sob	sock *	sod	spot
stop *	tock	top *	trot		

* means on the vocabulary list of national curriculum level 2 and ** means level 3.

Short-U sound /u/ as in duck

bluff	blunt	blush	brush	buck	bud
buff	bug	bum	bump	bunch	bunt
bus *	but *	buzz	chunk	club **	clump
clunk	clutch	crust	cub	cuff	cup *
cut *	drug	drum	duck *	dug **	dull
dump	dunk	dusk	dust	fluff	fun *
fuss	fuzz	glum	grub	gruff	gum
gust	hug	hum	hunt	hush	husk
hut	jug	jump *	just **	luck *	lunch *
lump	much *	muck	mud	mug	mush
musk	must *	mutt	nut	pluck	plug

续表

plum	plus	puff	pump	punt	pup
putt	rub	ruff	rug	run *	runt
rush **	rust	rut	shun	shrub	shut **
skunk	slug	slump	snub	snug	struck
strum	stub	stuck	stump	sub	such **
suds	sum	sun *	truck **	trust **	tub
tuck	tug	tusk	up *	us *	

* means on the vocabulary list of national curriculum level 2 and ** means level 3.

Diphthong /oi/ sound

/oi/ represented by OI

avoid **	boil **	choice **	coil	coin **	foil
hoist	join **	joint	moist	moisture	noise **
oil **	point **	poison	rejoice	soil **	spoil
toil	voice **				

/oi/ represented by OY

annoy	boy *	cowboy	coy	decoy	destroy
employ	enjoy **	joy **	joyful	loyal	ploy
royal	soy	toy *	voyage		

* means on the vocabulary list of national curriculum level 2 and ** means level 3.

Diphthong /ou/ sound

/ou/ represented by OU

about *	bounce	bound	cloud **	couch	count **
crouch	doubt **	flour	foul	found **	grouch
ground *	hound	house **	loud *	mound	mouth *
noun	ouch	out *	pouch	pound	pout
proud *	round	scout	shout *	snout	sour
south *	spout	sprout	trout		

/ou/ represented by OW

allow **	bow	brown *	brow	chow	cow *
crowd	crown	down *	drown	fowl	frown

续表

/ou/ represented by OW					
gown	growl	how *	howl	now *	owl
plow	powder	power	prowl	sow	towel
town **	vow	wow			
* means on the vocabulary list of national curriculum level 2 and ** means level 3.					

Variant vowel sound long /oo/

long /oo/ sound represented by-OO					
balloon **	bloom	boo	boom	broom	coo
cool *	coop	doom	food *	fool	gloom
goose	groom	hoof	hoop	hoot	igloo
kangaroo	loom	loop	loose	loot	moo
mood	moon *	moose	noon **	ooze	pool **
proof	roof	room *	root	school *	scoop
scoot	scooter	shampoo	shoo	shoot	sloop
smooth **	snoop	soon **	spook	spooky	spool
spoon **	stool	too *	tool **	toot	tooth **
troop	zoo *	zoom			
long /oo/ sound represented by-UE					
blue *	clue	due	glue **	sue	true **
long /oo/ sound represented by-EW					
blew **	brew	chew	crew	dew	drew **
flew **	grew **	knew **	new *	news **	screw
shrew	stew	threw **			
long /oo/sound in U-E pattern					
crude	June **	prune	rude	reduce **	
long /oo/ sound represented by-U					
junior **	solution	July **			
in this category, when long-U sound loses its /y/ part in /yoo/, the letter U sounds like long /oo/.					
* means on the vocabulary list of national curriculum level 2 and ** means level 3.					

Short-OO sound /oo/ as in book

short /oo/ sound represented by-OO					
afoot	book *	brook	cook *	cookie **	crook
foot *	football *	good *	goodbye *	hood	hoof
hook	look *	nook	notebook	rook	rookie
shook **	soot	stood **	took **	wood **	wooden
woof	wool				
* means on the vocabulary list of national curriculum level 2 and ** means level 3.					

Variant vowel sounds: Broad-O sound /or/

broad-O sound /or/ represented by AU					
audience	August **	author	autumn *	because *	caught **
cause **	clause	daughter **	dinosaur	fault	fraud
haul	haunt	launch	laundry	Paul	pause
sauce	sausage	taught **	vault		
broad-O sound /or/ represented by AW					
awful **	bawl	brawl	bawl	caw	crawl
dawn	draw *	drawn	fawn	flaw	gnaw
hawk	jaw	law **	lawn	lawyer **	paw
pawn	raw	saw **	shawl	slaw	sprawl
straw	strawberry **	thaw	yawn		
broad-O sound /or/ represented by AL (L)					
chalk **	stalk	talk *	walk *	call *	ball *
fall **	hall	mall **	small *	stall	tall *
wall *	halt	malt	salt *		
words in this category are also defined as L-influenced or L-controlled spellings by Bear et al. (2015)					
* means on the vocabulary list of national curriculum level 2 and ** means level 3.					

R-controlled vowel sound /air/

/air/ represented by AIR					
air *	chair *	fair **	flair	hair *	pair *
stair					

续表

/air/ represented by-ARE					
bare	blare	care **	dare	fare	flare
glare	hare	mare	pare	rare	scare
share *	spare **	square **	stare		
* means on the vocabulary list of national curriculum level 2 and ** means level 3.					
/air/ represented by-EAR					
bear *	pear **	tear	swear	wear *	
* means on the vocabulary list of national curriculum level 2 and ** means level 3.					

R-controlled vowel sound /ar/

/ar/ represented by AR					
arch	Arctic	ark	arm *	art *	artist **
article **	bar	bark	barn	car *	card *
cart	charge	charm	chart	guard **	harm **
dark *	dart	far *	farm *	garden *	hard *
harp	jar	lard	large **	march	mart
park *	part **	scar	scarf **	shark **	sharp
smart *	spark	star *	start	starch	tar
tart	yard **	yarn			
* means on the vocabulary list of national curriculum level 2 and ** means level 3.					

R-controlled vowel sound /ur/ as in bird, fern and burn

/ur/ represented by UR					
blur	burn *	burst	church	churn	curb
curl	curse	curve	fur	hurt *	nurse *
purple **	purr	purse	spur	surf	Thursday **
turkey	turn *	turtle	urge		
/ur/ represented by-IR					
thirst	twirl	squirm	whirl	bird *	birth **
birthday *	chirp	circle	circus	dirt	dirty *
fir	firm	first **	girl *	quirk	shirt *
sir *	skirt *	squirt	stir	swirl	third *

续表

/ur/ represented by-ER					
other **	over *	perch	perk	after *	better **
certain **	clerk	ever	fern	germ	her *
herd	jerk	letter *	merge	mother *	nerve
person **	river *	serve **	sister *	stern	swerve
term **	under *	verb	verge	verse	water *
winter *					
* means on the vocabulary list of national curriculum level 2 and ** means level 3.					

R-controlled vowel sound /or/

/or/ represented by OR					
bore	born **	chore *	chord	core	cork
corn **	door *	dorm	for *	force **	fork **
form **	fort	forth **	horn	horse *	more **
morning *	north **	or *	porch	pore	pork **
port	scorch	score **	shore	short	snore
sore	sort	sport *	store **	stork	storm **
sword	swore	sworn	thorn	torch	tore *
torn **	wore **				
/or/ represented by OAR					
aboard **	board **	coarse	hoard	oar	roar
soar					
* means on the vocabulary list of national curriculum level 2 and ** means level 3.					

Schwa /uh/ as in alarm

about *	above **	account **	adult **	afloat	afoot
afraid **	again *	ago *	agree **	ahead *	ajar
alarm **	alas	alone **	along **	American **	among **
anew	annoy	another **	apart	appear **	applause
ashamed	ashore	aside	asleep **	avoid **	await
awake **	aware **	away **	awhile		
* means on the vocabulary list of national curriculum level 2 and ** means level 3.					

Part Ⅲ Phonograms

Purpose: The following phonogram list can also be used to assist teachers in developing word lists for phonics or spelling instruction (Blevins, 2017) . For EFL teachers, the phonogram list can be referred to whenever analogy phonics instructions appear in textbooks. In China, "analogy phonics instruction" is included in several popular primary school textbooks.

Source: The list is based on Fry et al. (1993), which Blevins (2017) cites.

Explanation: This alphabetical list contains one-syllable words derived from vowel sounds. The alphabetical order begins with single consonants and progresses to clusters and digraphs.

Long-A sound /ai/ Phonograms

Phonograms	word list				
-ace	face *	lace	mace	pace	brace
	grace	place *	space *	trace	
-ade	fade	jade	made **	wade	blade
	glade	grade	shade	spade	trade
-age	age *	cage	gage	page **	rage
	sage	wage	stage **		
-aid	laid **	maid	paid **	raid	braid
-ail	bail	fail **	trail	hail	jail
	mail	nail	pail	quail	rail
	sail	tail *	wail	flail	frail
	snail				
-ain	main *	pain **	rain *	vain	brain **
	chain	drain	grain	plain	slain
	Spain **	sprain	stain	strain	train *
-aint	faint	paint **	saint	quaint	
-aise	praise **	raise **			
-ait	bait	gait	wait *	strait	trait
-ake	bake	cake *	fake	jake	lake *
	make *	quake	rake	sake	take *
	wake *	drake	flake	shake **	snake **
	stake	brake			

续表

Phonograms	word list				
-ale	bale	gale	male	pale	sale **
	tale	scale	stale	whale	
-ame	came **	dame	fame	game *	lame
	name *	same **	tame	blame	flame
	frame	shame **			
-ane	cane	jane	lane	mane	pane
	sane	vane	wane	crane	plane *
-ange	range	change **	grange	strange **	
-ape	cape	gape	nape	tape	drape
	grape *	scrape	shape **		
-ase	base	case **	chase		
-aste	taste **	baste	haste	waste **	paste
-ate	date **	fate	gate **	hate **	Kate
	late *	mate	rate	crate	grate
	plate **	skate	state **		
-ave	cave	gave **	pave	rave	save **
	wave	brave **	crave	grave	shave
	slave				
-ay	bay	day *	gay	hay	jay
	lay **	may *	nay	pay **	ray
	say *	way *	clay	fray	gray
	play *	pray	slay	spray	stay **
	stray	sway	tray		
-aze	daze	faze	gaze	haze	maze
	raze	blaze	craze	glaze	graze
-eak	break **	steak			
-eight	neigh	weigh **	sleigh		
-ey	hey	grey **	prey	they *	whey

* means on the vocabulary list of national curriculum level 2 and ** means level 3.

Long-E sound /ee/ Phonograms

-e	be *	he *	me *	we *	she *
-ea	pea	sea *	tea *	flea	plea
-each	beach *	leach	peach	teach **	bleach
	breach	preach			
-ead	bead	lead **	read **	knead	plead
-eak	beak	leak	peak	weak **	bleak
	creak	freak	sneak	speak *	squeak
	streak	tweak			
-eal	deal **	heal	meal **	peal	real **
	seal	teal	veal	zeal	squeal
	steal **				
-eam	beam	ream	seam	team *	cream
	dream **	gleam	steam	stream	
-ean	bean **	dean	jean	lean	mean **
	wean	clean *	glean		
-eap	-eap	leap	heap	reap	cheap **
-ear	dear *	fear	gear	hear *	near *
	rear	tear	year *	clear **	shear
	smear	spear			
-ease	cease	lease	crease	grease	
-east	beast	feast	least **	yeast	
-eat	beat **	feat	heat **	meat *	neat
	peat	seat **	bleat	cheat **	cleat
	pleat	treat **	wheat		
-eath	heath	sheath	wreath		
-eave	heave	leave **	weave	cleave	sheave
-ee	bee *	fee	knee **	see *	free *
	tee	wee	glee	flee	
	spree	three **	tree *		
-eech	beech	leech	breech	screech	speech **
-eed	deed	feed **	heed	need **	reed
	seed	weed	bleed	breed	creed
	freed	greed	speed **	tweed	

续表

-eek	leek	meek			
-eel	feel *	heel	kneel	peel	reel
	steel	wheel **			
-eem	deem	seem **	teem		
-een	keen	queen **	seen **	teen	green *
	screen **				
-eep	beep	deep **	jeep	keep *	peep
	seep	weep	cheep	creep	sheep *
	sleep *	steep	sweep *		
-eer	deer	jeer	peer	queer	sneer
	steer				
-eet	beet	feet *	meet *	fleet	greet
	sheet	skeet	sleet	street *	sweet **
	tweet				
-eeze	breeze	freeze	sneeze	squeeze	tweeze
	wheeze				
-iece	niece	piece **			
-ief	brief	chief	grief	thief	
-ield	field **	yield	shield		

* means on the vocabulary list of national curriculum level 2 and ** means level 3.

Long-I sound /igh/ Phonograms

-ibe	bribe	scribe	tribe		
-ice	dice	twice **	mice	nice *	rice *
	vice	price *	slice	splice	trice
-ide	hide **	ride **	side **	tide	wide **
	bride	glide	pride **	slide	snide
	stride				
-ie	die *	lie *	pie	tie **	vie
-ied	died **	lied **	cried **	dried **	fried
	spied	tried **			
-ier	brier	crier	drier	flier	

续表

-ies	dies **	lies **	pies	ties **	cries **
	dries **	flies **	skies **	spies	tries **
-ife	fife	knife **	life **	rife	wife **
	strife				
-igh	high **	nigh	sigh	thigh	
-ight	fight **	knight	light *	might **	night *
	right *	sight	tight	blight	bright **
	flight	fright	plight	plight	slight
-ike	bike *	pike	hike **	like *	spike
-ild	mild	wild **	child *		
-ile	file	mile **	smile **	pile	tile
	vile	while **			
-ime	dime	lime	mime	time *	chime
	grime	prime	slime		
-ind	bind	find *	hind	kind *	mind **
	rind	wind *	blind **	grind	
-ine	dine	fine *	line **	mine **	nine **
	pine	vine	shine **	shrine	spine
	swine	whine			
-ipe	pipe	ripe	wipe	gripe	snipe
	stripe	swipe			
-ire	fire *	hire	tire	wire	spire
-ise	guise	rise **	wise **		
-ite	bite	kite *	mite	quite **	rite
	site	white *	write *	sprite	
-ive	dive	five **	hive	jive	live *
	chive	drive **	strive	thrive	
-uy	buy *	guy			
-y	by *	my *	cry *	dry **	fry
	ply	pry	shy **	sky **	sly
	spy	try *	why *		
-ye	bye *	dye	eye *	lye	rye

* means on the vocabulary list of national curriculum level 2 and ** means level 3.

Long-O sound /oa/ Phonograms

-o	go *	no *	so *	pro	
-oach	coach	poach	roach	broach	
-oad	load	road **	toad		
-oak	soak	cloak	croak		
-oal	coal	foal	goal **		
-oam	foam	loam	roam		
-oan	loan	moan	groan		
-oast	boast	coast *	roast	toast	
-oat	oat	boat *	coat *	goat *	moat
	bloat	float	gloat	throat **	
-obe	lobe	robe	globe	probe	
-ode	code	lode	mode	node	strode
-oe	doe	foe	hoe	joe	toe
	woe				
-oke	coke	joke	poke	woke	yoke
	broke **	choke	smoke **	spoke **	stoke
-old	old *	cold *	fold	gold **	hold *
	mold	sold **	told **	scold	
-ole	dole	hole *	mole	pole	role
	stole **	whole **			
-oll	poll	roll	toll	droll	knoll
	scroll	stroll	troll		
-olt	bolt	colt	jolt	molt	volt
-ome	dome	home *	chrome		
-one	bone	cone	hone	lone	tone
	zone	clone	drone	phone *	prone
	shone	stone *			
-ope	cope	dope	hope **	mope	nope
	pope	rope **	scope	slope	
-ose	hose	nose *	pose	rose **	chose *
	close *	prose	those *		
-ost	host	most **	post **	ghost	

续表

-ote	note **	quote	rote	vote	wrote **
-ove	cove	wove	clove	drove	grove
	stove	trove			
-ow	bow	know *	low **	mow	row **
	sow	tow	blow **	crow	flow
	glow	grow **	show *	slow *	snow *
	stow				
-own	known **	mown	sown	blown **	flown **
	grown **	shown **	thrown **		

* means on the vocabulary list of national curriculum level 2 and ** means level 3.

Long-U sound /yoo/ phonograms

-ew	dew	few **	knew **	pew	
-ude	dude				
-ue	due	hue			
-uke	duke	puke			
-une	dune	tune			
-ube	cube	tube			
-ule	mule				
-ume	fume				
-ure	cure	pure			
-use	use	fuse	muse		
-ute	cute *	mute			

* means on the vocabulary list of national curriculum level 2 and ** means level 3.

Note: In British English, words like dude, tube, due, dune, tune, mute and duke belong to the Long-U sound group; in American English, they are classified as belonging to the long /oo/ sound group. Based on phonic decoding rules, those words are classified as belonging to the Long-U sound group.

Short-A sound / a/ Phonograms

-ab	cab	dab	gab	jab	lab
	nab	tab	blab	crab	drab
	flab	grab	scab	slab	stab

续表

-ack	back *	hack	Jack	knack	lack
	Mack	pack	quack	rack	sack
	tack	black *	clack	crack	shack
	slack	smack	snack	stack	track
	whack				
-act	fact **	pact	tact	tract	
-ad	bad *	dad *	fad	had **	lad
	mad **	pad	sad *	tad	clad
	glad **				
-aft	daft	raft	waft	craft	draft
	graft	shaft			
-ag	bag *	gag	jag	lag	nag
	rag	sag	tag	wag	brag
	crag	drag	flag	shag	snag
	stag				
-am	dam	ham	jam	ram	tam
	scam	scram	yam	clam	gram
	sham	slam	swam		
-amp	camp	damp	lamp	ramp	vamp
	champ	clamp	cramp	scamp	stamp
	tramp				
-an	ban	can *	fan *	man *	pan
	ran **	tan	van	bran	clan
	plan **	scan	span	than **	
-ance	dance *	lance	chance **	France **	glance
	prance	stance	trance		
-anche	ranch	blanch	branch		
-and	band **	hand *	land **	sand **	bland
	brand	gland	stand *	strand	
-ang	bang	fang	gang	hang **	pang
	rang **	sang **	clang	slang	sprang **

续表

-ank	bank **	lank	rank	sank **	tank
	yank	blank	clank	crank	drank *
	flank	plank	prank	spank	thank *
-ant	pant	rant	chant	grant	plant *
	scant	slant			
-ap	cap *	gap	lap	map *	nap
	rap	sap	tap	yap	chap
	clap	flap	scrap	slap	snap
	strap	trap	wrap		
-ash	bash	cash	dash	gash	hash
	lash	mash	rash	sash	brash
	clash	flash	slash	smash	stash
	thrash	trash			
-ask	ask *	cask	mask	task **	flask
-asm	chasm	plasm	spasm		
-asp	gasp	hasp	rasp	clasp	grasp
-ast	cast	fast *	last *	mast	past *
	vast	blast			
-at	bat	cat *	fat **	gnat	hat **
	mat	pat	rat	sat **	vat
	brat	chat **	flat	scat	slat
	slat	spat	that **		
-atch	batch	catch *	hatch	latch	match **
	patch	scratch	snatch		
-ath	bath **	math *	path	wrath	
-ax	**lax**	**tax**	**wax**	**flax**	

* means on the vocabulary list of national curriculum level 2 and ** means level 3.

Short-E sound /e/ phonograms

-ead	dead **	head *	lead **	read **	bread *
	dread	spread **	thread	tread	
-ealth	health **	wealth **	stealth		

续表

-eck	deck	heck	neck **	peck	check **
	fleck	speck	wreck		
-ed	bed *	fed **	led **	red *	wed
	bled	bred	fled	shed	shred
	sled	sped			
-edge	hedge	ledge	wedge	dredge	pledge
	sledge				
-eft	left *	cleft	theft		
-eg	beg	keg			
-eld	held **	meld	weld		
-elf	self	shelf **			
-ell	bell **	cell	dell	fell	jell
	sell *	tell *	well *	yell	
	dwell	shell	smell **	spell **	swell
-elp	help *	kelp	yelp		
-elt	belt	felt **	knelt	melt	pelt
	welt	dwelt			
-em	gem	hem	stem	them *	then *
-en	den	hen **	pen *	men *	ten **
	when *				
-ence	fence	hence	pence	whence	
-end	end **	bend	fend	lend **	mend
	send **	tend	vend	blend	spend **
	trend				
-ength	length	strength			
-ense	dense	sense **	tense		
-ent	bent	cent	dent	gent	
	lent **	rent	sent *	tent **	vent
	went **	scent	spent **		
-ep	pep	rep	prep	step	
-ept	kept **	wept **	crept	slept **	swept **
-esh	mesh	flesh	fresh		

续表

-ess	guess **	less **	mess **	bless	chess
	dress *	press	stress **		
-est	best *	jest	lest	nest	pest
	rest **	test **	vest	zest	blest
-et	bet	get *	jet	let *	met **
	net	pet *	set *	wet **	yet **
	fret				
-etch	fetch	sketch	wrench		
-ext	next *	text **			

* means on the vocabulary list of national curriculum level 2 and ** means level 3.

Short-I Phonograms

-ib	bib	fib	rib	crib	glib
-ick	kick **	lick	pick **	quick **	sick **
	tick	wick	brick	chick	click **
	flick	slick	stick **	thick **	trick
-id	bid	did **	hid *	kid *	lid
	mid	rid	grid	skid	slid
	squid				
-iff	cliff	sniff	stiff	whiff	
-ift	gift *	lift **	rift	sift	drift
	shift	swift	thrift		
-ig	big *	dig **	fig	jig	pig *
	wig	brig	sprig	swig	twig
-ilk	milk *	silk **			
-ill	ill *	bill	dill	fill **	gill
	hill *	kill **	mill	pill **	quill
	sill	till	will *	chill	drill
	frill	grill	skill **	spill	still **
	thrill	trill	twill		
-ilt	kilt	tilt	wilt	quilt	stilt

续表

-im	dim	him *	rim	brim	grim
	prim	slim **	swim *	trim	whim
-imp	limp	blimp	chimp	crimp	primp
	skimp				
-in	bin	fin	kin	pin	tin
	win *	chin	grin	shin	skin
	spin	thin *	twin		
-ince	mince	since **	prince **		
-inch	inch	cinch	finch	pinch	clinch
	flinch				
-ing	bing	ding	king **	ping	ring **
	sing *	wing **	bring *	cling	fling
	sling	spring *	sting	string	swing
	thing *	wring			
-is	is **	his *			
-ish	dish	fish *	wish *	swish	
-isk	disk	risk **	brisk	frisk	whisk
-isp	lisp	wisp	crisp		
-iss	hiss	kiss **	miss **	bliss	swiss
-ist	fist	list **	mist	wrist	twist
-it	bit	fit **	hit **	kit	knit
	lit **	pit	quit	sit *	wit
	flit	grit	skit	slit	spit
	split				
-itc	ditch	hitch	pitch	witch	switch
-ive	give *	live *			
-ix	fix **	mix **	six **		

* means on the vocabulary list of national curriculum level 2 and ** means level 3.

Short-O phonograms

-ob	cob	gob	job *	knob	lob
	mob	rob	sob	blob	glob
	slob	snob	throb		

续表

-ock	dock	hock	knock **	lock **	mock
	rock **	sock *	tock	block **	clock *
	crock	flock	frock	shock **	smock
	stock				
-od	cod	mod	nod	pod	rod
	sod	clod	plod	prod	trod
-oft	loft	soft			
-og	bog	cog	dog *	fog	hog
	jog **	log	clog	flog	frog
	smog				
-omp	pomp	romp	chomp	stomp	
-ond	bond	fond	pond	blond	
-op	bop	cop	hop	mop	pop
	sop	top *	chop	crop	drop **
	flop	plop	prop	shop *	slop
	stop *				
-ot	cot	dot	got **	hot *	jot
	knot	lot *	not *	pot	rot
	tot	blot	clot	plot	shot
	slot	spot	trot		
-otch	botch	notch	blotch	crotch	
-ough	cough **	trough			
-ox	ox	box *	fox **	lox	pox

∗ means on the vocabulary list of national curriculum level 2 and ∗∗ means level 3.

Short-U sound /u/ Phonograms

-ome	come *	some *			
-on	son **	ton	won **		
-ough	rough	tough	slough		
-ove	love *	glove **	shove	above **	
-ub	cub	dub	hub	nub	rub
	sub	tub	club	flub	grub
	scrub	shrub	snub	stub	

续表

-uch	much *	such **			
-uck	buck	duck	luck **	muck	puck
	suck	tuck	cluck	pluck	stuck
	struck **	truck **			
-ud	bud	cud	dud	mud	crud
	spud	stud	thud		
-uge	budge	fudge	judge **	nudge	drudge
	grudge	sludge	smudge	trudge	
-uff	buff	cuff	huff	puff	ruff
	bluff	fluff	gruff	scuff	sluff
	snuff	stuff			
-ug	bug	dug **	hug **	jug	lug
	mug	rug	pug	tug	chug
	drug	plug	shrug	slug	smug
	snug	thug			
-ulk	bulk	hulk	sulk		
-ull	cull	dull	gull	hull	lull
	mull	skull			
-um	bum	gum	hum	mum *	sum
	chum	drum	glum	plum	scum
	slum	strum	swum **		
-ump	bump	dump	hump	jump *	lump
	pump	rump	chump	clump	frump
	grump	grump	plump	stump	thump
	trump				
-un	bun	fun **	gun **	pun	run *
	sun *	shun	spun	stun	
-unch	bunch	hunch	lunch *	munch	punch
	brunch	crunch	scrunch		
-ung	hung **	lung	rung **	sung **	clung
	flung	sprung **	stung	strung *	swung **

续表

-unk	bunk	dunk	hunk	junk	sunk *
	chunk	drunk **	flunk	plunk	shrunk
	skunk	slunk	spunk	stunk	trunk
-unt	bunt	hunt	punt	runt	blunt
	grunt	stunt			
-up	cup *	pup	sup		
-us	bus *	plus	thus		
-ush	gush	hush	mush	rush **	blush
	brush **	crush	flush	plush	slush
	thrush				
-ust	bust	dust	gust	gust	just **
	must *	rust	crust	thrust	trust **
-ut	but *	cut *	gut	hut	jut
	nut	rut	glut	shut **	strut
-utch	hutch	clutch	crutch		
-utt	butt	mutt	putt		

* means on the vocabulary list of national curriculum level 2 and ** means level 3.

Diphthong /oi/ Phonograms

-oil	oil **	boil **	coil	foil	toil
	broil	spoil			
-oin	coin **	join *	loin	groin	
-oint	joint	point **			
-oise	noise **	poise			
-oist	foist	hoist	moist		
-oy	boy *	coy	joy **	toy *	soy

* means on the vocabulary list of national curriculum level 2 and ** means level 3.

Diphthong /ou/ Phonograms

-ouch	couch	pouch	vouch	crouch	grouch
	slouch				
-oud	loud **	cloud **	proud **		

续表

-ounce	bounce	pounce	trounce		
-ount	count **	mount			
-ound	bound	found **	hound	mound	pound
	round **	sound **	wound **	ground **	
-our	our *	hour *	sour	flour	scour
-ouse	house *	louse	mouse *	blouse **	spouse
-out	out *	about *	gout	tout	clout
	scout	snout	spout	sprout	stout
	trout				
-outh	mouth *	south **			
-ow	bow	cow *	how *	now *	vow
	brow	chow	plow		
-owl	fowl	howl	growl	prowl	scowl
-own	down *	gown	town **	brown *	clown
	crown	drown	frown		

* means on the vocabulary list of national curriculum level 2 and ** means level 3.

Variant vowel sound broad-O sound /or/ Phonograms

-all	all *	ball *	call *	fall **	mall **
	tall *	wall *	small *	squall	stall
-alk	balk	talk **	walk *	chalk **	stalk
-alt	halt	malt	salt **		
-aught	caught **	naught	taught **	fraught	
-aunch	haunch	launch	paunch	staunch	
-aunt	daunt	gaunt	haunt	jaunt	taunt
	taunt	flaunt			
-ault	fault	vault			
-aw	caw	gnaw	jaw	law **	paw
	raw	saw **	claw	draw *	flaw
	slaw	squaw	straw		
-awl	bawl	brawl	crawl	drawl	scrawl
	shawl				

续表

-awn	dawn	fawn	lawn	pawn	yawn
	brawn	drawn	prawn		
-ong	bong	dong	long	song	tong
	prong	strong *	wrong *		
-oss	boss	loss	moss	toss	cross
	cross	floss	gloss		
-ost	cost	lost **	frost		
-oth	moth	broth	cloth	froth	sloth
-ought	ought	bought **	fought **	sought **	brought **
	thought **				
* means on the vocabulary list of national curriculum level 2 and ** means level 3.					

Variant vowel sound short /oo/ Phonograms

-ood	good *	hood	wood *	stood **	
-ook	book *	cook *	hook	look *	nook
	brook	crook	shook **		
-oot	foot *	soot			
-ould	could **	would **	should **		
-ull	bull	full **	pull **		
-ush	bush	push **			
* means on the vocabulary list of national curriculum level 2 and ** means level 3.					

Variant vowels long /oo/ sound Phonograms

-ew	blew **	brew	crew	grew **	screw
-o	do *	to *	who *		
-oo	boo	coo	goo	moo	too *
	woo	zoo *	shoo		
-ood	food *	mood	brood		
-oof	goof	roof	proof	spoof	
-ool	cool *	fool *	pool	tool *	drool
	school *	spool	stool		

续表

-oom	boom	doom	loom	room *	zoom
	bloom	broom	gloom	groom	
-oon	boon	loon	moon *	soon *	croon
	spoon **	swoon			
-oop	coop	hoop	loop	droop	scoop
	sloop	snoop	stoop	swoop	troop
-oose	goose	loose	moose	noose	
-oot	boot	hoot	loot	moot	root
	toot	scoot	shoot		
-ooth	booth	tooth **			
-ooze	ooze	snooze			
-oup	soup *	croup	group **		
-ube	lube				
-uce	spruce	truce			
-ude	rude	crude			
-ue	blue *	clue	glue	true **	
-uke	fluke				
-ule	rule **				
-ume	plume				
-une	June **	prune			
-ure	lure	sure			
-use	ruse				
-ute	jute	lute	brute	chute	flute

∗ means on the vocabulary list of national curriculum level 2 and ∗∗ means level 3.

Note: In American English, words like dude, tube, due, dune, tune, mute and duke belong to the Long-U sound group and are classified in the long /oo/ group according to phonic decoding rules. These terms are classified as having a Long-U sound.

R-controlled sound /air/ phonograms

-air	air *	fair **	hair *	lair	pair *
	chair *	flair	flair	stair *	

续表

-are	bare	care *	dare	fare	hare
	mare	pare	rare	ware	blare
	flare	glare	scare **	spare **	snare
	square **	stare *			
-ear	bear *	pear **	wear *	swear	

* means on the vocabulary list of national curriculum level 2 and ** means level 3.

R-controlled vowel sound /ur/ phonograms

-earn	earn	learn *	yearn		
-erb	herb	verb			
-erge	merge	serge	verge		
-erk	jerk	clerk			
-erm	germ	term **			
-en	fern	stern			
-erve	nerve	serve	swerve		
-ir	fir	sir **	stir	whir	
-ird	bird *	third **			
-irk	quirk	shirk	smirk		
-irl	girl *	swirl	twirl	whirl	
-irt	dirt	flirt	shirt *	skirt *	
-irst	first **	thirst			
-irth	birth **	girth			
-ur	fur	blur	slur	spur	
-urb	curb	blurb			
-urge	urge	purge			
-url	curl	furl	hurl		
-urn	burn **	turn *	churn	spurn	
-urk	lurk	murk			
-urse	curse	nurse	purse		
-urt	curt	hurt *	blurt	spurt	

* means on the vocabulary list of national curriculum level 2 and ** means level 3.

R-controlled vowel sound /ar/ phonograms

-ar	bar	car *	far *	jar	mar
	par	tar	char	scar	spar
	star *				
-ard	card *	guard **	hard *	lard	yard
-arge	-barge	large **	charge		
-ark	bark	dark **	hark	lark	mark **
	park *	shark **	spark	stark	
-arm	arm *	farm *	harm **	charm	
-arn	barn	darn	yarn		
-arp	carp	harp	tarp	sharp	
-art	cart	chart	mart	part **	tart
	chart	smart **	start **		

* means on the vocabulary list of national curriculum level 2 and ** means level 3.

R-controlled vowel sound /or/ phonograms

-oar	boar	roar	soar		
-oor	door *	floor *			
-orch	porch	torch	scorch		
-ord	cord	ford	lord	chord	sword
-ore	bore	core	fore	gore	more **
	pore	sore	tore	wore	chore
	spore	force **	sore **	score **	store **
	gore	tore	shore	swore	
-ork	cork	fork **	pork **	stork	
-orm	dorm	form **	dorm	storm **	
-orn	born *	corn *	horn *	morn	torn *
	worn *	scorn	sworn	thorn	
-ort	fort	port	sort	short *	snort
	sport *				
-our	four *	pour			

* means on the vocabulary list of national curriculum level 2 and ** means level 3.

Part Ⅳ Sight Words List

The most Frequent 150 words

(in order of frequency according to American Heritage Word Frequency Book)

the *	could **	they *	use *	of *
no *	at *	may *	and *	make *
be *	water **	an *	than **	this *
go *	to *	first **	from **	good *
in *	been **	I *	new *	is **
long *	have *	write *	you *	little *
or *	our *	that *	very *	by *
used *	it *	after *	one **	me *
he *	word *	had **	man *	for *
called **	not *	too *	was **	just **
will *	any *	on *	his *	each **
day *	are *	most *	about *	same **
but *	know *	how *	right *	what *
get *	up *	look *	all *	through **
out *	think *	where *	back *	them *
such **	when *	much *	then *	here *
we *	before *	she *	take *	there *
also *	many *	why *	can *	around *
some *	thing **	find *	another *	so *
help *	your *	came **	these *	put *
which *	come *	would **	year *	their *
work *	other **	different *	said **	three **
its *	away **	if **	word *	who *
again *	do *	must *	now *	off *
into **	because *	people *	went **	has **
does **	my *	old **	more **	part **
made **	number **	her *	even **	over *
two **	place *	did **	like *	well *

续表

The most Frequent 150 words

(in order of frequency according to American Heritage Word Frequency Book)

down *	him *	as **	only **	see *
with *	way *	time *	his *	find *

* means on the vocabulary list of national curriculum level 2 and ** means level 3.

Dolch Basic Sight Words 220

a *	don't	in *	pick *	those **
about *	down **	into **	play **	three **
after *	draw *	is **	please **	to **
again *	drink **	it **	pretty *	today **
all *	eat *	its *	pull **	together **
always *	eight *	jump *	put *	too **
am *	every *	just **	ran **	try **
an *	fall **	keep *	read **	two **
and *	far *	kind *	red **	under *
any *	fast *	know *	ride *	up *
are *	find *	laugh **	right **	upon **
around *	first **	let *	round *	us *
as **	five **	light *	run **	use *
ask *	fly *	like *	said *	very *
at *	for *	little *	saw *	walk *
ate **	found **	live *	say *	want *
away **	four **	long *	see **	warm *
be *	from *	look *	seven **	was **
because *	full **	made **	shall *	wash *
been **	funny **	make *	she *	we *
before *	gave **	many *	show *	well *
best *	get *	may *	sing *	went **
better **	give *	me *	sit **	were **
big *	go *	much *	six *	what *
black *	goes **	must *	sleep *	when *

续表

Dolch Basic Sight Words 220

blue *	going	my *	small *	where *
both **	good *	myself **	so *	which *
bring *	got **	never *	some	white *
brown *	green *	new *	soon *	who *
but *	grow **	no *	start *	why *
buy *	had **	not *	stop *	will *
by *	has **	now *	take **	wish *
call *	have *	of *	tell **	with *
came **	he *	off *	ten **	work *
can *	help *	old *	thank **	would **
carry **	her *	on *	that **	write *
clean *	here *	once **	the **	yellow *
cold *	him *	one **	their **	yes *
come *	his *	only **	them **	you *
could **	hold **	open *	then **	your *
cut *	hot *	or *	there **	
did **	how *	our *	these **	
do *	hurt *	out *	they **	
does **	I *	over *	think **	
done **	if **	own **	this **	

* means on the vocabulary list of national curriculum level 2 and ** means level 3.

References

[1] Bald, J. Using phonics to teach reading and spelling [M]. Sage Publication Ltd, 2007.

[2] Bear, R. D., Invernizzi, M., Templeton, S., & Johnston, F. Words their way (6th ed.) [M]. Pearson Education, 2020.

[3] Bishop, M. M. The ABC's and all their tricks [M]. Dickinson Press, Inc, 1986.

[4] Blevins, W. Phonics from A to Z: A practical guide [M]. Scholastic Inc, 2017.

[5] Carroll, M. J., Crane, B. C., Duff, J. F., Hulme, C. & Snowling J. M. Developing language and literacy: Effective intervention in the early years [M]. John Wiley and Sons, Ltd, 2011.

[6] Department of Education, Science and Training. Teaching reading: Report and recommendations [EB/OL]. https://research.acer.edu.au/cgi/viewcontent.cgi?article=1004&context=tll_misc.

[7] Hepplewhite, D. Oxford phonics spelling dictionary [M]. Oxford, 2020.

[8] International Literacy Association. Explaining phonics instruction: An educator's guide [EB/OL]. https://literacyworldwide.org/docs/default-source/where-we-stand/ila-explaining-phonics-instruction-an-educators-guide.pdf. 2018.

[9] International Literacy Association. Meeting the challenges of early literacy phonics instruction [EB/OL]. https://www.literacyworldwide.org/docs/default-source/where-we-stand/ila-meeting-challenges-early-literacy-phonics-instruction.pdf. 2019.

[10] Papp, S. Phonics and literacy instruction for young learners in EFL. Part of the Cambridge papers in ELT series [M]. Cambridge University Press, 2020.

中文版词典

1	Phonics	自然拼读
2	Phonics Instruction	自然拼读教学
3	Consonant	辅音字母
4	Consonant Sound	辅音
5	Vowel	元音字母
6	Vowel Sound	元音
7	Phonemic Awareness	音素意识
8	Phonological Awareness	语音意识
9	Phonograms	拼读模块
10	Word Family	拼读模块
11	Word Chunk	拼读模块
12	Systematic Synthetic Phonics Approach（SSP）	系统综合自然拼读教学模式
13	Synthetic Phonics Instruction Approach	综合拼读教学模式
14	Analytic Phonics Instruction Approach	分析拼读教学模式
15	Analogy Phonics Instruction Approach	类比拼读教学模式
16	Speech Sound	音素
17	Phoneme	音素
18	Digraph	二合字母
19	Vowel Digraph	元音二合字母
20	Consonant Digraph	辅音二合字母
21	Onset	首音（声母）
22	Rime	尾音（韵母）
23	Onset-rime	首尾音（声母-韵母）
24	Diphthong	双元音音素

续表

25	Vowel Diphthong	双元音音素
26	Consonant Cluster	辅音字母连缀
27	Consonant Blends	辅音音素连缀
28	Syllable	音节
29	Open Syllable	开音节
30	Closed Syllable	闭音节
31	Stable Syllable	成音节
32	Final Stable Syllable	尾端成音节
33	Syllable Juncture Patterns	音节连接模式
34	Rhyme	韵
35	Alliteration	头韵
36	Assonance	谐音
37	Blending	混合音素
38	Segmentation	分割音素
39	Long-Vowel Sound	长元音
40	Short-Vowel Sound	短元音
41	Variant-Vowel Sound	变体元音
42	R-Controlled Vowel	受 R 影响的元音
43	Schwa	轻音
44	Hard Consonant	硬辅音
45	Soft Consonant	软辅音
46	Voiced Consonant	浊辅音
47	Unvoiced Consonant	清辅音
48	Voiceless Consonant	清辅音
49	Nasal Consonant	鼻（辅）音
50	Silent Consonant	不发音的辅音
51	Connected Text	可解码文本
52	Decodable Text	可解码文本
53	High Frequency Words	高频词
54	Sight Words	视觉词汇
55	Irregular Words	不规则词汇
56	Irregulars	不规则词汇

第1章 概述

本章旨在让读者掌握关于自然拼读相关的基本知识：

教学目标	本章主要讲授： 1. 自然拼读以及自然拼读教学的基本概念 2. 自然拼读相关的基本语音学知识 3. 音素意识的基本概念和技巧
具体目标	读者应该掌握： 1. 自然拼读的定义 2. 自然拼读教学的定义 3. 系统综合自然拼读教学模式（SSP Mode）的定义 4. 系统综合自然拼读教学模式的益处 5. 自然拼读技能与阅读理解的关系 6. 44 个基本音素 7. 语音学中与自然拼读相关的术语 8. 音素意识的基本概念与内涵 9. 音素意识的基本技能 10. 音素意识的培养与发展

1.1 自然拼读（Phonics）

自然拼读（Phonics），即英语语音拼读规则，研究的是字母和音素之间的对应关系，也是英语读写必备的技能。其规则本身不是一种特定的教学法或教学方式，相反，有几种教学方式来教授这种字母和音素之间的对应关系（Blevins, 2017; ILA, 2019）。本书后面章节会对自然拼读的不同教学方式进行详细介绍。

1.2 自然拼读教学（Phonics Instruction）

自然拼读教学（Phonics Instruction）指传授给学生字母和音素之间的对应关

系，以及如何在阅读和拼写中利用字母与音素之间的对应关系的教学活动。这一教学活动应包括师生双方（Blevins, 2017; ILA, 2019）。

1.3 自然拼读综合教学法（Synthetic Phonics Instruction）

自然拼读综合教学法（Synthetic Phonics Instruction）首先教授学生最基本的音素和字母之间的对应关系并引导学生运用音素意识将字母发音进行组合，从而拼读出单词的教学方法。这种方法能让英语初学者快速获得基本的单词拼读能力，为流利阅读打下基础。

1.4 系统综合自然拼读教学模式（Systematic Synthetic Phonics Instruction Mode.）

系统综合自然拼读教学模式（SSP Mode）是一种系统、全面、有计划的从最基本的字母—音素之间的关系开始学习，并逐步过渡到复杂、高级的字母组合发音的自然拼读教学模式（MMU, 2015）。

1.5 系统综合自然拼读教学模式的益处

系统综合自然拼读教学模式（SSP Mode）能让英语语言初学者迅速掌握基本音素和字母对应关系，即自然拼读中最基本的语音解码规则，从而顺利在阅读中对不认识的单词进行解码拼读。这种模式能够让学习者进一步成长为自信的独立阅读者。这种教学模式同时能培养学习者音素意识。音素意识对于自然拼读教学中具有关键作用（MMU, 2015）。

1.6 自然拼读和阅读之间的关系

为什么英语语言初学者有必要学习自然拼读？要回答这个问题，首先要理解自然拼读和早期英语阅读之间的关系。早期英语阅读包括两个阅读层面，第一是单词层面的阅读，第二是文本层面的阅读（Carroll et al., 2011）。

（1）单词层面的阅读：自然拼读教学能让初学者学会最基本的英语语音解码规则并将其运用在单词拼读中去识别陌生单词。随着初学者的拼读练习增多，所积累的视觉词汇（Sight Words）越多。视觉词汇指无须拼读，仅看一眼就能读出来的单词。日积月累，初学者在拼读练习及广泛的阅读中就能完成对视觉单词的积累，从而完成在单词层面的阅读任务。

（2）文本层面的阅读：随着初学者的视觉单词积累，文本阅读的流利度（Fluency）随之增加（Blevins, 2017; ILA, 2018, 2019）。这样学习者的阅读注意力就从单词识别转移到了上下文理解中，从而进一步促进阅读理解。

1.7　开始自然拼读教学的两个先决条件

开始自然拼读教学有两个关键的先决条件：第一是音素意识，第二是字母认知。

（1）音素意识。音素意识指学习者能意识到单个单词的发音是由不同的音素组成，并具有操控和驾驭音素的能力（Blevins，2017）。

（2）字母认知。在这里，字母认知主要指能够认识字母的名字和其所对应的主要发音。

以上两个先决条件都是早期阅读教学成功与否的重要因素。前述提到的系统综合拼读教学模式（SSP Mode）是英语作为外语学习者的最佳选择，因为这种教学模式在教授自然拼读语音解码规则的同时也培养了学习者的音素意识。

1.8　英语的 44 个音素

英语是由 26 个字母组成的语言。26 个字母对应 44 个不同的音素。当这些字母以各种不同的方式组合的时候，不同字母所对应的音素也根据特定的拼读规则组合起来成为单词的发音。在这 44 个基本音素中，有 25 个辅音音素和 19 个元音音素。如表 1.1 所示。

表 1.1

序号	辅音音素	元音音素
1	/b/ **b**at	/ai/ c**a**k**e**
2	/d/ **d**og	/ee/ f**ee**t
3	/f/ **f**an	/igh/ b**i**k**e**
4	/g/ **g**ate	/oa/ c**o**d**e**
5	/h/ **h**at	/yoo/ c**u**b**e**
6	/j/ **j**ump/**g**ym	/a/c**a**t
7	/**k**/ **k**ite/**c**at	/e/ b**e**d
8	/l/ **l**eaf	/i/ f**i**sh
9	/m/**m**op	/o/ f**o**g
10	/n/**n**et	/u/d**u**ck
11	/p/ **p**ig	/uh/ **a**larm
12	/r/ **r**ap	/air/ ch**air**
13	/s/ **s**un/**c**ent	/ir/ b**ir**d
14	/t/ **t**op	/ar/ c**ar**

续表

序号	辅音音素	元音音素
15	/v/ **v**ase	/or/ **for**
16	/w/ **w**agon	/oi/ b**oy**
17	/y/ **y**o-yo	/ou/ h**ou**se
18	/z/ **z**oo	long /oo/ m**oo**n
19	/ch/ **ch**eese	short /oo/b**oo**k
20	/sh/ **sh**ark	
21	/zh/ trea**s**ure	
22	voiced /th/ **th**e	
23	unvoiced /th/ **th**umb	
24	/hw/ **wh**y	
25	/ng/ ri**ng**	

注：除轻音音素/uh/摘自 Bear 等（2020）以外，都摘自 Hepplewhite（2020）版本的牛津拼写字典。

1.9 辅音字母

辅音字母（consonant/consonants）这个术语在本指南中指的是任何非元音字母（A、E、I、O、U）（Bear et al.，2020）。当书中出现辅音（consonant/consonants）的时候，会用大写字母来表示。

1.10 辅音音素

辅音音素是所对应的辅音字母的发音。发辅音的时候气流会部分或者全部中断。在本指南中，音素的发音用双斜线框起来，以区别于字母。

1.11 元音字母

元音字母包括 A、E、I、O、U 五个字母（Bear et al.，2020）。元音字母用以代表元音音素。在本指南中术语元音字母（vowel/vowels）将用大写字母 A、E、I、O、U 表示。

1.12 元音音素

当我们发元音的时候气流畅通无阻。通常元音音素由相应的元音字母代表（Blevins，2017）。而辅音字母里面的 W 和 Y 也经常扮演元音的角色，但是字母 W 和 Y 并不单独归于元音字母里，因此被称为半元音。当字母 Y 出现在单词或者音节末尾的时候，它起到了元音的作用。当字母 W 与另一个元音组合时，例如，在单词 few、how 以及 slow 中，字母 W 扮演了元音的角色（Blevins，2017）。

1.13 二合字母（Digraph）

二合字母由两个字母组成，每个字母代表一个声音。二合字母分为辅音二合字母和元音二合字母。例如，单词 ship 中的“SH”为辅音二合字母。单词 ocean 中的“EA”为元音二合字母。在英语中二合字母也被称为“digraph”，“letter team”，“letter pair”或者“spelling pattern”。

1.14 元音二合字母（Vowel Digraph）

元音二合字母指的是两个元音字母组合在一起却只代表一个元音音素。例如，单词 rain 中的“-AI”对应发音 Long-A（Bear et al.，2020）。在英语中，元音二合字母也被称为“vowel team”或者“vowel pair”（Bishop，1986；Blevins，2017）。

1.15 辅音二合字母（Consonant Digraph）

辅音二合字母（consonant digraph）指的是两个辅音组合在一起却只对应一个辅音音素，例如，单词 ship 中的“SH”，单词 chat 中的“CH”，单词 thin 中的“TH”，单词 why 中的“WH”，单词 photo 中的“PH”，单词 ghost 中的“GH”以及单词 sign 中的“NG”等（Bear et al.，2020；Bishop，1986；Blevins，2017）。在英语中，consonant digraph 又被称为 consonant team 或者 consonant pair。

1.16 双元音音素（Diphthong）

在语音学中，双元音指两个元音的联合。但这两个元音通常作为一个整体发音，在发音的过程中从第一个元音音素到第二个元音音素是平顺过渡的。换言之，双元音的发音过程从一种舌位平顺滑动到另一种舌位。英语中有两个双元音音素。一个是/oi/，例如，在对应单词 boy 中 OY 或者单词 coil 里 OI 的发音。另一个是/ou/，对应单词 house 里的 OU 或者 cow 里的 OW 的发音（Bear et al.，2020；Blevins，2017）。

1.17 辅音字母连缀（Consonant Cluster）

辅音字母连缀是两个辅音字母组合在一起发音，而每个辅音字母都保留其自身的音素发音。辅音字母连缀主要指的是辅音字母，而不是辅音音素。例如，单词 cluster 里的字母组合 CL，单词 skip 里面的字母组合 SK。辅音字母连缀和辅音二合字母是不一样的。辅音二合字母是两个辅音字母组合在一起代表一个音素。

1.18 辅音音素连缀（Consonant Blend）

辅音音素连缀（consonant blend）指的是辅音字母连缀（consonant cluster）所对应的音素组合，强调的是在音素层面的组合。例如，在单词 sloth 中辅音字母连缀 SL 对应的辅音音素连缀就是/sl/，在单词 skip 中辅音字母连缀 SK 所对应的辅音音素连缀就是/sk/。

1.19 首—尾音/声母—韵母（Onset-Rime）

首尾音（Onset-rime）指一个音节的两个组成部分，也被称为声母-韵母。尾音（Rime）指一个音节中元音字母以及其后的字母。通常一个音节中的首音（onset）在尾音（rime）前，而且首音（onset）是辅音字母、辅音字母连缀，或者是一个辅音二合字母。

更准确地讲，尾音（rime）可以被称为单词模块（Word Chunk）或者单词家族（Word Family）或者拼读模块（Phonogram）。例如，在单音节单词 tag 中，T 是首音，AG 是尾音。如果一个单词是双音节词，那么每个音节都包含一个首音-尾音，也就是说，这个双音节词包含两个首音-尾音。例如，双音节单词 classmate，第一套首音-尾音是 cl-ass，第二套首音-尾音是 m-ate。一些特殊的单词，例如，“at”“out”或者“up”就不具有首音。

1.20 拼读模块（Phonogram）

Phonogram 是一个或者一组字母，代表了一个音素、音节或者一组音素组合，而不具有任何实际意思经常被称作单词模块或者单词家族。从语言学角度来说，phonogram 也常常被称为一个单词里的“尾音”。例如，字母组合-AY 代表单词 ray 中的发音 long-A sound/ai/。再例如-ACK 代表了单词 back，hack，attack 以及 slack 中的发音/a/和/k/。由于四个单词都具有 phonogram-ACK，所以可以说它们具有同一个单词模块（Word Chunk）。

1.21 音节（Syllable）

音节是语言中单个元音音素和辅音音素组合发音的最小语音单位。单个的元音音素可以自成音节。简单来说，音节由单个或者一组辅音后紧接着的一个元音组成。

1.22 开音节（Open Syllable）

开音节指以元音结尾的音节，或者是一个元音字母加一个辅音字母（r 除外）再加一个不发音的字母 e 结尾的重读音节。通常在开音节中的元音字母，发音都是其所代表的长元音音素，长元音音素的发音其实是其字母音。换句话说，当一个音节以长元音音素结尾时，称为开音节。例如，在双音节单词 tiger 里，第一个音节“ti”就是个开音节（Bear et al.，2020）。

1.23 闭音节（Closed Syllable）

以辅音字母结尾的音节称为闭音节。换言之，闭音节通常以辅音字母结尾。在多音节单词中，闭音节指两个辅音中包夹着一个短元音，例如，多音节单词中的 rabbit，短元音/a/和短元音/i/分别被辅音/r/和/b/，以及辅音/b/和/t/包围。

1.24 成音节（Stable Syllable）

从语音学的角度讲，在某些多音节单词中，某些特殊的辅音可以与其他辅音构成一个音节，这种特殊的音节通常出现在单词结尾部分。成音节分为两大类。第一类成音节通常出现在一个单词的结尾。这是唯一不包括元音发音的音节。例如，单词 ta-ble 中的-ble，单词 bri-dle 中的-dle，单词 re-bel 中的-bel，单词 lo-cal 中的-cal，单词 un-cle 中的-cle，单词 cha-pel 中的-pel 以及单词 me-dal 中的-dal。很多末尾的成音节都由一个辅音+字母 L，以及字母 E 组成。他们之所以被称为尾端成音节（Final Stable Syllable），因为这些成音节都出现在单词末尾。这些成音节被称为稳定的成音节也是因为它们的发音相对比较固定。

第二类被称为其他尾端成音节（other Final Stable Syllable）。这一类成音节仅仅出现在单词的末尾，经常被当作单词模块（Phonogram/ word Chunk/word Family）。例如，单词 sta-tion 中的-tion，单词 vi-sion 中的-sion，单词 pic-ture 中的-ture，单词 plea-sure 中的-sure，单词 st-age 中的-age，单词 scrump-tious 中的-tious 以及单词 deli-cious 中的-cious。

1.25 音节连接模式（Syllable Juncture Patterns）

音节相交的地方通常是辅音（C）和元音（V）以不同模式的结合处。例如，在单词 read 中，其音节连接模式为“CVVC”。

1.26 四种基本单音节模式（Four Basic One-Syllable Patterns）

1.26.1 闭音节模式

这是最常见的音节模式。闭音节模式包括一个元音，并且以辅音结尾。大多数符合这种模式的单词都包含“短元音”发音，一共有十三种变式。如表 1.2 所示。

表 1.2

Patter	Example	Pattern	Example
CVCC	hand	CVCCC	match
CVC	cat	CVCCe	judge
CCVCC	fresh	CCVCC	crutch
CCVC	trip	CCVCCe	grudge
CCCVCC	script	VCC	add
VC	in	CCCVC	scrap
VCCC	inch		

1.26.2 元音二合字母模式

这是第二种常见的模式，一共有十二个变式。如表 1.3 所示。

表 1.3

模式	示例	模式	示例
CVVC	heat	CCVVC	treat
CVVCC	reach	CVV	pay
CCVV	play	CVVCe	leave
CCVVCC	bleach	CCVVCe	freeze
CCCVVC	sprain	VVC	oat
VVCC	each	CCCVV	three

1.26.3 元音-辅音-不发音的 E 模式

这是第三种常见模式，通常有四种变式。如表 1.4 所示。

表 1.4

模式	示例	模式	示例
CVCe	race	CCCVCe	strike
CCVCe	shave	VCe	ate

1.26.4 开音节模式

这是第四种常见的模式，只有两种变体：CCV 模式，例如，单词“she”；CV 模式，例如，单词“we”。了解以上音节连接模式能够帮助学习者确定单词中元音的发音是长元音还是短元音。

1.27 音素意识（Phonemic Awareness）

音素意识是语音意识（Phonological Awareness）的一个子集。音素意识指学习者在听到单词时，能够识别或者理解一个单词由一系列独立“发音”组成。学习者所听到的每一个发音都被称为一个音素。识别并会操控音素拼读出单词的意识和能力被称为音素意识。

1.28 语音意识（Phonological Awareness）

语音意识是能识别不同音素、音节、韵律的一种意识。语音意识能让学习者将口语中单词划分为音节、独立音素或者是学习者能读出来的拼读模块。语音意识是较为宽泛的概念，其中包括音素意识和音韵意识（ILA，2019）。若学习者具有语音意识，便能够分辨口语中的音节和音素。语音意识可以通过吟唱押韵歌谣、划分音节节拍或者将单词分割为独立音素等方式培养。

1.29 音素意识和语音意识之间的关系

如前文所述，音素意识是语音意识（Phonological Awareness）的一个子集。音素意识（Phonemic Awareness）的各方面都包含在语音意识中。语音意识（Phonological Awareness）分为深浅两个层面。浅层语音意识一般能够识别单词中的音节、首音和尾音。更深层的语音意识特指音素意识。初学者能利用音素意识去识别和操控单词里的音素，从而能进行单词拼读。

1.30 音素意识相关技能

1.30.1 押尾韵

能识别单词之间的尾韵，例如，cat/hat，can/man，以及 goat/coat。

1.30.2 押头韵

能识别单词中的头韵，例如，sun/sum，leaf/live。

1.30.3 识别谐音

能识别单词中的谐音，例如，单词里 leaf，bean 和 peach 中的“EA”的发音。

1.30.4 混合音素

当听到一个单词按字母顺序将单个音素读出来后能准确读出这个单词。通常混合音素有三子类别。

（1）混合音节：如听到 ta... ble，就能读出 table 这个单词。

（2）混合首音和尾音：如听到/p/... an 就能读出单词 pan。

（3）单个音素混合：注意到每一个音素的发音，例如，/s/ /a/ /t/，然后将这些单个音素组合在一起读出单词 sat。

1.30.5 语音分割：语音分割技能也包括以下三个子类别。

（1）口头音节分割：逐个音节地听单词，并能逐一口头表述出单词的音节。例如，听到单词 table，便能准确辨别和复述出音节 ta...ble。

（2）首音/尾音分割：例如，在听到单词 pan 的同时，首先注意到了首音/p/并准确复述出来，然后发出尾音 an。

（3）逐个音素的分割：例如，听到单词 sat 的时候能准确复述出 sat 并能口头发出/s/-/a/-/t/这三个连续的单个音素。

1.30.6 音素的操控

音素的操控一共包括 9 个子类别：

（1）首字母音素的替换：例如，将单词 mat 中的第一个发音/m/替换成发音/s/从而得到单词 sat。

（2）尾音音素的替换：例如，将单词 map 中的最后一个发音/p/替换成音素/t/从而得到单词 mat。

（3）元音音素的替换：例如，用音素/a/替换掉单词 mop 中间的音素/o/，从而得到单词 map。

（4）音节删除：例如，在读单词 baker 的时候，要求忽略首音节“ba-”只发出音节“-ker”。

（5）词头音素删除：例如，在读单词 sun 的时候，忽略掉词头音素/s/，只发出韵母“-un”。

（6）尾音删除：例如，在读单词 hit 的时候，忽略掉音素/t/，只发出/h/与/i/得到 hi-。

（7）删除辅音音素连缀中的首音：例如，在读单词 step 的时候，忽略位于单词开头首音音素/s/，只发出/tep/得到 tep。

（8）删除辅音音素连缀中的尾音：例如，在读单词 best 的时候，忽略尾音/t/，只发出/bes/从而得到 bes。

（9）删除辅音音素连缀中的第二个音素：例如，在读单词 frog 的时候，忽略第二个音素/r/，只发出/fog/从而得到 fog。

1.31 音素意识的发展

音素意识（Phonemic Awareness）是动态发展的，是可以通过上述提到的音素操控技能练习而培养的。系统的综合自然拼读教学模式能够培养和加强学生的音素意识，因为这种自然拼读教学模式融合了“音素混合在一起发音从而拼读出单词”的技能。如果一定要单独教授音素意识的话，利用儿童读本中的韵文以及音素操控相关训练活动是十分有效的。

1.32 音素意识的重要性

音素意识（Phonemic Awareness）是自然拼读教学的先决条件之一。音素意识较弱的学生可能很难学会拼读，或者说他们的拼读和阅读能力不尽如人意。若缺乏音素意识，他们可能难以区分单词中包含的音素或者无法理解音素的含义。此外，他们在学习过程中还必须能够对单词例如 sit /s/-/i/-/t/进行音素分割，才能正确拼读和拼写该词。

一旦初学者具备了音素意识，他们就能进入词汇层面的阅读。反过来，词汇层面的阅读也能进一步增强音素意识（Blevins，2017）。

第 2 章　自然拼读规则

本章旨在帮助学习者掌握最基本、最常见的语音解码规则。

教学总目标	本章旨在帮助学习者掌握： 1. 常见语音解码规则 2. 常见的拼读模块
具体目标	学习者将能够掌握： 1. 常见的元音解码规则 2. 常见的辅音解码规则 3. 常见的拼读模块

本章将着重介绍字母与其相应的发音。英语包含 26 个字母和 44 个音素。44 个音素包括 25 个辅音音素和 19 个元音音素。本章将这些音素进行分类讲解。换言之，本章将分门别类地详细介绍辅音音素连缀、辅音二合字母、变体元音、元音二合字母以及拼读模块（Phonograms）。

注意：在本指南中，带有斜线的字母（如/k/）指音素发音而不是单词或者字母。例如，单词 kitten 中的音素/k/由字母 K 代表。同时，破折号“-”用于字母或者拼读模块前，表示拼读模块或者字母所代表的音素并非处于单词初始位置。例如，-CK 和-Y 表示拼读模块 CK 和字母 Y 在代表各自相对应的音素时，在单词中并非处于首位。

2.1　元音音素

元音音素可以被分为三类：长元音音素、短元音音素、其他类别元音音素，如图 2.1 所示。

- 元音音素
  - 长元音音素
  - 短元音音素
  - 其他元音音素
    - 元音组合
      - /oi/boy
      - /ou/how
    - 变体元音
      - short/oo/look/oo/
      - long/oo/moo
      - /or/ball,hawk,haul
    - 轻音/uh/
    - R控制的元音音素
      - /or/ for
      - /ur/ fur, bird, her
      - /ar/ far
      - /air/ hair

图 2.1

在介绍元音音素前，首先介绍两个特殊的元音字母 E 和 U。这两个字母在单词中可以不发音。

不发音的 E：当字母 E 是单词中最后一个字母且在它之前还有另一个元音字母时，它通常不发音，例如，单词 rope，dense 和 cheese 中的最后一个字母 E 就不发音。

不发音的 U：当字母 U 出现在字母 G 和字母 E/ I/ Y 时，例如，单词 guess，plague，guide 和 guy 中的 U 不发音。

2.1.1　长元音音素

长元音 A（Long-A sound /ai/）发同名字母 A 的音

规则 1：如同在单词 lake 中，元音字母 A 后面紧跟一个辅音字母，辅音字母后面紧跟一个不发音的字母 E，那么字母 A 的发音为长元音 A/ai/。简单的规则是在字母组合模式 A-E 或者是在 CVCe 或者 VCe 结构中不发音的字母 E 让字母 A 发长元音，例如，在单词 lake 和 ate 中。

规则 2：字母组合"-AY"在单词中通常发长元音 A，例如，在单词 way 和 okay 中。

规则 3：元音字母组合"-AI"在单词中通常发长元音 A，例如，在单词 paid，wait 和 claim 中。

规则 4：当字母 A 独立出现在一个音节的结尾的时候即开音节中，例如，在单词 ba-by 中，字母 A 的发音为长元音 A，例如，在单词 a-corn，A-pril 中。

规则 5：有时元音组合"-EA"也发长元音 A，例如，在单词 break，great 和 steak 中。

规则 6：当字母组合"-EY"在词根结尾时，代表长元音 A，例如，在单词

obey 和 prey 中。

需要注意的是当字母组合“-EY”出现在一个音节中的时候，通常被写作“-EI”，但仍发长元音 A，例如，在单词 their，eight 和 veil 中。

长元音 E（Long-E sound /ee/）发同名字母 E 的音

规则 1：元音字母组合“EE”代表长元音 E，例如，在单词 meet，queen 和 bee 中。

规则 2：字母组合“EA”代表长元音 E。例如，单词 mean 和 cream 中的字母组合 EA 就发长元音 E。大多数时候常见的长元音 E 都由字母组合 EA 或者 EE 代表。

规则 3：当长元音 E 以 E_E 的形式出现时，便构成了 VCe 或者 CVCe 结构。在这种结构中，不发音的字母 E 让单词结构中的第一个元音 E 发长元音 E，例如，在单词 eve，here 和 mere 中。

规则 4：有时候元音字母组合“-IE”也代表长元音 E，例如，在单词 believe 和 chief 中。

规则 5：长元音 E 在单词中可以由单个的字母 E 代表。这种情况通常字母“-E”位于一个音节的末尾，也就是开音节的末尾。例如，在单词 she，be，me 和 fe-ver 中。

规则 6：当单词以字母“-Y”结尾且组成单词的字母数量大于 3 时，“-Y”有时候代表长元音 E，例如，在单词“majesty”和“puppy”中。

规则 7：当字母组合“-EY”在一个单词中扮演后缀的角色时，所代表的发音和单词 puppy 中的字母“Y”是一致的，都代表长元音 E。例如，在单词 turkey，honey 和 valley 中。

长元音 I（Long-I sound /igh/）发同名字母 I 的音

规则 1：当字母 I 以“I_E”的形式，即出现在 CVCe 或者 VCe 结构中，不发音的字母 e 让前面的字母 I 发长元音 I，例如，在单词 hike，ice 和 bike 中。

规则 2：当字母 I 或者 Y 是所在音节的最后一个字母时，字母 I 或者 Y 代表着长元音 I，例如，在单词 hi，idea，I，my，sky 和 tyrant 中。通常，在三个字母组成的以字母 Y 结尾的单词，即当单词以“__y”的形式出现的时候，字母 Y 通常发长元音 I。例如，单词 fly，fry，cry，spy，why，shy，try 和 dry。

规则 3：当元音字母组合“-IE”出现在词根的末尾的时候通常代表被重读的长元音 I，例如，在单词 pie，tie 和 die 中，虽然并不常见，但在三个字母组成的单词中，通常形式是_ie 的情况下，ie 发长元音 I。

规则 4：拼读模块“-igh”在单词中通常也代表长元音 I 的发音，例如，在单词 high, fight, sigh, might 和 right 中。

长元音 O (Long-O sound /oa/ sounds) 发同名字母 O 的音

规则 1: 当字母 O 在单词中以“O_E”的形式出现时，即是在 VCe 或者 CVCe 结构中，单词末尾不发音的字母 E 标志着前面的元音字母 O 发出长元音 O，例如，在单词 home 或者 code 中。

规则 2: 元音字母组合“OA”通常在单词中代表长元音 O，例如，在单词 boat, oat 和 goat 中。

规则 3: 当字母 O 是所在音节中的最后一个字母时，例如，在单词 o-ver, o-kay 和 go 中，单个字母 O 也代表长元音 O。

规则 4: 元音字母组合“-OW”在单词中代表长元音 O，例如，在单词 low, mow 和 bowtie 中。

规则 5: 元音字母组合“-OE”在单词中代表长元音 O，例如，在单词 toe 和 doe 中。

长元音 U (Long-U sound /yoo/ sounds) 发同名字母 U 的音

规则 1: 当字母 U 在单词中以“U_E”的形式出现时，即在通常所说的 VCe 和 CVCe 结构中，单词末尾不发音的字母 E 让前面的元音字母 U 的发音为长元音 U，如同在单词 mule 和 cube 中一样。

规则 2: 当字母 U 为所在音节的最后一个字母时，即在开音节中单个字母 U 也发长元音 U，例如，在单词 hu-go 和 fu-el 中。

规则 3: 当字母 U 是所在音节的最后一个字母，并且字母 U 前面紧邻着字母 R 或者 L 的时候，字母 U 虽然应该还是长元音 U，但出来的音是单词 food 中的音素/oo/，例如，在单词 flu 和 rumor 中。

2.1.2　短元音音素

短元音音素经常位于单词的开头或者中间以及闭音节内，但偶尔也会出现在词尾的位置。

短元音 A (Short-A Sound /a/ as in cat)

规则: 当字母 A 出现在闭音节中时，通常字母 A 代表着短元音 A，例如，在单词 cat, rap, that 中。

短元音 E (Short-E Sound /e/ as in bed)

规则 1: 当元音字母 E 出现在闭音节中的时候，代表着短元音 E 的发音，例如，在单词 fled，pet，felt 中。

规则 2： 当元音字母 E 位于单词的首位，且在同一个音节中紧接一个辅音字母时，字母 E 发短元音 E，例如，在单词 egg，end，ef-fort，es-timate 以及 ex-tra 中。

规则 3： 元音字母组合“-EA”有时候会代表短元音 E，例如，在单词 head，meant，health 以及 pleasure 中。

短元音 I（Short-I Sound /i/ as in fit）

规则 1： 当元音字母 I 或者 Y 出现在闭音节中时，元音字母 I 或者 Y 代表短元音 I，例如，在单词 bit，sym-bol，pig 和 dim-ple 中。

规则 2： 当元音字母 I 位于单词首位且在同一个音节中，I 后面紧跟着一个辅音时，字母 I 的发音是短元音 I。例如，在单词 it 和 ig-loo 中。

短元音 O（Short-O sound /o/ as in fox）

规则 1： 当元音字母 O 出现在闭音节中的时候，元音字母 O 代表着短元音 O 发音，例如，在单词 dot，soft，pop 和 cost 中。

规则 2： 当元音字母 O 为一个单词的首字母且在同一个音节中字母 O 后面紧接一个辅音字母时，字母 O 代表着短元音 O 的发音，例如，在单词 off，of-fice 和 oc-topus 中。

短元音 U（Short-U sound /u/ as in duck）

规则 1： 当元音字母 U 出现在闭音节中时代表短元音 U，例如，在单词 dust，hush 和 but 中。

规则 2： 当元音字母 U 为一个单词的首字母，且在同一个音节中后面紧跟一个辅音字母时，字母 U 代表着短元音 U 的发音，例如，在单词 up，ut-most 和 ug-ly 中。

2.1.3 其他元音音素

如前文所述，其他元音音素这一类别包括双元音音素（Vowel Diphthong），变体元音音素（Variant Vowels），受 R 控制的元音音素（R-controlled Vowels）以及轻音音素（Schwa）。

双元音音素： 指元音组中两个元音一起发声的同时，发音从第一个元音平滑过渡到第二个元音的音素。其中，最典型的双元音音素有单词 boy 中-OY 的发音/oi/，以及单词 house 和 cow 中-OU 和-OW 的发音/ou/。

以下是代表双元音音素的字母组合列表：

双元音音素/ou/（Diphthong /ou/ as in house）

字母组合 OU 和 OW 是最经常代表双元音音素/ou/的两个字母组合，例如，在单词 house 和单词 cow 中。

规则 1：字母组合-OU 是典型代表英语中双元音音素/ou/的字母组合。发音/ou/在单词中间的时候，例如，单词 shout，通常所听到的双元音音素/ou/由字母组合 OU 代表，而不是由字母组合 OW 代表。

规则 2：字母组合-OW 也能代表双元音音素/ou/，但 OW 组合通常出现在词根的末尾。例如，在单词 how，plow 以及 allow 中。

规则 3：字母组合 OW 经常出现在单词末尾的字母 L，N 或者 D 之前，代表双元音音素/ou/，例如，单词 owl，crowd 和 frown。当字母组合-OW 前面紧挨着一个辅音时，-OW 应该改写成字母组合-OU，例如，单词 couch 和 loud。

然而，有时仅凭眼睛无法断定字母组合-OW 到底是不是代表着双元音音素/ou/，需要学习者积累词汇以及经验根据上下文对陌生词汇的读音进行判断。

双元音音素/oi/（Diphthong /oi/ as in toy）

对应双元音音素/oi/最常见的字母组合是“-OY”和“OI”，例如，在单词 toy 和 oil 中。

规则 1：元音字母组合“OI”经常在单词中代表双元音音素/oi/，例如，在单词 point 中。元音字母组合“OI”位于词根的中间。如果在词根的末尾“OI”就被写作“OY”，例如，在单词 boy 中。但在一个特殊的单词 tortoise 中，双元音音素/oi/被弱化了。

规则 2：字母组合“-OY”在词根的末尾经常代表双元音音素/oi/，例如，在单词 boy，toy 以及 enjoy 中。反之，如果双元音音素/oi/出现在词根中间，则由元音字母组合“OI”代表。

2.1.4 变体元音音素

在变体元音音素这一小节里，代表短元音/oo/音素和长元音/oo/音素的字母组合“OO”以及代表宽音/o/的字母组合“AW”，“AU”及“AL（L）”都将被一一介绍。

短元音音素/oo/（Short /oo/ sound as in good）

短元音音素/oo/ 指的是元音字母组合 OO 所代表的短元音的发音，最常见的拼写规则如下：

规则 1：元音字母组合 OO 代表着短元音音素/oo/，例如，在单词 book，

cook，foot，took，shook 中。

规则 2： 拼写模块-OUL 也可以代表短元音音素/oo/。例如，在单词 “could” 和 “would” 中。

规则 3： 字母 U 在特定音节中也能代表短元音音素/oo/，例如，在单词 bull，pull 以及 bush 中。

长元音音素/oo/（Long /oo/ sound as in moo）

长元音音素/oo/表示在发出/oo/音素时声音应该拖得长一些，很多时候长元音音素/oo/由元音字母组合 OO 所代表。长元音音素/oo/常见的拼写规律总结如下：

规则 1： 元音字母组合 OO 也代表长元音/oo/，例如，在单词 moon，boom 和 zoo 中。

规则 2： 当长元音音素/oo/出现在词根末尾时，也可以被元音组合-UE 代表，因为-UE 本身代表的发音/yoo/中的/y/弱化了，因此发出的是长元音/oo/，例如，单词 true 和 glue。

规则 3： 如规则 2 所述，当字母 U 代表的长元音 U 的发音/yoo/中的音素/y/失去之后，就只能发长元音/oo/的音，尤其是在一些 CVCe 或者 VCe 的结构中，例如，单词 flute，rule 和 dude（美式发音）。

规则 4： 在一些单词中，长元音/oo/也可以被代表长元音 U 的字母所代表，尤其是在长元音 U /yoo/中失去发音的/y/ 时。例如，在单词 ruby 以及 truth 中。

规则 5： 字母组合-EW 本来是代表长元音 U /yoo/的，例如，在单词 few 中。但当长元音 U 的发音受到单词里字母 L 或者 R 的影响时，长元音 U 发音/yoo/变成了长元音/oo/，例如，在单词 flew，grew，brew 和 strew 中。

规则 6： 在一些特殊的单词里，例如，在单词 soup，cougar，through，coup 和 tourism 中，元音字母组合 OU 也代表着长/oo/音素。.

宽元音 O（Broad-O sound /or/ as in law，haul and tall）

宽元音 O 实际上指发音/or/，但代表发音/or/的字母组合 OR 将在稍后的 R-控制的元音中进行讲解。这里将介绍最常见的代表宽音 O 的三个字母组合 AL（L），AU 和 AW。

规则 1： 如同在单词 sauce 里一样，元音字母组合 AU 代表了宽音 O 的发音。在一个词根的中间的时候，宽音 O 一般由字母组合 AU 代表，而不是 AW 代表。

规则 2： 如同在单词 jaw 里一样，元音字母组合 AW 代表着音素宽音 O。通常字母组合 AW 位于词根的末尾时代表宽音 O，例如，单词 saw，law，straw。

规则 3：代表宽音 O 的字母组合 AW 通常出现在单词中结尾的 L，K 以及 N 前面，例如，在单词 crawl，pawn 和 hawk 中。但是，当宽元音 O 出现在其他辅音前面时，代表宽音 O 的字母组合是 AU 而不是 AW，比如在单词 pause，autumn 和 audio 中。

2.1.5　受 R 控制的元音音素

本章主要讨论受 R 控制的元音音素。字母 R 通常出现在单词末尾或者 R 后紧跟不同的辅音，而字母 R 会改变单词中它前面的元音字母的发音。

/air/ sound as in hair

/air/发音最常见的对应的拼写是字母组合 AIR，如单词 chair；字母组合 ARE，如单词 bare；字母组合 EAR，如单词 wear。

规则 1：音素/air/可以被拼读模块-AIR 代表，例如，单词 air，fair，hair 和 stair。

规则 2：音素/air/可以被拼读模块-ARE 代表，例如，单词 are，care 和 glare。

规则 3：音素/air/可以被拼读模块-EAR 代表，例如，单词 bear，pear 和 swear。

/ar/ sound as in hard

音素/ar/是受 R 控制的元音音素，通常由字母组合 AR 代表。

规则：音素/ar/通常由字母组合 AR 代表。很多时候字母 R 出现在单词的末尾，比如在单词 far 中。有时候字母组合 OR 经常后面紧接着一个辅音，例如，在单词 hard 中。而字母 A 在音节中间通常表示短元音/a/，但当这个短元音/a/被字母 R 所影响时，短元音/a/代表着宽元音发音/ar/。

/or/ sound as in porch

音素/or/被划分为宽元音 O，通常由字母组合 AW，AU 以及 AL（L）代表。而在受 R 字母控制的时候，/or/被 OR 所代表。

规则 1：很多时候，/or/被字母组合 OR 所代表。R 字母经常出现在单词后，例如，在单词 for 中。有时候字母 OR 后面也紧接着一个辅音字母，例如，在单词 torn 中。

规则 2：音素/or/经常被字母组合 OAR 所代表，例如，在单词 board，coarse 和 oar 中。

/ur/ sound as in bird, fur and her

音素/ur/也是受到 R 影响的音素。经常被字母组合 ER，IR 以及 UR 所代表。例如，在单词 her，bird 以及 fur 中。

规则1：字母组合-IR可以代表发音/ur/。原本字母I在音节中间应该发短音/i/，但当I后紧接着一个字母R情况下或者字母I后面紧接着字母R和另一个辅音字母时，Ir代表/ur/的音，例如，在单词fir，bird和dirty中。

规则2：字母组合UR代表音素/ur/，例如，在单词fur和turn中。通常字母U在音节中发短音U，但这个短音U受到字母U后面的字母R或者是R和后面紧接着的辅音的影响发/ur/，例如，在单词blur，burn和hurry中。

规则3：如同在单词her中一样，字母组合ER也能代表音素/ur/。通常字母E在音节中发短音E，但这个短音E受到字母E后面的字母R或者是R和后面紧接着的辅音的影响从而发/ur/，例如，在单词refer和herd中。同时，字母组合ER也是常见的后缀。

规则4：如同在单词learn中一样，字母组合EAR也能代表音素/ur/。通常在字母组合EAR中，字母EA受到后面的字母R或者是R和后面紧接着的辅音的影响从而发/ur/。

2.1.6 轻音/uh/

轻音/uh/是元音之一，经常出现在非重读音节中。在非重读音节中尤为显著。例如，轻音/uh /出现在单词about的第一个音节中，单词definition的第二个音节中，单词doctor和table的最末尾的音节中。

语言学家认为，这是由于在单词中，非重读音节引起的音素变体，因此被称为弱化音（Murmur）或者中和音（Neutral Sound）。例如，单词alarm中的轻音/uh/可以理解为一种语音音素变体或者同位异音。事实上，教授这一读音在实际课堂教学中是一种挑战。

轻音音素/uh/能被下述任何元音字母所代表：A，E，I，O和U，比如，在单词alone，happen，direct，gallop和circus中。

许多以非重读音节开始的多音节单词都包含轻音/uh/，表2.1对此类单词进行了归类总结。

表2.1

about *	again *	along	appear	awake
above **	ago *	American *	applause	aware **
account **	agree **	among **	ashore	away **
adult **	ahead	aside	afloat	annoy
asleep **	awoke *	alarm	another **	avoid **
afraid **	alone **	apart	await	

注：*表示新课标中的二级词汇；**表示新课标中三级词汇。

2.2　辅音音素

2.2.1　硬辅音和软辅音

术语“硬辅音”和“软辅音”仅限用于指字母 C 和 G 的发音音素。

当字母 C 是软辅音时，代表发音/s/，和字母 S 在单词 soft 中的发音一样，例如，在单词 city 中。

当字母 C 是硬辅音时，代表发音/k/，和字母 K 在单词 kite 中的发音一样，例如，在单词 crisis 中。

当字母 G 是软辅音时，代表音素/j/，和字母 J 在单词 jeep 中的发音一样，例如，在单词 gymnast 中。

当字母 G 是硬辅音时，代表音素/g/，如同在单词 goat 中。

规则 1：软辅音字母 C 的规则是当字母 C 恰好在字母 I，E，Y 前面时，即代表音素/s/，例如，在单词 cent 中。

规则 2：硬辅音字母 C 的规则是当字母 C 恰好不在字母 I，E，Y 前面时，即在字母 A，O，U 以及其他辅音字母前面时，字母 C 为硬辅音代表音素/K/，例如，在单词 cracker 中。

规则 3：软辅音字母 G 的规则是当字母 G 恰好在字母 I，E，Y 前面时，即代表音素/j/，例如，在单词 gym 中。

规则 4：硬辅音字母 G 的规则是当字母 G 恰好不在字母 I，E，Y 前面时，即在字母 A，O，U 以及其他辅音字母前面时，字母 G 为硬辅音，代表音素/g/，例如，在单词 goat 中。

2.2.2　清辅音、浊辅音以及鼻音

辅音音素是通过闭口方式限制或者完全中断发音产生的，而元音音素是通过张口方式产生的。因此，辅音音素的发音分类在于发音时阻断发声气流的程度，分为浊辅音、清辅音和鼻音。

不同辅音的分类如表 2.2 所示。

表 2.2

分类	定义	辅音发音
清辅音	发音的时候声带不振动的辅音	/p/
		/t/
		/k/
		/f/
		/s/

续表

分类	定义	辅音发音
清辅音	发音的时候声带不振动的辅音	/ch/
		/sh/
		/th/ (thing)
		/h/
浊辅音	发音的时候声带振动的辅音	/b/
		/d/
		/g/
		/v/
		/z/
		/j/
		/zh/
		/w/
		/th/ (this)
		/r/
		/l/
		/y/
鼻（辅）音	发鼻音的时候口腔中的气流通路被阻塞，气流通过鼻腔发音	/m/
		/n/
		/ng/

注：值得注意的是，清辅音除了被称为 unvoiced consonant，也可以称作 voiceless consonant。

2.2.2.1 浊辅音发音规则

B /b/ as in bat

浊辅音 B/b/ 对应的清辅音是 P /p/。

规则 1：字母 B 最经常用来代表浊辅音音素/b/，例如，在单词 cab，bat 以及 bag 中。这种字母发音的关系非常可靠，因为字母 B 基本上不代表其他辅音音素。

规则 2：当辅音字母 B 紧跟在字母 M 后的时候，辅音字母 B 不发音。例如，在单词 lamb 和 climb 中。换言之，在字母组合 MB 中，B 不发音。

规则 3：当辅音字母 B 出现在辅音字母 T 前，且两字母紧挨着的时候，字母 B 不发音，例如，在单词 debt 和 doubt 中。换言之，在字母组合 BT 中，B 不发音。

规则 4：当字母 B 在一个单词中重叠出现的时候，其中一个字母 B 不发音，例如，在单词 lobby 和 rubber 中。

D /d/ as in dog

浊辅音 D/d/对应的清辅音是 T/t/

规则 1：字母 D 通常都代表音素/d/，例如，在单词 dog，dive 和 duck 中，D 字母和音素/d/之间的关系很可靠。

规则 2：字母 D 有时候也代表音素/t/，尤其是在后缀-ED 中。当一个单词中的后缀-ED 前紧邻的辅音是清辅音的时候，后缀-ED 代表着清辅音音素/t/。例如，在单词 liked 和 hoped 中。

规则 3：字母 D 偶尔也代表音素/j/，例如，在单词 graduate，soldier，badge，schedule 和 education 中。在所列举的例子中，非重读字母 I，或者长元音 U /yoo/中的/y/ 将字母 D 对应的发音/d/变成了/j/。

规则 4：当字母 D 在一个单词中重叠出现的时候，其中一个字母 D 不发音，例如，在单词 ladder 和 daddy 中。

G /g/ as in gate

浊辅音 G/g/对应的清辅音是 K /k/。

规则 1：字母 G 经常代表音素/g/，例如，在单词 gate，goat 和 bag 中。这种情况下，/g/称为硬辅音音素，而字母 G 称为硬辅音。但这种字母音素对应关系并不完全可靠，因为字母 G 有时候也可以代表其他音素。

规则 2：当字母 G 后紧接字母 I，E 或者 Y 时，通常字母 G 是软辅音，代表音素/j/，例如，在单词 gentle，gem，gym，magic，agent，age 和 page 中。

规则 3：当字母 G 后没有紧接字母 I，E 和 Y 的同时，字母 G 后面紧接着字母 A，O 和 U 或者是其他辅音时，字母 G 代表音素/g/，例如，在单词 game，goat，gust 和 groom 中。

规则 4：字母 G 虽然代表的发音/g/和/j/，但也有很多不规则的单词，例如，单词 girl，get，gill，get 和 gift。

规则 5：当字母 G 刚好在字母 H 前面形成字母组合 GH 时，字母 G 不发音，例如，在单词 light，night，might，tight，eight 和 sleigh 中。

规则 6：当字母 G 刚好在字母 N 前面形成字母组合 GN 时，字母 G 不发音，例如，在单词 sign，reign，design 和 gnat 中。

规则 7：字母组合 GH 有时候也代表音素/f/，例如，在单词 tough，rough，

enough，cough，slough 和 roughen 中。

V /v/ as in vase

浊辅音 V/v/对应的清辅音是 F/f/。

规则：字母 V 经常代表音素/v/，例如，在单词 vase，vegetable 和 viva 中。V 字母和音素/v/间的对应关系很可靠，因为字母 V 基本不代表其他音素。

Z /z/ as in zoo

浊辅音 Z/z/ 对应的清辅音是 S/s/。

规则 1：字母 Z 通常代表音素/z/，例如，在 zebra，zoom 以及 zipper 中。

规则 2：当字母 S 在两个元音字母之间的时候通常代音素/z/，例如，在单词 easy，raisin，nose 和 music 中。

J /j/ as in jet

浊辅音 J/j/对应的清辅音是 CH/ch/。

规则 1：字母 J 通常代表发音/j/，例如，在单词 jam，January 和 jump 中。字母 J 和音素/j/的对应关系相当可靠。同时，当字母 G 紧挨出现在字母 I，E 和 Y 前时，也能代表音素/j/。

规则 2：字母 J 基本上不会出现在单词的结尾。但当音素/j/出现在单词末尾时被字母组合-DGE 或者 GE 所代表，例如，在单词 huge 中。

W /w/ as in wagon

音素/w/算半元音，也归于浊辅音一类，语音学上称为 voiced semivowel。

规则 1：字母 W 经常代表音素/w/，例如，在单词 warm，wasp 和 water 中。字母 W 和/w/间的对应关系并不可靠，因为字母 W 经常出现在元音二合字母 OW 中，例如，在单词 throw 中。

规则 2：当字母 Q 后面紧跟着字母 U 时，字母 U 就会代表音素/w/，而字母 Q 代表音素/k/，例如，在单词 quack 中。在英语中，字母 Q 总是和 U 成对出现。

规则 3：当字母 W 出现在字母组合 WR 中时，W 不发音，例如，在单词 write，wrap 和 wrack 中。

规则 4：字母 W 在字母组合 WH 中，在大多数地区的英语发音中代表音素/w/，而在有些地区的英语中，则代表清辅音音素/hw/。

规则 5：当字母 W 作为辅音并在音节中出现在字母 A 前面的时候，字母 W 能将字母 A 所代表的短音 A 变成短元音 O，例如，在单词 wash 和 want 中。

规则 6：当字母 W 作为辅音并在音节中出现在字母 O 前面时，字母 W 能将字母 O 所代表的短音 O 变成短元音 U，例如，在单词 won 和 wonder 中。

TH /th/ as in this (voiced)

规则 1：二合字母 TH 经常用于表示浊辅音/th /，例如，在单词 the 或者 that 中。这种发音对应关系相对可靠。但值得注意的是，在英语中，二合字母 TH 代表浊辅音多于 TH 所代表的清辅音。例如，在单词 thin 中，二合字母 TH 代表着清辅音。

规则 2：特殊情况下，在个别的单词中，TH 的发音为/t/，例如，在单词 Thomas 和 thyme 中。

R /r/ as in rock

在大多数美式英语中 R/r/归于浊辅音一类。

规则 1：辅音字母 R 通常在单词开头都代表音素/r/，例如，在单词 reap，ring 中。这个对应关系非常可靠而且不涉及其他音素。

规则 2：字母 R 经常影响同一个音节内短元音的发音，并把这些短元音变为受到 R 控制的元音，例如，单词 far，fork，bird 以及 hurt 中。

规则 3：当字母 R 位于两个元音之间，也就是说，当 R 后面紧接着一个元音时，字母 R 扮演辅音的角色进入下一个音节和 R 后面的元音一起发音，这样一来，字母 R 前面的元音就能保持原来应有的发音了。例如，在单词“car-ry”，“hur-ry”，“ber-ry”和“bor-row”中。在这些单词里，当两个字母 R 一起出现，前一个 R 不发音，后面一个 R 进入下一个音节扮演辅音的角色。

规则 4：RH 是音素/r/的字母组合，来源于拉丁文。也就是说，在 RH 字母组合中，字母 H 是不发音的，例如，在单词 rhinos，rhyme 中。

规则 5：WR 字母组合也代表音素/r/。也就是说 W 是不发音的，例如，在单词 write，wrist 和 wrap 中。

L /l/ as in leaf

字母 L 代表的浊辅音音素/l/。

规则 1：通常音素/l/在单词词首由字母 L 所代表。例如，在单词 look，live 和 sleep 中。

规则 2：当字母 L 在单词中叠加出现的时候，或者字母 L 出现在单词或者音节末尾的时候，不仅不再代表音素/l/，而且几乎不发音。例如，在单词 bell，hell 和 hall 中时。

规则3：在同样一个音节里面，字母L在字母F，M，K前面也不发音。例如，在单词calf，calm以及could中。

Y /y/ as in yo-yo

音素/y/也是一个半元音。

规则1：音素/y/由字母Y代表，例如，在单词yellow，beyond和yes中。这条规则并不完全可靠，因为字母Y并不总是代表音素/y/，其可靠概率只有3%。通常只有当字母Y扮演辅音的角色并且在一个单词或者是一个音节的起始位置的时候才代表音素/y/。

规则2：大多数情况下，据统计，大约有97%的概率字母Y并不处于单词的开头或者是音节的起始端，因此很多时候字母Y的发音是长元音I/igh/，长元音E/ee/以及短音I/i/。

规则3：当字母Y正好处于音节中间时，通常代表着短元音I/i/，例如，在单词gym和symbol中。

规则4：当字母Y在一个单词的词根或者是一个音节的最后时，例如，在单词by，cry，fly和deny中，字母Y代表的是长元音I /igh/。

规则5：在拼读模式Y_E中，字母Y代表长元音I /igh/，例如，在单词type，style和analyze中。

规则6：在元音组合YE中，字母Y也是代表长元音I/igh/，例如，在单词bye和rye中。

规则7：当字母Y作为一个单词的后缀并且位于一个包含三个字母以上的单词最末尾时，代表着长音E/ee/，例如，在单词can-dy，hap-py以及histo-ry中。

注：Bishop（1986）指出，有些字典或者专家学者指出字母Y所代表的长音E应归于短音I。但是因为初学者很多时候无法从单词中听出短音I的这个发音，尤其是在非重读音节中，因此Bishop认为如果把字母Y所代表的短音I发成长元音E，更有利于初学者识别出字母Y所代表的发音。

/zh/ sound as in treasure

音素/zh/从来不会被字母组合ZH所代表，因为在英文中根本就没有字母组合ZH。在英语单词中，很多时候只有后缀-S，-SI和-GE，代表音素/zh/。

规则1：如同在单词leisure，pleasure和treasure中，后缀-S就代表着音素/zh/。也就是说，如果字母S前面有字母R或者后面紧接着一个元音字母，这个字母S就代表着音素/zh/。

规则2：音素/zh/在单词confusion，decision和illusion中，在成音节-SION

中，由-SI所代表。这一类词，如Bishop（1986）所提到的，都源自于拉丁文。

规则3：音素/zh/也可以被后缀-GE所代表，如同在单词beige，collage，garage和montage中一样。这一组词汇基本上源自于法语。

2.2.2.2 清辅音的发音规则

P /p/ as in pig

清辅音P/p/所对应的浊辅音是B /b/。

规则1：字母P大多数时候是代表音素/p/，例如，在单词pen，play和pin中。这种对应关系是高度可靠的，因为字母P基本上不代表其他音素。

规则2：当字母P紧接在字母N，S或者T后面的时候，例如，在单词pneumonia，psychology中，字母P通常不发音。

规则3：当字母P叠加出现在一个单词中的时候，例如，在单词supper，happy和floppy中，其中一个字母P不发音。

规则4：字母P经常出现在辅音二合字母PH中。PH作为辅音二合字母，通常代表着音素/f/，例如，单词phone中的PH就代表音素/f/。

T /t/ as in tin

清辅音T/t/所对应的浊辅音是D /d/。

规则1：字母T经常代表着音素/t/，例如，在单词top和cat中。这种对应关系相当可靠。

规则2：字母T在法语外来词中经常被忽略，也就是不发音，例如，在单词bouquet，debut和ballet中。

规则3：当字母T在一个单词中叠加出现，例如，在单词little中，其中一个字母T不发音。

规则4：拼读模块“-TCH”，例如，在单词watch中，字母T不发音。也就是说，拼读模块-TCH的发音同辅音二合字母CH/ch/。

规则5：当字母T夹在字母S和后缀-LE或者-EN之间的时候，字母T不发音，例如，在单词hasten，often，nestle，castle和hustle中。

规则6：字母T也出现在辅音二合字母TH中，例如，在单词this或者thing中。

规则7：辅音字母连缀TR中也包括字母T，例如，在单词tree中。

规则8：当字母T恰好在一个非重读的长音U/yoo/之前，字母T代表着音素/ch/。因为长元音U /yoo/中的发音/y/将字母T的发音变成了/ch/，例如，在单词nature，picture和actual中。

规则9：如果字母T刚好在一个包括非重读字母I的后缀前面，并且这个字母I后面刚好又紧接着一个元音字母，那么这个非重读字母I便将字母T的读音转化成了音素/sh/。也就是说，字母T在成音节-TION中代表音素/sh/，例如，在单词nation，motion，partial和patient中。

K /k/ as in kin

清辅音K/k/所对应的浊辅音是G /g/。

规则1：有时候，字母K代表着音素/k/，例如，在单词kid和kind中。这种对应关系是相对可靠的，因为字母K也几乎不代表其他音素。

规则2：很多情况下，辅音二合字母CK也代表音素/k/，例如，在单词sock中。

规则3：当字母K后紧接着字母N的时候，例如，在单词know，knock和knot中，字母K通常不发音。换句话说，在字母组合KN中，K不发音。

规则4：字母Q也时常代表着音素/k/，但字母Q无法独立代表音素/k/，字母Q是和字母U组合出现形成QU组合而代表音素/k/，例如，在单词queen，quilt和quack中。

规则5：当字母C后面紧接一个辅音字母或者是字母“A，O，U”的时候，字母C代表着音素/k/，例如，在单词cat，cut，cold和cluster中。

F /f/ as in fin

清辅音F/f/对应的浊辅音是V/v/。

规则1：字母F就代表着音素/f/，例如，在单词find，beef和fan中，这种对应关系相对可靠，因为基本上字母F不代表别的音素。

规则2：辅音字母组合PH也可以代表音素/f/，例如，在单词phone和pharmacy中。

规则3：当辅音二合字母GH位于一个单词末尾且GH前面是元音组合AU或者OU时，也可以代表音素/f/，例如，在单词laugh和enough中。换言之，GH在拼读模块-AUGH和-OUGH中代表着音素/f/。

规则4：当音素/f/出现在一个单词末尾时，也可以被辅音字母组合FF所代表。通常辅音字母组合-FF紧接在短元音之后出现。值得注意的是其中一个字母F不发音，例如，在单词cliff和off中。

规则5：字母F也可以代表音素/v/，例如，在单词“of”中。

S /s/ as in sink

清辅音S/s/所对应的浊辅音是Z/z/。

规则 1：在单词 sing，sun 和 loss 中，音素/s/是被字母 S 所代表的。这种对应关系不太可靠，因为音素/s/经常被其他字母所代表。

规则 2：音素/s/可以被单词词根中短元音后面紧接着的后缀-SS 所代表，但其中一个 S 是不发音的，例如，在单词 hiss，bliss 和 kiss 中。

规则 3：在英语中音素/s/也可被后缀-SS 所代表，例如，在后缀-LESS，-NESS，-RESS 和-ESS 中。这些后缀也出现在单词 hopeless，sadness，actress 和 princess 中。值得注意的是，同上，当两个字母 S 叠加出现时，有一个 S 不发音。

规则 4：音素/s/也可以被字母 C 所代表，尤其是当字母 C 后面紧接着字母"I，E，Y"时，例如，在单词 city，cent 和 cyber 中，字母 C 代表着音素/s/。

规则 5：当辅音字母连缀 SC 后面紧接着字母"I，E，Y"时，字母 C 是软辅音 C，代表着音素/s/，例如，在单词 scene 和 science 中。

规则 6：当辅音字母连缀 SC 后面紧接着字母"A，O，U"或者其他辅音字母时，字母 C 代表着音素/k/，因此连缀 SC 代表着辅音音素连缀/sk/，例如，在单词 scatter，scoop 和 script 中。

CH /ch/ as in cheese

清辅音 CH /ch/所发出的音实际上是音素/t/和音素/sh/的结合，其所对应的浊辅音是 J/j/。

规则 1：如同在单词 cheese 和 lunch 中，音素/ch/被辅音二合字母 CH 所代表。这种音素与字母对应的关系不是很可靠，因为二合字母 CH 有时候也代表音素/k/，例如，在单词 chemical 和 character 中。

规则 2：辅音二合字母也可以代表单词 Greek 中的音素/k/。这种对应关系体现在受希腊语影响的词根中，例如，在字母组合 CHR-，CHL-和 SCH-中，CH 都代表音素/k/，例如，在单词 christ，chloride 和 school 中。

规则 3：音素/ch/也由词根后缀-TCH 所代表，例如，在单词 ditch，pitch 和 hatch 中。

SH /sh/ as in shot

清辅音音素/sh/所对应的浊辅音是/zh/。

规则 1：辅音二合字母 SH 经常代表音素/sh/，例如，在单词 shark，ship 和 fish 中，这种对应关系是相对可靠的。

规则 2：偶尔，音素/sh/也可以被其他字母所代表，比如被字母 S 代表，例如，在单词 sure 和 sugar 中。

规则 3：音素/sh/在成音节中也可以被字母-TI 所代表，例如，在单词 nation，option，diction 和 function 中，这些带有-TION 成音节的词很多源自拉丁语。

规则 4：在源自法语的英语词汇中，音素/sh/被辅音二合字母 CH 所代表，例如，在单词 Chicago，chef，chiffon 和 chic 中。但通常仅凭肉眼，很难区分出二合字母 CH 究竟代表着音素/sh/或者是 /ch/。

规则 5：在单词 special，glacier，racial 和 official 中，音素/sh 被字母-CI 所代表。这一类单词来源于拉丁文。具体来讲，由字母 I 所代表的非重读音短音/i/被软辅音 C 所影响，从而发出了/sh/的音。

规则 6：如同在单词 passion 里一样，音素/sh/被字母-SSI-所代表。这种对应关系也源自拉丁语。换言之，由字母 I 所代表的非重读音短音/i/将由字母 SS 所代表的音素/s/ 转化成了/sh/，例如，在单词 session，profession，confession 和 procession 中。

WH /hw/ as in wheel

音素 WH /hw/基本上已经被音素/w/所取代。

规则 1：辅音二合字母 WH 可以用来代表音素/hw/，而且这个二合字母通常出现在单词或者音节的开头。

规则 2：有时候二合字母 WH 也代表着音素/h/，例如，在单词 who，whose 和 whole 中。

TH /th/ as in thumb

规则：二合字母 TH 通常代表着音素/th/，例如，在单词 thin，thing 和 bath 中。这种对应关系相对可靠，因为二合字母 TH 大多数时候只代表清辅音音素/th/，例如，在单词 thick，thirsty 和 thread 中。有时候，二合字母 TH 也代表着浊辅音音素/th/，例如，在单词 the，their 和 there 中。总体来说，字母 TH 代表清辅音音素/th/的概率比其代表浊辅音音素/th/的概率低。

H /h/ as in hut

字母 H 所代表的音素/h/是清辅音，而且发音仅仅只是“送气”。

规则 1：字母 H 通常代表着音素/h/，例如，在单词 hat，hey 和 hike 中。当字母 H 出现在单词首位时，这种对应关系是相对可靠的。

规则 2：字母 H 在一组源自法语或者拉丁语的外来词汇中通常不发音，例如，在单词 hour，honor，vehicle 和 exhaust 中。

规则 3：在源于拉丁语的英文单词，例如，在单词 rhyme，rhinoceros 和 myrrh 中，字母 H 不发音。

规则 4：有时音素/h/也被字母组合 WH 所代表，例如，在单词 who，whole，whom 和 whose 中。

2.2.2.3 鼻辅音的发音规则

M /m/ as in moon

规则 1：字母 M 通常代表着音素/m/，例如，在单词 mat，mop 和 ham 中。当字母 M 出现在单词首位时，这种对应关系非常可靠。

规则 2：MB 和 MN 这两个很常见的辅音字母组合中字母 B 和 N 都不发音，也就是说 MB 和 MN 都代表着音素/m/，例如，在单词 lamb，comb 和 column 中。

规则 3：当字母 M 在单词中叠加出现的时候，有一个字母 M 不发音，另一个字母 M 代表音素/m/，例如，在单词 hammer，common 和 summer 中。

N /n/ as in net

规则 1：字母 N 经常代表着音素/n/，例如，在单词 name，nod 和 can 中，这种对应关系相当可靠，因为字母 N 也就只代表音素/n/。

规则 2：字母组合 KN，PN，ND 和 GN 都可以代表音素/n/，例如，在单词 knife，pneumonia，handsome 和 sign 中。

规则 3：当字母 N 在单词中叠加出现时，例如，在单词 funny，sunny，kennel 和 dinner 中，有一个字母 N 不发音，另一个字母 N 代表音素/n/。

NG /ng/ as in ring

规则 1：二合字母-NG 是特殊的辅音字母组合，通常代表音素/ng/，通常二合字母 NG 都不出现在单词首位或者音节首位。

规则 2：二合字母 NG 所代表的音素/ng/经常出现在一个单词的元音后面，例如，在单词 flying，strong 和 length 中。

2.2.3 辅音字母连缀

辅音字母连缀（Consonant Cluster）是辅音音素连缀（Consonant Blend）的书面形式。辅音音素连缀是两三个字母结合在一起所形成的辅音字母连缀的发声单位。辅音字母连缀通常出现在单词首位，偶尔会出现在单词末尾。辅音字母连缀中，每个字母所对应的音素都保留着自己的独立的发音。如表 2.3 所示。

表 2.3

Cluster	Blend	Examples
CL	/kl/	As in words cliff, close and clement
DR	/dr/	As in words dress, drive and dream
FL	/fl/	As in words flower, flee and fly
SN	/sn/	As in words snap, snore and snail
SP	/sp/	As in word spring, splash and wasp
ST	/st/	As in words stamp, sting and best
TR	/tr/	As in tree, trip and travel
GR	/gr/	As in green, grape and ground
GL	/gl/	As in glad, glue and glee
SK	/sk/	As in ski, skunk and frisk
BR	/br/	As in broom, bride and bright
BL	/bl/	As in blood, bloom and blame
CR	/kr/	As in crab, creepy and climb
SC	/sk/	As in scooter, scope and scan
SM	/sm/	As in smile, smell and smoke
FR	/fr/	As in frog, fry and free
SL	/sl/	As in slim, slide and sleep
PR	/pr/	As in prince, price and present
PL	/pl/	As in plus, please and play
SW	/sw/	As in swing, swim and sweet
TW	/tw/	As in twin, two and twist
QU	/kw/	As in queen, quill and quiet
SCR	/skr/	As in scream, script and scramble
SPL	/spl/	As in splash, splendid and split
SPR	/spr/	As in spring, spread and sprawl
STR	/str/	As in street, stripe and string
CHR	/kr/	As in Christmas, chrome and Christ
THR	/thr/	As in throw, thrive and three
SHR	/shr/	As in shrug, shrink and shred
PHR	/fr/	As in phrase

2.2.4 辅音二合字母

辅音二合字母（Consonant Digraph）指两个辅音字母组合在一起却只对应一个辅音音素，如表 2.4 所示。

表 2.4

Digraph	Sound	Examples
TH	/th/	As in this
TH	/th/ voiceless	As in thing
WH	/w/ or /hw/	As in what
CH	/ch/	As in cherry
CH	/k/	As in Christ
PH	/f/	As in photo
SH	/sh/	As in shoe
-GH	/gh/	As in laugh
GH	/g/	As in ghost
NG	/ng/	As in ring

2.2.5 不发音的辅音

很多字母在单词里面有时候不发音，只是平时我们没有刻意留心过。通常，这些不发音的字母都是辅音。一些特定的辅音字母虽然拼写方式没有变化，但它们的发音随着时间的推移而改变。这种不发音的辅音经常出现在外来词中。一些辅音字母不发音的原因归结于字母间的交互作用，有些来自字母本身发音的变化。常见的不发音辅音的分类列表，如表 2.5 所示。

表 2.5

Categories	Silent consonant	Rules	Examples
1. Letter Interactions		When a native English suffix beginning with vowels is added to roots that contain a short vowel followed by a single consonant letter, the consonant letter is doubled to keep the initial vowel short, while the additional consonant is silent.	rub-rub**b**ed, hop-hop**p**ed big-big**g**er fun-fun**n**y fat-fat**t**est top-top**p**ing

续表

Categories	Silent consonant	Rules	Examples
1. Letter Interactions	Silent L	When LL or L follows a single A or O, the short A becomes an AW sound, as in "bald" and "ball," and the short O becomes a long O sound, as in "cold" and "roll." L is not silent at this point. However, if the final letter is K or M, the L becomes silent, as in "talk" or "calm."	calm talk folk
	Silent T	When the words end in "–st" before the suffix "–le".	hust–le cast–le nes–tle
		When the words end in "–st" or "–ft" before suffix "–en".	soft–en fast–en hast–en
2. Obsolete consonant sounds	KN–	K is always silent before N at the beginning of a root word.	know knock knee
	WR–	W is always silent before R at the beginning of a root word.	write wrist wrench
	GN	G is silent before letter N, either at the beginning or at the end.	sign gnaw
	–MB	When letter B is after letter M in a word, letter B is silent.	lamb climb crumb
	–MN	When letter N is after letter M, letter N is silent.	environment condemn autumn
	–GH	In other words, when the vowel preceding "GH" is a long vowel, "GH" is silent in spoken language. When short vowels precede "GH," "GH" is pronounced as a /f/ sound.	eight right fight night though

续表

Categories	Silent consonant	Rules	Examples
3. Individual Silent Consonant	Silent H	Sometimes, "H" is silent in root words borrowed from French.	hour, exhibition, oh, honor, heir, hourly, dishonesty, herbal, heiress
		"H" is silent after the prefix ex-	exhibit exhibition
		"H" is silent after "G" at the beginning of the syllable.	ghetto, spaghetti, ghost, ghastly
	Silent P	"P" is always silent at the beginning of the words if the consonant after "P" cannot be blended with "P".	pneumonia
4. Scholarly Insertion	Silent B		debt
	Silent C		muscle
	Silent S		island

2.2.6 特殊的辅音字母

2.2.6.1 Letter Q

严格来说，字母 Q 其实可以从英语字母表里面移除了，因为它的发音基本上已经被字母 K 所代表的音素所取代，而且字母 Q 总是和字母 U 成对出现。

字母组合 QU 代表着/kw/发音，例如，在单词 queen，quiet 和 quail 中。这种拼写模式源自拉丁文。

如同在单词 antique，mosquito 和 bouquet 中，二合字母组合 QU 只代表着音素/k/，而字母 U 不发音。这几个词源于法语。

2.2.6.2 Letter X

通常，字母 X 代表三种发音：

（1）X 可以代表辅音连缀/ks/，例如，在单词 fox，box，ox 和 wax 中。

（2）X 可以代表辅音连缀/gz/，例如，在单词 exact 中。规律是当字母 X 位于一个非重读音节末尾而且后面紧跟着一个元音或者是不发音的 H 时。

（3）X 可以代表音素/z/，当时 X 位于单词头，例如，在单词 xylophone 中。

2.3 拼读模块

2.3.1 定义

拼读模块（Phonogram，Word Family，Word Chunk，Word Pattern）指拼读组

合，从语言学角度来讲，拼读模块，即表音符号就是首音（onset）和尾音（rime）的组合。尾音指一个音节中元音字母以及其后的字母。通常一个音节中的首音在尾音前，而且首音通常是单个辅音字母、辅音字母连缀或者是辅音二合字母。例如，在单音节单词 tag 中，T 是首音，AG 是尾音。语音拼读模块自 17 世纪起被用于拼读教学（Bear et al.，2020；Blevins，2017）。

2.3.2　学习拼读模块的优势

学习者利用拼读模块，例如，单词 fat 里面的“-at”，能准确读出拼读练习书中的单词 sat，pat 以及 rat。由于这些单词拼读模块出现在许多早期阅读书籍中，因此掌握这些词汇模块对于提高阅读流利性至关重要。当早期阅读者在阅读中遇到更多的多音节单词时，他们能更明白这些词汇所包含不同的表音模块，例如，前缀、后缀或者更小一些的发音单元，这种洞察力能帮助他们快速有效解码单词。

相较而言，拼读模块具有规律性和一致性。研究显示，在初级阅读文本中出现的 286 个表音模块中有 95%也就是 272 个非常稳定的拼读模块出现在 1473 个单词中。因此，研究人员和教育工作者注意到使用拼读模块可以帮助初学者读出更多单词。表 2.6 是 Blevins（2017）总结出的小学阶段常见的含有 37 个常见拼读模块的 500 个词汇。

表 2.6

-ack as in lack	-ank as in frank	-eat as in beat	-ill as in bill
-ock as in block	-ump as in lump	-ail as in tail	-ap as in nap
-ell as in bell	-in as in bin	-oke as in broke	-unk as in trunk
-ain as in train	-ash as in lash	-est as in nest	-ine as in dine
-op as in hop	-ake as in cake	-at as in bat	-ice as in dice
-ing as in sing	-or as in for	-ale as in gale	-ate as in fate
-ick as in lick	-ink as in blink	-ore as in bore	-ame as in blame
-aw as in law	-ide as in hide	-ip as in hip	-uck as in duck
-an as in fan	-ay as in hay	-ight as in night	-ir as in tapir
-ug as in jug			

2.3.3　拼读模块的不足之处

拼读模块经常通过类比教学法（Analogy Instruction Approach）教授，第 3 章将详细介绍类比教学法。研究表明，拼读模块确实可以帮助到初学者阅读和拼写。然而 Blevins（2017）也提出了不一样的看法。他认为，拼读模块不应该成为对初学者自然拼读教学中的重点。因为对于初学者来说，他们的单词分解能力有限，如果依赖于拼读模块识别单词，将影响初学者语音意识的发展和单词结构分析能力。虽然初学者通过记忆拼读模块识别单词比较有效率，但在教授拼读模块的过程中，单一的字母与音素间的对应关系却被忽略了，这可能会阻碍学习者语音意识和语音能力的培养与发展。因此，不太建议在自然拼读教学的初始阶段利用类比教学法给初学者教授拼读模块，相反，更建议先使用系统综合语音教学法（Synthetic Instruction Approach）循序渐进地为初学者教授单个的音素。表 2.7~表 2.25 是 Blevins（2017）和 Fry 等（1993）总结出的一些拼读模块。

（1） Short-A sound /a/ phonograms，如表 2.7 所示。

表 2.7

-**ab** as in cab	-**ack** as in lack	-**act** as in fact	-**ad** as in mad	-**aft** as in raft
-**ag** as in bag	-**am** as in ham	-**amp** as in camp	-**an** as in fan	-**ance** as in dance
-**anch** as in ranch	-**and** as in land	-**ang** as in fang	-**ank** as in bank	-**ant** as in pant
-**ap** as in map	-**ash** as in cash	-**ask** as in mask	-**asm** as in spasm	-**asp** as in gasp
-**ast** as in cast	-**at** as in mat	-**atch** as in match	-**ath** as in math	-**ax** as in tax

（2） Short-E sound /e/ Phonograms，如表 2.8 所示。

表 2.8

-**ead** as in head	-**ealth** as in health	-**eath** as in death	-**eck** as in deck	-**ed** as in bed
-**edge** as in hedge	-**eft** as in left	-**eg** as in beg	-**eld** as in held	-**elf** as in self
-**ell** as in bell	-**elp** as in help	-**elt** as in belt	-**em** as in them	-**en** as in den
-**ence** as in hence	-**ench** as in bench	-**end** as in bend	-**ength** as in length	-**ense** as in dense
-**ent** as in dent	-**ep** as in step	-**ept** as in kept	-**esh** as in mesh	-**ess** as in less
-**est** as in nest	-**et** as in bet	-**etch** as in fetch	-**ext** as in next	

（3） Short-I sound /i/ phonograms，如表 2.9 所示。

表 2.9

-**ib** as in bib	-**ick** as in lick	-**id** as in bid	-**iff** as in cliff	-**ift** as in lift
-**ig** as in big	-**ilk** as in milk	-**ill** as in bill	-**ilt** as in tilt	-**im** as in him
-**imp** as in limp	-**in** as in fin	-**ince** as in mince	-**inch** as in finch	-**ince** as in mince

续表

-**ing** as in sing	-**ing** as in hinge	-**ink** as in mint	-**ip** as in hip	-**is** as in his
-**ish** as in fish	-**ive** as in five	-**ix** as in fix	-**isk** as in risk	-**isp** as in crisp
-**iss** as in hiss	-**ist** as in list	-**it** as in fit	-**itch** as in pitch	-**ive** as in five
-**ix** as in fix				

(4) Short-O sound /o/ phonograms，如表 2.10 所示。

表 2.10

-**ob** as in mob	-**ock** as in mock	-**od** as in nod	-**oft** as in loft	-**og** as in hog	-**omp** as in stomp
-**ond** as in bond	-**op** as in hop	-**ot** as in lot	-**otch** as in blotch	-**ough** as in cough	-**ox** as in fox

(5) Short-U sound /u/ phonograms，如表 2.11 所示。

表 2.11

-**ome** as in come	-**on** as in son	-**ough** as in rough	-**ove** as in dove
-**ub** as in hub	-**uch** as in much	-**uck** as in duck	-**ud** as in mud
-**uff** as in buff	-**ug** as in bug	-**ulk** as in bulk	-**udge** as in judge
-**ull** as in dull	-**um** as in	-**umb** as in thumb	-**ump** as in lump
-**un** as in bun	-**unch** as in bunch	-**ung** as in lung	-**unk** as in junk
-**unt** as in blunt	-**up** as in pup	-**us** as in bus	-**ush** as in rush
-**utt** as in butt	-**utch** as in hutch	-**ut** as in but	-**ust** as in dust

(6) Long-A sound /ai/ phonograms，如表 2.12 所示。

表 2.12

-**ace** as in face	-**ade** as ni made	-**age** as in cage	-**aid** as in laid
-**ail** as in sail	-**ain** as in main	-**aint** as in faint	-**aise** as in raise
-**ait** as in wait	-**ake** as in bake	-**ale** as in male	-**ame** as in name
-**ane** as in lane	-**ange** as in range	-**ape** as in cape	-**ase** as in base
-**aste** as in taste	-**ate** as in late	-**ave** as in cave	-**ay** as in day
-**aze** as in maze	-**eak** as in break	-**eigh** as in neigh	-**ey** as in hey

（7）Long-E sound /ee/ phonograms，如表 2.13 所示。

表 2.13

-**e** as in be	-**ea** as in pea	-**each** as in peach	-**ead** as in lead	-**eak** as in beak
-**eal** as in heal	-**earm** as in beam	-**ean** as in mean	-**eap** as in heap	-**ear** as in dear
-**ease** as in lease	-**east** as in beast	-**eat** as in feat	-**eath** as in heath	-**eave** as in leave
-**ee** as in bee	-**eech** as in beech	-**eed** as in feed	-**eek** as in leek	-**eel** as in feel
-**eem** as in deem	-**een** as in been	-**eep** as in beep	-**eer** as in deer	-**eet** as in feet
-**eeze** as in breeze	-**iece** as in niece	-**ief** as in brief	-**ield** as in field	

（8）Long-I sound /igh/ phonograms，如表 2.14 所示。

表 2.14

-**ibe** as intribe	-**ice** as in dice	-**ide** as in hide	-**ie** as in pie
-**ied** as in cried	-**ier** as in drier	-**ies** as in ties	-**ife** as in wife
-**igh** as in high	-**ight** as in fight	-**ike** as in bike	-**ild** as in mild
-**ile** as in mile	-**ime** as in dime	-**ind** as in find	-**ine** as in fine
-**ipe** as in wipe	-**ire** as in fire	-**ise** as in rise	-**ite** as in bite
-**ive** as in five	-**uy** as in buy	-**y** as in by	-**ye** as in bye

（9）Long-O sound /oa/ phonograms，如表 2.15 所示。

表 2.15

-**o** as in go	-**oach** as in coach	-**oad** as in road	-**oak** as in soak
-**oal** as in foal	-**oam** as in foam	-**oan** as in loan	-**oast** as in toast
-**oat** as in goat	-**obe** as in robe	-**ode** as in code	-**oe** as in foe
-**oke** as in coke	-**old** as in fold	-**ole** as in dole	-**oll** as in doll
-**olt** as in bolt	-**ome** as in home	-**one** as in bone	-**ope** as in cope
-**ose** as in rose	-**ost** as in host	-**ote** as in note	-**ove** as in stove
-**ow** as in row	-**own** as in known		

（10）Long-U sound /yoo/ phonograms，如表 2.16 所示。

表 2.16

-**ew** as in few	-**ube** as in tube	-**ue** as in cue	-**uke** as in puke
-**une** as in tune	-**ute** as in mute		

注：在英式英语中，dude，tube，due，dune，tune，mute 和 duke 这一类单词被归于长元音 Long-U 组中，可是在美式英语中，根据语音解码规则，虽然它们也被归于长元音 Long-U 组中，但是它们的发音确实存在长元音/oo/，如同在单词 goose 中一样。

（11）Diphthong /oi/ phonograms，如表 2.17 所示。

表 2.17

-**oil** as in boil	-**oin** as in coin	-**oint** as in point
-**oise** as in noise	-**oist** as in moist	-**oy** as in boy

（12）Diphthong /ou/ phonograms，如表 2.18 所示。

表 2.18

-**ouch** as in pouch	-**oud** as in loud	-**ounce** as in ounce
-**ount** as in count	-**ound** as in found	-**our** as in our
-**out** as in about	-**outh** as in mouth	-**ouse** as in mouse
-**own** as in down	-**owl** as in howl	-**ow** as in bow

（13）Variant Vowel long /oo/ phonograms，如表 2.19 所示。

表 2.19

-**ew** as in flew	-**o** as in do	-**oo** as in boo	-**ood** as in mood
-**oof** as in hoof	-**ool** as in pool	-**oom** as in room	-**oon** as in noon
-**oop** as in loop	-**oose** as in loose	-**oot** as hoot	-**ooth** as in booth
-**ooze** as in snooze	-**oup** as in soup	-**ube** as in lube	-**uce** as in spruce
-**ude** as in rude	-**ue** as in cue	-**uke** as in luke	-**ule** as in mule
-**ume** as in fume	-**une** as in dune	-**ure** as in cure	-**uth** as in truth
-**ute** as in cute			

注：在英式英语中，dude，tube，due，dune，tune，mute 和 duke 这一类单词被归于长元音 Long-U 组中，可是在美式英语中，根据语音解码规则，虽然它们也被归于长元音 Long-U 组中，但是它们的发音确实存在长元音/oo/，如同在单词 goose 中一样。

（14）Variant Vowel short /oo/ phonograms，如表 2.20 所示。

表 2.20

-**ood** as in good	-**ook** as in look	-**oot** as in foot
-**ush** as in bush	-**ull** as in bull	-**ould** as in could

（15） Variant Vowel sound /or/ （Broad O sound） phonograms，如表 2.21 所示。

表 2.21

-**all** as in ball	-**alk** as in talk	-**alt** as in salt	-**aught** as in taught	-**aunch** as in launch
-**aunt** as in haunt	-**ault** as in fault	-**aw** as in law	-**awl** as in crawl	-**awn** as in fawn
-**ong** as in long	-**oss** as in boss	-**ost** as in cost	-**oth** as in sloth	-**ought** as in ought

（16） R-controlled vowel sound /air/ phonograms，如表 2.22 所示。

表 2.22

-**air** as in fair	-**are** as in fare	-**ear** as in pear

（17） R-controlled vowel sound /ur/ phonograms，如表 2.23 所示。

表 2.23

-**earn** as in learn	-**erb** as I herb	-**erge** as in merge	-**erk** as in clerk
-**erm** as in term	-**ern** as in fern	-**erve** as in nerve	-**ir** as in fir
-**ird** as in bird	-**irk** as in smirk	-**irst** as in first	-**irt** as in dirt
-**irth** as in birth	-**ur** as in fur	-**urb** as in curb	-**urge** as in urge
-**urse** as in curse	-**url** as in curl	-**urn** as in burn	-**urk** as in lurk
-**urt** as in hurt			

（18） R-controlled vowel sound /ar/ phonograms，如表 2.24 所示。

表 2.24

-**ar** as in far	-**ard** as hard	-**arge** as in large	-**ark** as in bark
-**arm** as in farm	-**arn** as in barn	-**arp** as in sharp	-**art** as in dart

（19） R-controlled vowel sound /or/ phonograms，如表 2.25 所示。

表 2.25

-**oar** as in boar	-**oor** as in door	-**orch** as in porch	-**ord** as in ford	-**ore** as in core
-**ork** as in fork	-**orm** as in norm	-**orn** as in corn	-**ort** as in fort	-**our** as in four

第 3 章　自然拼读规则的教学方式

本章旨在让学习者了解不同的自然拼读教授方法。

总目标	本章旨在帮助受训者掌握以下两点内容： 1. 三种不同的自然拼读教学方式的异同 2. 系统综合教学模式的教学范围和顺序
分目标	在本章中，受训者应该掌握以下八点内容： 1. 自然拼读教学的必要性 2. 三种不同的教学方式：系统综合模式、类比模式、分析模式 3. 高效系统综合教学模式的特点 4. 自然拼读教学的准备条件 5. 字母认知的必要性和教学方式 6. 可解码初级阅读文本的益处 7. 常见词汇、高频词汇、不规则词汇之间的关系 8. 不规则词汇教学方式

3.1　拼读教学的必要性

本书讨论了如何通过系统综合模式进行自然拼读教学模式。Bald（2007）指出，拼读是实现英语早期阅读的必要条件而非充分条件，因为英语中字母与发音的对应关系并不是百分之百的准确，但拼读为语言学习者提供了成长为进阶阅读者和写作者的最直接途径。

国际阅读协会（2019）发表报告称，英语是由 26 个字母组成的语言。26 个字母分别代表着 44 个音素。虽然只有 84%的英文单词是完全符合拼读规则的，但教授和学习最基本的拼读规则对于初学者来说依然是大有裨益的。因为一旦他们掌握了最基本的拼读规则，大多数书面文字就能顺利转变为常见的听力口语单词，从而继续转变为容易理解的书面文字。这种能对书面文字进行解码并转化为日常听力口语单词的能力对于初学者发展成为高阶阅读者至关重要。当初学者获得自动解码识字的能力时，他们的大脑精力将更多地投入到上下文的理解中，从而进一步提升阅读理解能力和文字欣赏能力。这也是为什么本书专注于利用最基本的系统综合自然拼读教学模式来提升初学者的单词拼读能力从而实现流利阅读。正如前文所述，自然拼读指字母和其所代表音素间的关系，是初级语言学习和写作的必备知识。掌握自然拼读解码规则对于所有英语语言学习者都有益处，包括以英语为外语的中国学生。例如，对于有阅读障碍或者在进入小学以前没有接触过英语书籍，或者是没有英语听力口语环境的英语语言学习者来说，教授和学习自然拼读解码规则是至关重要的。而在中国，以英语为外语的初学者正好符合这一情况。因此，自然拼读解码规则的学习能够帮助中国的英语学习者加深字母和发音之间对应关系的理解，从而发展出自动解码单词的能力并实现流利阅读。因此，本书的重点将放在对系统综合自然拼读模式的解读上。

3.2　自然拼读教学模式介绍

自然拼读或者英语语音解码规则本身并不是一种教学方法，不能直接将自然拼读（Phonics）称为自然拼读教学法，相反，有很多教学模式或者方法可以教授自然拼读语音解码规则。

自然拼读教学（Phonics Instructions）一词特指教授自然拼读解码规则的教学活动。按照Blevins（2017）的说法，主流的三种教学模式是综合自然拼读教学模式（Synthetic Phonics Instruction Approach）、类比教学模式（Analogy Instruction Approach）及分析教学模式（Analytic Instruction Approach）。其中，系统综合法和分析法是目前应用最广泛的教学模式。类比教学模式相对侧重于拼读模块的教学，通常与系统综合法或者是分析教学法搭配使用。

多年来，在英语为母语的国家，哪种自然拼读教学模式的教学效果最好一直是争论的焦点。例如，究竟是系统综合模式好还是分析教学模式好？目前，在以英语为母语的国家中，业内专家们一致认为虽然两种教学模式各有其优点，但更建议使用系统综合教学模式。系统综合教学模式首先要求教学内容应该循序渐进且清楚明晰。换言之，字母与音素间的对应关系即拼读规则应该有系统性地、有规划地、由简到繁地、直截了当地、明确地讲授给学习者。此外，系统化的教学意味着在教学过程中需要重视对已经教授过的规则、知识的复习，并螺旋式地推进教学进度，以确保学习者所掌握的知识得以巩固，并能顺利进阶学习。因此，清晰明了的系统综合自然拼读教学模式被认为是最直接、最高效的语音拼读规则教学模式。与让学生自己去发现总结规律的分析模式来说，系统综合教学模式的教学效率更高，教学效果更好。

3.3 综合自然拼读教学模式

3.3.1 定义

综合自然拼读教学模式，顾名思义，指在拼读的过程中将单个的音素整合起来发音的方式。这种语音教学模式被认为是清晰而系统的。这种教学模式能提供具体的拼读例子供学生理解字母和音素间的关系，并进一步认知书面文字和单词发音之间关系。

3.3.2 解读综合自然拼读教学模式

综合自然拼读教学模式要求学习者将单个的字母发音组合起来发音并读出单词。例如，如果学习者学到了字母 T 代表发音/t/，而字母组合 EA 的发音为长元音 E，他们能顺利拼读出单词 T-EA /tea。

大多数的综合自然拼读教学课程都是从教授字母发音所对应的辅音字母、元音字母、辅音二合字母（例如 sh，th 或者 wh）以及辅音字母连缀（例如 bl，st）开始的。然后讲授更复杂的拼读规则如长元音音素、R 控制的元音音素、变体元音音素以及元音二合字母等。

然而，这也不是一成不变的模式，只要教学设计能针对不同的学情，教学设计清晰明了、由浅入深、具有系统性，就可以满足学习者的需求。

3.3.3 综合拼读教学模式的特点

（1）综合拼读教学是从教授字母发音到教授字母所对应的音素再到拼读整体单词的一种渐进式、自下而上、从局部到整体的一种具有逻辑性的拼读规则教学模式。

（2）这种教学模式教学周期短，教学节奏合理，通常一个学期能完成整个教学。

（3）通过不断的练习，学习者将掌握到将单个音素组合发音读出单词。

（4）在掌握字母发音的同时学习到音素，并能将单个音素组合拼读成为单词。

（5）学习者在获得拼读能力的同时获得拼写能力。

（6）教学可以通过使用具有吸引力的资源及活动实习，如游戏故事活动或者是韵律歌曲。

（7）这种教学模式可以为学习者的语言发展和综合阅读能力发展奠定基础。

（8）这是相对全面的自然拼读学习方案，有利于以英语为外语的学习者、缺乏英语环境、缺乏视觉词汇的学习者以及在早期初级阅读中比较吃力的学习者。

(9) 这种教学模式可以同时培养并进一步发展学习者的音素意识和英语单词解码能力。

3.3.4 综合教学模式的教学顺序

(1) 教授字母名。

(2) 教授和复习每个字母所对应的发音。

(3) 详细教授和解读特定的发音规则。

(4) 教授将音素进行整合拼读并发出单词音的方式。

(5) 为学习者提供拼读上下文中不熟悉单词的机会。

3.3.5 综合自然拼读教学模式的范例

(1) 在黑板上写出字母"S"。

(2) 向学生解释字母"S"代表单词 sit 中的音素/s/,但是勿将音素符号/s/写出来。

(3) 在黑板上写下单词"sit",请一位学生圈出字母 S。

(4) 缓慢地用手指逐个指着单词中的字母并带领着学生读出单个音素并拼读出单词 sit。

(5) 引导学生思考并说出一些 S 开头的单词并由教师将单词写在黑板上。

(6) 引导学生圈出黑板上以 S 开头单词中的字母 S。

(7) 教师提供一些 S 开头简单的包含前述学过的音素并符合拼读规则的单词,让学生练习拼读。

3.4 自然拼读分析教学模式

3.4.1 定义

自然拼读分析教学方法(Analytic Instruction Approach)也称为间接教学模式(Indirect Model)或者发现型教学模式(Discovery Model)。通过这种从整体到部分的教学方法,学生从整个单词开始观察,并在教师引导下推断出单词中字母与其所对应的音素(发音)间的联系,这是本小节的重点内容。

3.4.2 关于分析型教学模式的解读

在以英语为母语的国家,分析型教学模式获得了很多教师的青睐,因为教师们认为,如果学习者自己发现和总结出这些规律,他们能够更好地将这些知识内化。然而,这种教学模式一定程度上依赖于学生较高水平的语音意识以及大量的已有视觉词汇,因此,这种教学模式不太适合缺乏英语环境的以英语为外语的学习者或者是有英语阅读障碍的学生。此外,如果要采用这种教学模式,首先应该对学习者进行语音意识以及音素意识的培养,让学习者初步具备听单词分辨音素的能力,才能为分析型自然拼读教学模式做好准备。

在早期英语阅读教学中，如果以分析教学模式替代综合教学模式，由于分析教学模式建立在大量的视觉词汇和引导学生去发现单词拼读规律上，这种教授拼读规律的模式需要很长时间，有研究称，这种教学模式甚至可以长达五六年。

3.4.3　分析型教学模式的特点

（1）字母与其发音之间的联系并不表示按照特定的顺序，例如，字母顺序、元音-辅音的顺序进行教授。

（2）拼读模块或者是拼读规则的教授是基于对整个单词的拆分分析。

（3）教学周期较长，最长可达五六年。

（4）在初始阶段，并不教授学习者如何将单个音素组合发音读出单词。

（5）需要学习者拥有大量已经建立好的视觉词汇作为词汇中音素拆分分析的基础。

（6）这种教学模式需要学习者具有不错的音素意识来分辨听力词汇中的音素，因此这种教学模式并不能帮助学习者建立音素意识。

3.4.4　分析型教学模式的教学顺序

（1）根据事先设计好的具有共同音素的单词列表，老师可以用粉笔写在黑板上：pen，pity，pat 等单词。

（2）教师引导学习者仔细观察这一组单词以期找到这一组单词所共有的音素。

（3）一旦识别出这一组单词共有的音素，教师可与学生讨论并进一步解释音素发音及其规则。

（4）教授给学习者字母 P 所代表的音素为/p/，并加以练习。

3.5　自然拼读类比教学模式

3.5.1　定义

类比自然拼读教学模式（Analogy Instruction Approach）能够让学习者利用学过的拼读模块而读出拥有相同拼读模块（Phonogram）的陌生单词，拼读模块也被称为词族（Word Family）或者是表音模块（Word Chunk）。

3.5.2　解读类比拼读教学模式

顾名思义，类比拼读教学模式与拼读模块有关。学习者可以通过识别单词中的拼读模块以确定单词的发音。类比教学模式经常与综合拼读教学模式共同使用，也是综合拼读教学模式的有益补充，以解决英语中不规则词汇的拼读问题。例如，学习者熟悉拼读模块“-ould”就能准确读出单词 could，would 和 should。

类比拼读教学模式可以帮助学习者理解更复杂的拼读模块。国际阅读协会（2018）指出，拼读的第一层次是字母层。这一层次涉及综合语音教学所教授的最基本字母-音素对应关系。第二层是模块层次，这一层次可以利用类比拼读教学模式教授拼读模块。简言之，首先鼓励学习者通过综合语音拼读模式学习最基本的音素及其发音规则，其次利用类比拼读教学模式学习发音模块以解决不规则英语单词拼读问题，这样有助于早期阅读教学的顺利进行，这也是为什么类比教学模式是综合拼读教学模式的有益补充。

此外，Blevins（2017）认为，类比拼读教学模式不适合拼读初学者。如果使用类比拼读教学法教授初学者利用视觉去记忆拼读模块则会忽略最基本的字母-音素之间的联系，可能会影响初学者习得拼读最基本的拼读规则，并阻碍学习者音素意识的发展。虽然类比拼读教学模式在拼读教学中有其独特的优势，但应该谨慎使用。在我国，常见的拼读模块经常出现在主流教材中。

3.5.3 类比教学模式的教学顺序

（1）将目标拼读模块写在黑板上，例如，写上拼读模块“-ight”。

（2）紧接着，教师教授并引导学生讨论目标读音的发音。

（3）教师在黑板上写几个含有同样拼读模块的词汇，并重点强调拼读模块的读音，并带领学生进行拼读学习。

（4）教师鼓励学生讨论并说出更多的含有拼读模块“-ight”的词。

3.6 高效的系统综合拼读教学模式的特点

除了明确性和系统性，高效的系统综合拼读教学模式还应该具有以下七个特征：

3.6.1 技能习得前的准备

在学习拼读规则以前，学习者至少应该能进行字母认知，并具备音素意识。

3.6.2 范围和顺序

学习者在已有知识的基础上，由浅入深地、有系统性地学习语音解码规则。综合拼读教学模式的教学顺序鼓励尽早让学习者拼读出尽可能多的单词，并专注于教授给学习者实用的拼读技能。虽然，并没有放之四海而皆准的教学顺序和范围，只要能通过一系列的由浅入深、由简到繁的阶梯式的教学方式，都能最大限度地提高学生的学习成功率。一般来说，拼读课程所教授的拼读规则的内容顺序、广度和深度均可以根据学情进行调整。

3.6.3 混合音素的技能

如前文所述，明确而系统的综合语音教学法可以在教授学习者语音解码规则的同时培养学习者的音素意识。这取决于将音素组合在一起发音的技能，简称混音技能（Blending Skill）。混音是教授学习者将音素组合在一起进行拼读发音的主要策略之一，学习者必须经常练习混音技能。这种技能也在学习者从单音节词阅读到多音节词阅读过程中发挥着重要作用，因此，混音技能是早期语音拼读教学的重点。

3.6.4　听写

为了帮助学习者将正在发展的语音拼读技能有效地转化拼写技能，听写是关键的一环。听写可以帮助学习者提高他们拼写能力和对常见英语单词拼写模式的理解，并且帮助他们在拼写中运用到拼读规则。这样，学习者将有越来越多的机会练习和发展他们的语音拼读拼写能力，从而助力于下一步的英语书面表达。

3.6.5　单词意识

拼读单词和按照所包括的不同音素给单词分类是提高学习者单词意识（Word Awareness）的关键活动。例如，教师给学习者提供一堆打乱顺序的字母，并要求学习者按照教师指令用所给出的字母拼出一系列不同的目标单词。同时，教师也可以给定学习者一些包含不同音素的单词，并要求学习者按照教师给出的指令，根据单词所包含的不同音素对单词进行分类。这些活动不仅可以帮助学习者分析单词的音素组成、熟悉英语单词的拼读及拼写规律，还有助于学习者从单音节词的学习过渡到多音节词的学习。

3.6.6　可解码文本的阅读

自然拼读教学的目的是帮助学习者培养独立阅读文本的能力。在阅读教学的初始阶段，可解码文本能帮助学习者培养对文本阅读的舒适感和自信心，是早期拼读教学的重要学习工具，这种可解码文本可以反复阅读，用以提高学习者的阅读理解能力。

3.6.7　高频词汇

英语中出现频率最高的视觉词汇（Sight Word）称为高频词（High Frequency Word）。某些视觉词汇是不规则的，也就是说，这些词汇并不遵循英语的拼读规则。有些视觉词虽然出现频率高，但遵循拼读规则。学习者应该能在阅读过程中迅速识别视觉词汇，从而无须花费额外时间在拼读高频出现的视觉词汇上。

3.7　系统综合拼读教学模式的教学范畴和顺序

系统综合拼读教学法的教学范围和顺序是动态而灵活的，可根据学情进行调整。尽管如此，这也是自然拼读教学与研究领域一个颇具争议的点。一些学者认为，应该先教授长元音，因为长元音比短元音更容易区分。此外，长元音的发音与字母名相同，更便于初学者记忆。而部分学者认为，长元音规则相较于短元音来说相对复杂，因此应在学习者利用学习短元音时掌握了拼读方法后再教授，而且他们认为短元音的结构 CVC 很容易被学习者掌握，因此这一部分学者主张一开始教授短元音。对此，自然拼读专家 Blevins（2017）推荐如下讲授顺序：

（1）首先教授短元音的发音，因为短元音相对容易学习且学习效率相对较高，其次短元音的结构大多是CVC结构。

（2）将辅音和短元音结合起来讲授，以便学习者尽可能早地进行拼读，从而生成单词。

（3）尽可能早地把辅音字母连贯地教授完毕。

（4）可以选择一个教授拼读规则的顺序，以保证尽可能在讲解和练习中最大限度地囊括更多单词。

（5）从简单拼读规则过渡到更复杂的拼读规则。

1）短元音和辅音。

2）辅音二合字母（ch，sh，th，wh）。

3）辅音字母连缀（r-blends，s-blends，l-blends）。

4）单词末尾的不发音的字母E（a_e，e_e，i_e，o_e，u_e）。

5）长元音。

6）变体元音音素（oo，au，aw）以及双元音音素（ou，ow，oi，oy）。

7）不发音的字母以及附加结尾（-ed，-s，-ing）。

3.8 字母认知的要求

由于英语是字母组合形成的语言，字母代表着一系列的发音音素，所以学习者有必要首先认知字母。学习者应该能够在上下文中识别最基本的大小写字母。

另外，学习者能够迅速识别没有按照顺序排的字母，同时知道每个字母最常关联的发音。

研究显示，能够准确迅速识别字母的学习者比那些识别字母有困难的学习者更容易习得自然拼读规则中字母和音素之间的联系。因为在阅读过程中，能迅速识别字母的学习者能将更多的精力投入到字母和音素间的关系中，从而进一步迅速识别并读出单词成为流利读者。因此可以说，字母认知的准确性和快速性都反映了学习者对字母知识的掌握。

3.9 字母教学的指南

（1）首先教授学习者字母名称，知道字母名以后教师能够利用字母名帮助学生掌握字母名和音素间的联系。

（2）向学习者介绍字母形状及其字母名。

（3）根据学习者需求定制字母讲授课程。

（4）帮助学习者识别字母间的区别和相似之处。

（5）要利用典型的例子和详细的讲解来解释拼读规则。

（6）教学节奏能根据学习者的需求进行调整。

（7）教学要涵盖多感官的活动。

（8）字母类儿童绘本很重要。

3.10 字母类绘本的优势

字母绘本按照字母顺序呈现了字母表中的字母，许多字母绘本都以能激发学习者兴趣的主题为中心，字母绘本用于加强学习者对字母的识别能力，同时有助于词汇量的拓展。这类字母绘本对于缺乏词汇积累的以英语为外语的初学者来说是一个很好的选择。具体来说，其优点如下：

（1）有助于初级阅读者的口语发展。

（2）有助于学习者记住字母顺序。

（3）有助于初学者将字母及其发音联系起来。

（4）有助于初学者在发展词汇量的同时扩展通识知识。

（5）帮助以英语为外语的学生拓展词汇量。

（6）能吸引对全文字书籍有阅读恐惧的学习者。

3.11 利用字母绘本教授字母的技巧点拨

（1）以中等偏慢的语速朗读字母绘本，让学习者感受到语言的魅力并欣赏插图。

（2）再朗读一次目标绘本并与学习者共同讨论一些他们感兴趣的点，例如，讨论插图中以该字母所代表的物体。注意在整个讨论过程中要保持轻松愉快的氛围。

（3）使用字母表中的单词和图去创造一张有字母有图有单词的练习，让学习者将单词、图片以及发音进行匹配。

（4）指导学习者根据课堂上所教授的模式制作自己的字母绘本。

3.12 视觉词汇、高频词汇以及不规则词汇

视觉词汇是成为流利阅读者的必备条件。视觉词汇包括高频词，其中很多词汇是不符合拼读规则的。有研究显示，学习者习得不规则词汇的速度不如习得规则词汇迅速。因此，必须引导学习者利用视觉词汇的方式来熟悉不规则词汇，将不规则词汇演变成视觉词汇。

3.13 英语里的不规则词汇

在英语中，大约84%的单词拼写遵循特定的拼写规律。也有研究报道说，据

不完全统计，英语中有50%~85%的单词是遵循拼写规则的，不同的统计方法有不同的答案。根据这个估计，在剩下的16%的单词中，只有3%是高度不符合拼读规则的。这些所谓的不遵循拼读规则的词汇，可以通过拼读模块（Phonogram）进行学习或者在教师的指导下通过可解码文本阅读而将这些不规则词汇变成自己的视觉词汇。因此，在学习了最基本的字母-音素联系后，学习者可以通过继续学习拼读模块（Phonogram）掌握这些不符合拼读规则的词汇。比如说，拼读模块“ough”是最常见的不规则读音模块，它代表着好几种发音，因此带有拼读模块“ough”单词可以分类讲授：

（1）“ought”：fought，brought，sought，wrought。

（2）“ough”：tough，rough，enough。

（3）“ough”：though，dough，although。

3.14　高频词的建议教学步骤

（1）朗读目标词汇并将这个高频词放入一个合适的句子中进行讲解准备。

（2）一边朗读句子，一边将句子写在黑板上并强调高频词。

（3）讨论目标词汇以及其可能包含的拼读特点。

（4）教师用手指着每一个字母或者拼读模块引导学习者大声拼读出该单词。

（5）当学习者在纸上写下单词的时候，请他们大声读出来。

3.15　常见高频词表

表3.1总结了由美国传统高频词书中总结出的最常见的150个高频词，这些词汇也是新课标所规定的单词。

表3.1

the **	could **	they *	use *	of *
no *	at *	may *	and *	make *
be *	water *	a *	than *	this *
go *	to *	first *	from *	good *
in *	been **	I *	new *	is *
long *	have *	write *	you *	little *
or *	our *	that *	very *	by *
used *	it *	after **	one **	me **
he *	words *	had *	man *	for *
called **	not *	too *	was *	just *

续表

will *	any *	on *	where **	each *
day *	are *	most *	about *	same *
but *	know *	how *	right *	what *
get *	up *	look *	all *	through *
out *	think *	where *	back *	them *
such *	when *	much *	then *	here *
we *	before *	she *	take *	there *
also **	many **	why *	can **	around *
some *	things *	an *	another *	so *
help *	your *	came **	these *	put *
which *	come **	would *	years *	their *
work **	other *	different *	said **	three *
its *	away *	if *	word *	who *
again *	do *	must *	now *	off *
into *	because *	people *	went **	has **
does **	my *	old *	more *	part *
made *	number *	her *	even *	over *
two *	place *	did **	like *	well *
down *	him *	as **	only *	see *
with *	way *	time *	his *	find *

注：* 表示新课标中的二级词汇；** 表示新课标中三级词汇。

3.16 可解码文本的定义

可解码文本是初学者进入普通文本阅读的桥梁，因此被称为连接性文本、桥梁文本。可解码文本围绕着重复的语音特征进行编写，有利于初学者复习巩固特定的自然拼读规则。

3.17 可解码文本的特点

可解码文本在以下几个方面可以提供非常好的阅读体验：

（1）有符合拼读规则的可解码的文字。

（2）句子长度循序渐进地增加，通常由一页一个句子慢慢增加到两个句子甚至更多。

（3）单词的复杂程度通常由单音节词过渡到双音节合成词。

（4）涵盖了专有名词、普通名词及名词的复数形式。

（5）涵盖了代词尤其是人称代词。

（6）涵盖了动词的现在时和过去时。

（7）涵盖了形容词和副词短语。

（8）书中的气泡对话涵盖了直接引语。

（9）逗号、介词、连词、疑问句以及其他标点符号都提供了正确的语法示例。

3.18　可解码文本的好处

（1）这一类书允许初学者将他们所学习到的单词拼读规则付诸实践，并能阅读到许多类似的单词。

（2）正如 Johnson 和 Watson（2007）所建议的那样，拼读课程应该和文本阅读活动相结合，这为学习者提供了操练拼读规则和提高他们语音拼读技能的机会。

（3）可以使用与所教授的音素对应的可解码文本来帮助学习者阅读由所教授的音素组成的句子或者文本材料。

（4）如 Carroll 等（2011）指出，阅读可解码文本可以作为在上下文中加强和练习解码规则以及增强信心的一种手段。

（5）阅读可解码文本对在早期阅读中打下更坚实的基础至关重要，当面对水平较低的读者时更是如此。

（6）可解码文本包括高频词以及不规则拼读词汇，因此可解码文本的使用能让学习者顺利将不规则词汇转化为高频视觉词汇。

3.19　综合语音教学模式小结

（1）首先教授字母认知。

（2）单独教授字母与音素之间的关系，即由浅入深教授自然拼读解码规则，推荐的顺序如下：

1）单个辅音。

2）辅音二合字母。

3）辅音字母连缀。

4）不发音的字母。

5）短元音。

6）长元音。

7）其他元音：双元音；变体元音；由 r 控制的元音；轻音（可选择）。

（3）可解码文本与高频词（对于以英语为外语的学生，根据学情可选）。

（4）拼读模块以及不规则词汇（对于以英语为外语的学生，根据学情可选）。

第 4 章　教学指南与系统综合教学模式的示例

本节旨在加强受训者在系统综合教学模式下的语音教学知识和教学技能：

主要目标	本章旨在帮助受训者掌握以下两方面内容： 1. 字母表、解码规则、视觉词汇教学的一些基本原则 2. SSP 模式的具体教学过程：字母表、拼读规则和视觉词
具体目标	在本章中，学员将能学到并展示以下技能： 1. SSP 模式中字母识别的教学过程 2. SSP 模式中单辅音的教学过程 3. SSP 模式中辅音二合字母的教学过程 4. SSP 模式中辅音字母连缀的教学过程 5. SSP 模式中不发音辅音字母的教学过程 6. SSP 模式中短元音的教学过程 7. SSP 模式中长元音的教学过程 8. SSP 模式中其他元音的教学过程 9. SSP 模式中读音模块、视觉词汇以及不规则词汇的教学过程 10. SSP 模式教学过程中的一些注意事项

4.1　字母认知的教学过程

4.1.1　教学目标

（1）帮助学习者记忆字母顺序。

（2）帮助学习者掌握字母与音素之间的联系。

（3）帮助学习者发展音素意识。

（4）帮助学习者口语发展。

（5）帮助学习者拓展词汇和相关通识知识。

4.1.2 指南

（1）选择合适的字母顺序来进行教授，比如按照字母歌顺序。

（2）根据学生的认知能力确定是先教授大写字母还是小写字母或者二者同时教授。

（3）从教授字母名开始，然后字母形以及其最常见的发音。

（4）帮助学习者区分相似字母，例如，字母 B 或者 D 的小写形式。

4.1.3 课程示例

（1）导读阶段。

1）教师在黑板上写下目标字母的大小写。

2）如果有任何与目标字母相似的字母，也将其写下来进行比较。

3）评估学习者对字母发音的熟悉程度以及认知以目标字母开头的单词的能力，例如，Letter F is for flamingo，更进一步地，可以利用图片让学习者指认目标字母所代表的物体。

4）介绍故事中的人物以及名称，让学习者推测作者选择这种动物以及其名称的原因。

5）展示本书的封面和插图，以引发学习者的预测与讨论。

（2）正式阅读阶段。

1）第一次大声朗读故事，让学习者熟悉本书语言和故事情节。

2）重读故事，并指导学习者用目光搜索和识别目标字母，允许学习者在听到单词首字母的时候指出来。

3）在随后的阅读中，引导学习者找出书中以目标字母开头的物品，并尝试将书中出现的物品与页面上的单词相匹配。

（3）读后阶段。

1）指导学习者找到这本书中以目标字母开头的所有物品，并欣赏字母吟唱（如果有）。

2）教师创建一个以目标字母发音开头的词汇列表，然后玩一个快速找单词的游戏以强化所学习到的目标字母、音素及包含目标字母及音素的单词。

4.2 SSP 模式下辅音字母讲授过程

4.2.1 教学目标

（1）让学习者熟悉每一个辅音最常见读音。

（2）让学习者熟悉与每个字母相关的常见字母发音。

4.2.2 指南

（1）指导学习者记住每一个辅音最常见的发音与写法。

（2）在课程中优先选取CVC结构单词来教授辅音，而不要一开始就教授辅音字母连缀或者辅音二合字母。

（3）在字母K之后，字母C和G可以成对讲解。

（4）字母Q可以独立于字母K之外讲授。

4.2.3 课程示例

单辅音

（1）拼读规则：字母S代表发音/s/。

（2）步骤1：复习，字母R。重读包括先前所教授的字母R的发音的故事或者段落，同时指导学习者练习口头将以字母R开头的单词按照音素拼读出来以培养音素意识。

（3）步骤2：讲授字母与音素之间的联系。

1）向学习者解释字母S代表单词sock里面的音素/s/。

2）在黑板上写下单词sock。

3）然后老师用手指在字母下方滑动并带领学生将sock这个单词中的音素连接拼读出来。

4）让一位志愿者来突出强调字母S及其读音/s/。

5）通过指着字母S来强调其读音/s/来引起学生们的注意。

6）继续让学习者小组合作创建一个包括字母S及音素/s/的词汇列表。

7）将列表中含有字母S及音素/s/的词汇逐一写在黑板上，一边引导学生拼读一边配以图片释意。

（4）步骤3：混合音素拼读成单词。

1）在黑板上写下以目标字母S开头的一些简单词汇。

2）再写出几个已经学过的简单的词汇和带有目标字母的词汇进行比较。

3）写一两个包含这些词和其他高频词的句子。

例如：Sat，sad，sock。

Mat，mad，rock。

Sam is sad。

I sat on the rock。

4）引导学习者使用字母a，o，l，s，t和m尽可能多地去构建所学过的单词。

（5）步骤4：文字识别和声音的辨别。在黑板上写下一些含有目标字母S和其所对应的音素/s/的简单单词，然后教师随机大声朗读这些单词，请学习者识别教师当前正在朗读的单词。

（6）步骤5：可解码文本（以英语为外语的学习者可选）。基于学习者之前已经学过的词汇并根据目标字母及其对应的音素，为学习者提供可解码的文本进行阅读练习，这个步骤是根据学情进行取舍的。

（7）步骤6：听写（以英语为外语的学习者可选）。听写当日课程中的简单词汇，并将答案记录在黑板上。此活动旨在帮助学习者学习按照音素分割单词并将单词读音和拼写联系起来。对于以英语为外语的学习者来说，还可以展示相应的图片，以帮助他们将单词和意思联系起来。这一步骤也是根据学情进行取舍的。

4.3 SSP模式下的辅音二合字母教学过程

4.3.1 教学目标

（1）让学习者熟悉辅音二合字母的发音。

（2）帮助学习者快速识别单词中的二合字母。

4.3.2 原则

（1）在一个词中同时出现的两个辅音字母代表一个音素发音的时候，这两个辅音字母被称为辅音二合字母。

（2）学习者掌握所有单辅音后，可以紧接着教授辅音二合字母。

4.3.3 教学范例

辅音二合字母

（1）拼读规则：常见的辅音二合字母“SH”代表着单词shoot中的发音/sh/。

（2）步骤1：复习，再次阅读包含先前所教授的字母发音关系的故事或者段落，并让学习者练习将音素进行混合拼读出所学过的词汇以培养音素意识。

（3）步骤2：字母发音关系介绍。

1）向学习者解释字母S和H所组成的辅音二合字母所代表的音素/sh/。

2）在黑板上写下单词ship并配以图片。

3）教师用手指在单词字母下方滑动带领学习者拼读出单词ship。

4）让一名志愿者勾画并强调二合字母SH。

5）教师指着二合字母SH并让学生说出其代表的发音/sh/。

6）继续让学生说出包含二合字母SH及其音素/sh/的单词并列在黑板上。

7）一边列包含有二合字母SH的单词一边为学习者提供插图以释义。

（4）步骤3：混合音素成单词。

1）在黑板上写下以目标二合字母SH开头的单词。

2）写出已经学过的简单词汇与目标单词进行比较。

3）写一两个包含目标词汇、简单词汇和其他高频词汇的句子。

例如：Sock，shock，sop，shop。

Fish，dish，hush，rush。

The ship is big。

I wish I had a red dish。

4）引导学习者使用字母 a、o，l，sh，m，f 和 p，建构更多的已知单词。

（5）步骤4：单词识别和音素辨别。教师在黑板上写下带有目标二合字母 SH 及其所对应的音素/sh /的简单词汇列表并随机大声朗读，让学习者识别教师当前正在朗读的单词。

（6）步骤5：可解码文本（以英语为外语的学习者可选）。基于学习者之前已经学过的词汇并根据目标字母及其对应的音素，为学习者提供可解码的文本进行阅读练习，这个步骤是根据学情进行取舍的。

（7）步骤6：听写（以英语为外语的学习者可选）。听写当日课程中的简单词汇，并将答案记录在黑板上。此活动旨在帮助学习者学习按照音素分割单词并将单词读音和拼写联系起来。对于以英语为外语的学习者来说，还可以展示相应的图片，以帮助他们将单词和意思联系起来。这一步骤也是根据学情进行取舍的。

4.4 SSP 模式下辅音字母连缀的教授

4.4.1 教学目标

（1）让学习者熟悉辅音字母连缀的发音。

（2）帮助学习者识别单词中的辅音字母连缀。

4.4.2 原则

（1）辅音字母连缀（Consonant Cluster）是由两到三个辅音字母组合在一起出现在一个单词中并且保留各自独立音素的字母组合。辅音字母连缀所代表的音素则为辅音音素连缀（Consonant Blend）。

（2）辅音字母连缀的发音是相对可靠的，几乎总是代表着固定的辅音音素连缀。

（3）辅音字母连缀有一个例外的组合就是字母 SC 组合。这个字母组合可以代表单词 scare 里面的/sk/音，或者如同在单词 science 里面一样不发音。

（4）辅音字母连缀可以分为三大类和三小类，如表 4.1 所示。

表 4.1

由 r 控制的连缀	br, cr, dr, fr, gr, pr, tr
由 l 控制的连缀	bl, cl, fl, gl, pl

续表

由 s 控制的连缀	sc，sk，sl，sm，sn，sp，st，sw
其他连缀	tw，qu
三字母连缀	str，spt，thr，
	chr，phr，shr（digraph+consonant）
四字母连缀	ngth as in strength（digraph+digraph）

（5）在单个的辅音和二合字母教授完毕之后，可以教授辅音字母连缀。

（6）在教授辅音字母连缀的时候，更建议按照类别教授，而非逐个讲授。

（7）辅音字母连缀的讲授对于以英语为外语的学习者来说是可选择的，具体教授与否或者教授哪一些均取决于学情、学习者的音素意识发展和具体的课时安排，因为辅音字母连缀中的辅音字母都保留了其原有的发音，具有良好音素意识的学习者能自己读出来。

4.4.3 课程示例

辅音字母连缀

（1）拼读原则：以字母 S 开头的辅音字母连缀。

（2）步骤 1：复习，重读包含先前教授的辅音字母连缀的故事或者段落，并让学习者练习将音素进行混合拼读出所学过的词汇以培养音素意识。

（3）步骤 2：字母发音关系介绍。

1）在黑板上写下单词 snake，stone 以及 spot。

2）画出每个单词里的辅音字母连缀“SN，ST 以及 SP”。

3）提醒学习者这几个辅音字母连缀的读音分别是/sn/，/st/ and /sp/（请不要在黑板上写出表音符号）。

4）用手指着单词并带领学习者大声地将单词中的音素进行混合并拼读出单词。

5）请一位志愿者勾画出单词中所包含的辅音字母连缀“SP，ST 和 SN”。

6）用手指着不同单词中的辅音字母连缀并请学习者们同时大声说出目标辅音字母连缀所代表的音素。

7）让学习者创建一个包含目标辅音字母连缀词汇的单词表。

8）将含有目标辅音连缀的单词表写在黑板上并配上图片释义。

（4）步骤 3：混合音素拼读成单词。

1）在黑板上写下以目标字母开头的单词。

2）写出已经学过的简单词汇与目标单词进行比较。

3）写一两个包含这些词和其他高频词的句子。

例如：Sock，shock，sop，shop。

Spot，stop，spit，snap。

I spot a sock/shop。

4）鼓励学习者用字母 a，o，e，s，m，t，p 和 sh 创造更多的单词。

（5）步骤4：单词识别和音素辨别。在黑板上写下带有目标字母和读音的简单词汇列表，让学习者识别教师当前正在朗读的单词。

（6）步骤5：可解码文本（以英语为外语的学习者可选）。基于学习者之前已经学过的词汇并根据目标字母及其对应的音素，为学习者提供可解码的文本进行阅读练习，这个步骤是根据学情进行取舍的。

（7）步骤6：听写（以英语为外语的学习者可选）。听写当日课程中的简单词汇，并将答案记录在黑板上。此活动旨在帮助学习者学习按照音素分割单词并将单词读音和拼写联系起来。对于以英语为外语的学习者来说，还可以展示相应的图片，以帮助他们将单词和意思联系起来。这一步骤也是根据学情进行取舍的。

4.5　SSP 模式中不发音辅音字母的教学（可选）

字母表中大多数的辅音字母偶尔在单词中不发音。辅音经常有不发音的情况，因此单词的发音随着时间的推移而改变拼写却相对稳定。同时，不发音的辅音字母也出现在外来词汇中，只是在阅读过程中我们不一定能意识到。

4.5.1　教学目标

（1）帮助学习者辨识单词中不发音的辅音字母。

（2）帮助学生理解单词中不发音的辅音的规则。

4.5.2　准则

（1）在 170000 个常用词中出现频率最高的不发音的辅音字母有 15 个（Burmeister，1971；Blevins，2017）。

如表 4.2 所示，黑体字母为不发音的辅音字母。

表 4.2

1. **t**ch /ch/ as in ha**t**ch	2. **d**g /j/ as in lo**d**ge	3. **w**r /r/ as in **w**rite
4. **k**n /n as in **k**now	5. **g**n/n/ as in sign	6. m**b**/m/ as in lam**b**
7. **p**s/s/ as in **p**sychology	8. **l**k /k/ as in talk	9. **l**m /m/ as in calm
10. r**h** /r/ as in r**h**ino	11. **d**j/j/ as in a**d**just	12. w**h**/h/ as in **w**ho
13. **b**t /t/ as in deb**t**	14. g**h**/g/ as in g**h**ost	15. m**n**/m/ as in hym**n**

（2）当教师觉得有必要给学习者教授不发音的辅音字母时，应先教授单个辅音，辅音字母连缀以及辅音二合字母。或者当中高阶学习者在阅读练习中遇到不发音的辅音字母的时候再教授给他们比较合适。

4.5.3 课程示例

不发音的辅音字母

（1）拼读原则：字母组合 WR 中字母 W 不发音。

（2）步骤 1：复习，重读包含先前教授的辅音字母连缀的故事或者段落，并让学习者练习将音素进行混合拼读出所学过的词汇以培养音素意识。

（3）步骤 2：字母发音关系介绍：

1）向学习者解释，有时候一个字母并不代表一个音素，有时候不发音。

2）在黑板上写下单词 write，并且强调当字母 W 和 R 在一起的时候字母 W 不发音。

3）然后教师用手指划过单词并带领学习者拼读出单词 write。

4）请一位志愿者上来勾画出目标字母 WR 并指出字母 W 不发音。

5）让学习者指出字母组合 WR 并说出其代表的发音/r/。

6）继续让学习者创建一个包含目标辅音字母 WR 的单词表，并在课本和教室中找找能否找到包含 WR 字母组合的单词。

7）将包括 WR 字母组合的单词写在黑板上并配以图片释义。

（4）步骤 3：混合音素拼读成单词。

1）在黑板上写下以目标字母开头的单词。

2）写出已经学过的简单单词与目标单词进行比较。

3）写一两个包含这些词和其他高频词的句子。

例如：Rap，wrap，wing，wring。

Wreck，wrong，wrist，wrinkle。

I wrap the wings。

4）鼓励学习者用更多的字母，例如，用字母 wr，a，e，I，s，t，p 和 ck 尽可能多地写出一些单词。

（5）步骤 4：单词识别和音素辨别。在黑板上写下含有目标字母和其所代表的音素的简单词汇列表并让学习者识别教师当前正在朗读的单词。

（6）步骤 5：可解码文本（以英语为外语的学习者可选）。基于学习者之前已经学过的词汇并根据目标字母及其对应的音素，为学习者提供可解码的文本进行阅读练习，这个步骤是根据学情进行取舍的。

（7）步骤 6：听写（以英语为外语的学习者可选）。听写当日课程中的简单词汇，并将答案记录在黑板上。此活动旨在帮助学习者学习按照音素分割单词并将单词读音和拼写联系起来。对于以英语为外语的学习者来说，还可以展示相应的图片，以帮助他们将单词和意思联系起来。这一步骤也是根据学情进行取舍的。

4.6 SSP 模式中短元音的教学模式

4.6.1 教学目标

帮助学习者识别特定的短元音字母的发音关系。

4.6.2 原则

借助简单的 CVC 结构的词，比如 cat，sun 和 big 教授短元音发音，如表 4.3 所示。

表 4.3

Short-A sound /a/	Short-E sound /e/	Short-I sound /i/	Short-O sound /o/	Short-U sound /u/
bad*	bed*	bib	box**	bud
bag**	bet	big**	cob	bug
cat**	fed	bit*	cot	bun
cab	get**	did**	dog**	bus**
can**	hen	dig*	fog	but**
cap**	jet	dip	fox	cub
cat**	led	fix*	got**	cup*
dad**	leg**	fit*	hog	cut*
fan	let**	hid*	hop	dug**
fat*	men**	him**	hot**	fun*
gas	met	hip	job*	gun*
had**	net	hit*	jog	hug
has**	pen**	kid**	lot*	hut
hat	pet*	kit	mom**	jug
jam	red**	lid	mop	mud
lab*	set	lip	not**	mug
mad*	ten**	lit**	pod	nut
man**	vet	pig**	pop	pup

续表

Short-A sound /a/	Short-E sound /e/	Short-I sound /i/	Short-O sound /o/	Short-U sound /u/
map **	web	pin	pot	rub
mat	wet *	pit	rod	rug
pad	yes **	rib	son **	run **
pal	yet *	rid	top *	sub
pan		rip		sum
pat		sit **		sun
rag		six **		tub
ram		tip		tug
ran **		wig		
rap		win *		
rat		zip		
sad **				
sat				
tag				
tan				
tap				
van				
wag				

注：＊表示新课标中的二级词汇；＊＊表示新课标中三级词汇。

4.6.3 课程示例

短元音发音

（1）拼读原则：字母 A 代表着单词 cat 中的短元音发音/a/。

（2）步骤 1：复习，重读包含先前教授的辅音字母连缀的故事或者段落，并让学习者练习将音素进行混合拼读出所学过的词汇以培养音素意识。

（3）步骤 2：字母-音素对应关系介绍：

1）与学习者共同探讨字母 A 代表短音/a/的规律。

2）将单词 cat 写在黑板上并配以图片。

3）然后教师用手指划过单词 cat 并带领学习者拼读出单词 cat。

4）请一位志愿者来勾画出字母 A 并对其发音加以强调。

5）请学习者说出字母 A 对应的短元音的读音/a/。

6）请学习者继续写出一些带有字母 A 并且发短元音的单词。

7）将含有目标字母 A 与其所对应的短元音/a/的词汇列表写在黑板上并配上图片释义。

（4）步骤 3：混合音素拼读成单词。

1）在黑板上写下包括目标字母的单词。

2）写出已经学过的简单单词与目标单词进行比较。

3）写一两个包含这些词和其他高频词的句子。

例如：At，sat，mat，cat。

Am，mad，lap，sad。

Cat sat on the mat。

I am mad。

4）鼓励学习者用字母 a，s，t，m，c，d 和 p 尽可能多地写一些已知单词出来。

（5）步骤 4：单词识别和音素辨别。在黑板上写下带有目标字母和其所代表的音素的简单词汇列表并让学习者识别教师当前正在朗读的单词，例如，单词 ham，lamb，fab 以及 nap。

（6）步骤 5：可解码文本（以英语为外语的学习者可选）。基于学习者之前已经学过的词汇并根据目标字母及其对应的音素，为学习者提供可解码的文本进行阅读练习，这个步骤是根据学情进行取舍的。

（7）步骤 6：听写（以英语为外语的学习者可选）。听写当日课程中的简单词汇，并将答案记录在黑板上。此活动旨在帮助学习者学习按照音素分割单词并将单词读音和拼写联系起来。对于以英语为外语的学习者来说，还可以展示相应的图片，以帮助他们将单词和意思联系起来。这一步骤也是根据学情进行取舍的。

4.7 SSP 模式下长元音教学模式

4.7.1 教学目标

帮助学生掌握长元音的字母与音素对应关系。

4.7.2 原则

（1）通过简单的单音节词开始介绍长元音。建议使用 CVCe 结构（辅音-元音-辅音-e）开始教学。这种模式下，长元音发音较为可靠，而且这个结构中末尾的字母 E 也是不发音的 E。在一些教材里，这个不发音的 E 被称为变音标记。

需要提醒学习者注意末尾不发音的 E 前面的元音是长元音。

（2）CVC 和 CVCe 模式之间的对比可以用来说明不发音的字母 e 是如何改变字母发音的。

表 4.4 是 CVC 结构和 CVCe 模式对比参考表。

表 4.4

Contrast of CVC and CVCe pattern word list			
bit/bite	past/paste	can-cane	us-use
cod/code	rag/rage	cub-cube	Fat-fate
dim/dime	rip-ripe	fad-fade	not-note
fin/fine	scrap-scrape	glob-globe	fin-fine
grad/grade	slid-slide	hat-hate	pal/pale
hop-hope	spin-spine	kit-kite	shin-shine
man-mane	twin-twine	mat-mate	pan-pane
mad-made	wag-wage	rob-robe	hid-hide
tap-tape	not-note	rod-rode	slop-slope
van-vane			

用以教学的 VCe 结构单词表有 4 个。

VCe 结构中的长元音 A，如表 4.5 所示。

表 4.5

VCe Words List：Long-A sound /ai/ A_E pattern				
ace	age *	bake	base	blade
blame	blaze	brace	brake	brave **
cage	cake *	came **	cane	cape
case	cave	chase	crane	crate
date *	daze	drape	face *	fade
fake	fame	flake	flame	game *
gate **	gave **	gaze	glaze	grace
grade	grape *	grate	grave	haste
hate **	haze	jade	lace	lake *
lame	lane	late *	made **	make *

续表

VCe Words List：Long-A sound /ai/ A_E pattern				
male	mane	mate	name *	pace
page **	pale **	pane	paste	pave
place *	plane *	plate **	quake	race **
rage	rake	rate	rave	safe *
sake	sale **	same **	save **	scale
scrape	shade	shake **	shame **	shape **
shave	skate	slate	snake **	space *
spade	stage	stake	stale	state **
take *	tale	tame	tape **	taste **
trace	trade **	vane	vase	wade
wage	wake *	wave **	waste **	whale **
EXCEPTIONS：Advantage, are, average, breakage, cabbage, climate, courage, delicate, furnace, have, manage, message, palace, passage, private, purchase, senate, separate, surface and village				

注：* 表示新课标中的二级词汇；** 表示新课标中三级词汇。

VCe 结构中的长元音 I，如表 4.6 所示。

表 4.6

Long-I sound /igh/ I_E pattern			
bike *	bite	bride	chime
crime	dice	dime	dine
dive	drive *	file	fine *
five *	glide	hide **	hike **
hive	kite *	lice	life **
like *	lime	pine	pipe
price **	pride **	rice *	ride **
ripe	rise **	shine	side **
slice	slide	slime	smile **
spice	spike	spine	stride
strike	stripe	swine	tide
tile	time *	twice	twine
vine	while **	white *	wide **

续表

Long-I sound /igh/ I_E pattern			
wife **	wipe	wise **	write *
EXCEPTIONS: Active, aggressive, automobile, determine, engine, expressive, favorite, figurine, give, justice, live, machine, magazine, massive, native, notice, office, opposite, police, practice, promise, representative, routine, service			

注：* 表示新课标中的二级词汇；** 表示新课标中三级词汇。

VCe 结构中的长元音 O，如表 4.7 所示。

表 4.7

Long-O sound /oa/O_E pattern				
bone	broke **	choke	chose	code
cone	dome	drove **	globe	hole **
home *	hope **	hose	joke **	lone
mole	nose *	note **	poke	pole
role **	rode **	rope **	rose **	slope
smoke **	spoke **	stole **	stone **	stove
stroke	those **	tone	vote	whole **
woke **	zone			
EXCEPTIONS: Above, become, come, done, glove, gone, improve, lose, love, lovely, move, movement, none, purpose, remove, shove, some, something, welcome, whose				

注：* 表示新课标中的二级词汇；** 表示新课标中三级词汇。

VCe 结构中的长元音 U，如表 4.8 所示。

表 4.8

Long-U sound /yoo/ U_E pattern					
cube	cute *	cure	fuse	mule	use *
EXCEPTIONS: Assure, conclude, crude, flute, include, June, measure, pleasure, prune, rude, rule, sure, treasure					

注：* 表示新课标中的二级词汇；** 表示新课标中三级词汇。

（3）除 VCe 模式和不发音的字母 E 作为标记以外，许多元音字母组合，即元音二合字母（vowel digraph）例如，“AI，AY，EE”代表着长元音音素。如表 4.9 所示。

表 4.9

元音二合字母	对应的音素	示例	可靠度（%）
AI	Long-A sound /ai/	rain	74
EI		rein	40
-AY		say	96
-EY		convey	20
EA	Long-E sound /ee/	seat	51
EE		bee	86
-EY		key	58
-IE		chief	51
OA	Long-O sound /oa/	boat	94
OW		snow	50
EW	Long-U sound /yoo/	few	95

4.7.3　课程示例

长元音音素

（1）拼读原则：字母组合“EA”和“EE”代表着长元音 E 音素，例如，在单词 Bee 和 peach 中。

（2）步骤 1：复习，重读包含先前教授的辅音字母连缀的故事或者段落，并让学习者练习将音素进行混合拼读出所学过的词汇以培养音素意识。

（3）步骤 2：字母与音素之间的关系介绍：

1）与学习者共同探讨字母组合 EE 和 EA 代表长元音 E 的规律。

2）将单词 bee，seat，field 写在黑板上并配以图片释义。

3）教师用手指划过这些单词并带领学生拼读出 bee，seat 以及 field。

4）请一位志愿者来勾画出字母组合 EE 和 EA 并加以强调其读音为长元音 E/ee/。

5）请学习者说出字母组合 EE 以及 EA 对应的长元音读音为/ee/。

6）请学习者继续写出一些带有字母组合 EE 和 EA 并且发长元音 E 的单词。

7）将含有目标词汇的单词表写在黑板上并配上图片释义。

（4）步骤 3：混合音素拼读成单词。

1）在黑板上写下以目标字母开头的单词。

2）写出已经学过的简单单词与目标单词进行比较。

3）写一两个包含这些词和其他高频词的句子。

例如：Bet，beat，fed，feed。

Leaf，need，flea，bee。

The bee is on the leaf。

4）鼓励学习者用字母 ee，ea，s，d，t，p，k，以及 l 写出更多的已知单词。

（5）步骤 4：单词识别和音素辨别。在黑板上写下带有目标字母和其所代表的音素的简单词汇列表并让学习者识别教师当前正在朗读的单词。

（6）步骤 5：可解码文本（以英语为外语的学习者可选）。基于学习者之前已经学过的词汇并根据目标字母及其对应的音素，为学习者提供可解码的文本进行阅读练习，这个步骤是根据学情进行取舍的。

（7）步骤 6：听写（以英语为外语的学习者可选）。听写当日课程中的简单词汇，并将答案记录在黑板上。此活动旨在帮助学习者学习按照音素分割单词并将单词读音和拼写联系起来。对于以英语为外语的学习者来说，还可以展示相应的图片，以帮助他们将单词和意思联系起来。这一步骤也是可以根据学情进行取舍的。

4.8 SSP 模式下其他元音的教学过程

4.8.1 教学目标

（1）让学习者熟悉双元音的拼读规则。

（2）让学习者熟悉变体元音的拼读规则。

（3）让学习者熟悉 r 控制元音的拼读规则。

（4）让学习者熟悉轻音的拼读规则。

4.8.2 原则

（1）双元音：双元音是由嘴巴滑动产生的元音音素（Blevins，2017；Bear et al.，2020）。双元音音素/oi/由字母组合 OY 或者 OI 所代表，例如，在单词 boy 和 oil 中；双元音音素/ou/由字母组合 OU 或者 OW 所代表，例如，在单词 cow 和 blouse 中。

（2）变体元音：某些元音二合字母并不被归类于长元音或者短元音，这些元音被称为变体元音，如表 4.10 所示。

表 4.10

变体元音音素	所对应的二合字母	示例	可靠度（%）
/ou/	OU	house	35
	OW	how	48

续表

变体元音音素	所对应的二合字母	示例	可靠度（%）
Long /oo/	UI	fruit	53
	OO	food	59
Short /oo/	OO	look	36
/or/（broad-O sound）	AW	hawk	100
	AU	haul	94

注：①宽音 O 或者是音素/or/在上表中归类于受 R 控制的元音；②二合字母 OO 所代表的发音虽然有长有短，但其代表的长音会多一些，但是只凭眼睛是无法分辨出长短音的，读者只能凭日常积累来分辨。(Adapted from Blevins, 2017)

（3）R 控制的元音：R 控制的元音被称为受 R 影响的元音。字母 R 控制着它前面的元音的发音。具体而言，当字母 R 出现在一个单词的最后并且恰好在另一个辅音字母前，字母 R 将前面的短元音变为 R 控制的元音，例如，在单词 bird, fork 和 burn 中。R 控制的元音列表如表 4.11 所示。

表 4.11

R 控制的元音音素	对应的字母组合	示例
/ur/	-ER	her, fern, herb, perfect
	-IR	bird, first, girl, stir
	UR	urn, purse, burn, curl
	EAR	earn, learn, pearl, search
/ar/	AR	far, barn, harsh, arm
/or/	OR	fork, horn, for, horse
	OAR	board, coarse, oar, soar
/air/	AIR	hair, fair, pair, stair
	-ARE	care, aware, share, scare
	-EAR	bear, pear, tear, wear

（4）Schwa。一些语言学家认为，轻音不是一个独特的声音，相反，它应该是一个元音变体而且无须重读。因此可以被称为轻音。要教授轻音很难，通常轻音的习得需要日常的阅读听力词汇积累，因此对于以英语为外语的学生来说，是否要学习取决于学情以及教学计划。

4.8.3 课程示例

Diphthong /oi/

（1）拼读原则：字母组合 OY 和 OI 代表着双元音音素/oi/，例如，在单词 boy 和 oil 中。

（2）步骤 1：复习，重读包含先前教授的辅音字母连缀的故事或者段落，并让学习者练习将音素进行混合拼读出所学过的词汇以培养音素意识。

（3）步骤 2：字母与音素之间的关系介绍：

1）向学习者介绍，字母组合 OY 和 OI 代表着双元音音素/oi/，例如在单词 boy 和 oil 中。

2）将单词 boy 和 oil 写在黑板上并配图解释。

3）教师用手指划过所写单词的每个字母并带领学生拼读出单词 boy 和 boil。

4）请一位志愿者来勾画出单词中的字母组合“OY” and “OI”。

5）请学习者说出字母组合 OY 和 OI 对应的音素为/oi/。

6）继续让学习者写出一些带有音素/oi/并包括字母组合 OY 或者 OI 的单词。

7）将含有目标词汇的单词表写在黑板上并配以图片释义。

（4）步骤 3：混合音素拼读成单词。

1）在黑板上写下包含目标字母的单词。

2）写出已经学过的简单单词与目标单词进行比较。

3）写一两个包含这些词和其他高频词的句子。

例如：Boy，point，boil，toy。

Joy，oyster，join，noise。

The boy enjoys the toy。

4）鼓励学习者用字母 oi，oy，b，l，n，c 和 j 写出更多的单词。

（5）步骤 4：单词识别和音素辨别。在黑板上写下带有目标字母和读音的简单单词列表并让学习者识别教师当前正在朗读的单词。考虑一下单词 toy，join 以及 boy。

（6）步骤 5：单词识别和音素辨别。在黑板上写下带有目标字母和其所代表的音素的简单词汇列表并让学习者识别教师当前正在朗读的单词。

（7）步骤 6：可解码文本（以英语为外语的学习者可选）。基于学习者之前已经学过的词汇并根据目标字母及其对应的音素，为学习者提供可解码的文本进行阅读练习，这个步骤是根据学情进行取舍的。

（8）步骤 7：听写（以英语为外语的学习者可选）。听写当日课程中的简单词汇，并将答案记录在黑板上。此活动旨在帮助学习者学习按照音素分割单词并将单词读音和拼写联系起来。对于以英语为外语的学习者来说，还可以展示相应的图片，以帮助他们将单词和意思联系起来。这一步骤也是可以根据学情进行取舍的。

4.9　不规则词汇，常见词汇以及拼读模块的教学

如前文所述，理论上学习者已经具备了最基本的语音解码规则知识和音素意识，学习者应该进一步阅读可解码文本来增强他们的阅读自信心，巩固他们所学到的语音解码规则。同时在阅读中也能频繁遇见不符合拼读规则的词汇。这些不符合拼读规则的词汇既可以通过阅读积累成为读者的视觉词汇，也可以由教师在学习者阅读过程中遇见的拼读模块（Phonogram）的时候进行教学指导。正如 Blevins（2017）指出的一样，拼读模块不适合初学者，因为初学者可能更喜欢通过类比的方式拼读出单词，而不是通过字母-音素关系拼读单词，这样会削弱初学者建立字母-音素之间的联系以及音素意识的发展。相反，在掌握了最基本的字母-音素关系后，有了一定视觉词积累后再总结拼读模块，对于提高阅读流利性来说非常重要。如前文所提到的，英语有84%的词汇是可解码的，而剩下16%的单词可以通过拼读模块或者视觉词的方式获得。因此：

（1）拼读模块，特别是使用频率较高的拼读模块应该教授给学生。

（2）可以通过可解码文本或者分级阅读来帮助学生积累视觉词汇。

（3）拼读模块和视觉词汇都可用于教授不规则词汇。

由于2022年版本义务教育新课标要求学生掌握最基本的字母-音素对应关系，在第三章里包括最基本的自然拼读语音规则，这些内容是本书最基本的内容，因此拼读模块将归纳在附录中。

4.10　关于规则概括的讨论

通过系统明确的综合拼读教学模式，学习者的注意力从单个字母转移到了字母与音素对应的关系上，包括混合和分割单词中不同的音素或者拼读模块，并且随着不断的拼读练习，语音解码规则在他们脑海里会分类、内化，从而助力于他们的阅读理解。值得一提的是，虽然学习这些语音拼读规则有利于学习者的拼读、拼写以及早期阅读，但不应该过分强调拼读规则的绝对性，因此以下方针供教师参考：

（1）避免在语音教学中过分强调语音拼读规则，因为拼读规则只是一种工具，可以帮助学习者专注于通过语音解码识别生词。

（2）只需要教授给学习者最常见的拼读规则，并且避免在教授过程中使用特别专业的词汇。

（3）应该多注重所教授的规则的应用，而不是局限于口头复述规则。一旦学习者了解了如何应用规则，就没有必要反复强调规则。

（4）要选择适当的时机引入语音拼读规则，便于学习者理解和应用。

（5）避免绝对化规则，要告知学生规则之外也有例外。

表4.2是一些规则实用度的总结，本书只总结了超过95%可靠度的拼读规则。

表4.12

类别	规则	示例	实用度（%）
辅音规则	1. When letter C is before O or A, it has /k/ sound.	cat	100
	2. When-CK at the final position of a word, it has /k/ sound.	cock	100
	3. In spelling pattern-ight, letter tam “gh” is silent.	right	100
	4. In letter team “KN”, K is silent.	knock	100
	5. In letter team “WR”, W is silent.	write	100
	6. When one consonant letter is doubled in a word, one letter is silent.	berry	99
	7. When letter C is before I or E, it has /s/ sound.	cent	96
元音规则	8. Letter team “EE” represent long-E sound /ee/.	bee	98

4.11 语音课应该避免做的事情

Blevins（2017）在长期的课堂观察总结后提出了语音课应该避免的事情供教师们参考：

（1）应该避免让学习者在课堂上感到不知所措，而应该让学习者明确教师们本堂课的教学目标。

（2）避免立即纠正学习者的错误，应该提供给学习者自我监察和自我更正的机会。

（3）避免在课堂上使用特殊例子来解释正在教授的规则。

（4）避免使用含混不清的术语进行教授，例如：

1）应该避免说：“你看清了什么声音?”而应该说：“您听清了这个单词的发音吗?”

2）应该避免说：“字母T发的是/t/”而应该说：“字母T代表着音素/t/。”

3）应该避免说：“字母OI是双元音音素”，而应该说字母组合OI代表着双元音音素/oi/。

4.12 自然拼读课程应该做的

Blevins（2017）在长期的课堂观察总结后提出了语音课应该做的事情供教师们参考。

（1）授课应该有逻辑顺序。

（2）讲授拼读规则的时候应该表述明确、准确。

（3）课程应该按教学周持续进行。

（4）每堂课应该有明确目标和重点。

（5）每堂课的设计从学习者已有知识开始。

（6）每堂课应该有对上一次课的复习，尤其是对上次课所学的音素进行混合发音练习并提供可解码的阅读的材料。

（7）讲授的范畴和顺序应该根据不同学情有所裁剪。

（8）每堂课应该有听写或者拼写游戏来巩固所学。

附录　供教学参考的单词表

第一部分　辅音音素词汇表

下表分为两类：

（1）为了教学方便，2022 版新课标所要求的单词已经按照字母顺序罗列出来。

（2）单词列表包括 Blevins（2017）和 Hepplewhite（2020）所列出来的词汇。

单词表的使用建议如下：

（1）可供学习者进行拼读练习。

（2）可供学习者造句和教师用来编撰可解码文本。

（3）可用于词汇游戏。

（4）可用于拼读练习和听写。

/b/ as in bat

Words begin with /b/ sound in National Curriculum					
baby *	back *	bad *	bag *	ball *	banana *
basketball *	be *	bear *	beautiful *	bed *	before *
begin *	beside *	between *	big *	bike *	bicycle *
bird *	birthday *	black *	blackboard *	blue *	boat *
body *	book *	box *	boy *	bread *	breakfast *
bring *	brother *	brown *	bus *	busy *	but *
by *	background	balloon **	bamboo **	banana *	bank **
basic **	basket **	bathroom **	beach *	bean **	beat **
because *	become **	bedroom **	beef **	believe **	bell **
below **	beast	better **	bill **	birth **	biscuit **
bit **	bully **	burn **	blind **	block **	blood **

续表

Words begin with /b/ sound in National Curriculum					
blouse **	blow **	board **	bored	boring **	born **
boss **	borrow **	both **	bottle **	bottom **	bowl **
brain **	brave **	break **	bridge **	bright **	Britain **
British **	brush **	build **	building **	burn **	business **
/b/ represented by B in initial position					
back *	bad *	badge	bag *	bait	bake
ball *	balloon **	ban	band **	bank **	bar
barn	base *	basket **	bass	bat **	batch
bath **	bathe	beach *	bead	beak	beam
bean	bear *	beast	bed **	bee *	beef **
been **	beet	beg	bell **	belt **	bench
bend	bent	best **	bet	bib	bid
big *	bike *	bill **	bin **	bind	birch
bird *	bit **	bite	boar	boast	boat *
bog	boil **	bold	bone	book *	boom
boost	boot	bop	born **	boss **	botch
both **	bottle **	bound	bow	bowl **	box *
boy *	buck	bud	budge	bug	bull
bum	bump	bun	bunch	bunk	bunt
burn *	burst	bus *	but *	butterfly	button
buzz	by *				
/b/ represented by B in final position					
bib	cab	cob	club **	crab	crab
crib	cub	grab	job *	knob	lab **
rib	rob	rub	scrub	sob	sub

＊表示 2022 版新课标中二级词汇；＊＊表示 2022 版新课标中三级词汇。

/d/ as in dog

Words begin with /d/ sound in National Curriculum					
dad	dance *	day *	dear *	desk *	difficult *
dinner *	dirty *	do *	doctor *	door *	down *
duck *	daily **	danger **	dangerous **	dark **	date **

续表

Words begin with /d/ sound in National Curriculum					
daughter **	dead **	deaf **	deal **	dear *	December **
decide **	decision	deep **	degree **	delicious **	depend **
describe **	desk *	develop **	development	dialogue **	diary **
dictionary **	die **	difference **	different **	difficult *	difficulty
dig **	dining **	discover **	direct *	direction *	director *
discovery *	discuss **	discussion	divide **	dish **	dollar **
double **	doubt **	dream **	drive **	drop **	dry **
dumpling **	during **				
/d/ represented by D in initial position					
dad	debt	dig **	disk	door *	dune
damp	deck	deep **	deer	den	dent
desk *	dew	did **	die **	dig **	dill
dim	dime	dine	ding	dip	dirt
dirty *	dish **	disk	dive	do *	dock
doe	dog *	doll *	dollar	dome	done *
door *	dose **	dot	down *	doze	duck *
due	dug	dull	dump	dune	dunk
dusk	dust	dye			
/d/ represented by D in final position					
bad *	bead	bed *	bid	bird *	braid
bread *	bud	cloud **	cod	creed	did **
fad	fed	feed **	food *	freed	glad **
good *	greed	hand *	hid **	hood	kid *
lad	laid *	lead **	led **	lid	load
loud **	mad **	mood	mud	need **	nod *
pad	paid **	plead	plod	pod	pond
raid	read *	red *	rid	road **	rod
sad *	said **	seed	sled	slid	sod
speed *	spud	stead	steed	stood **	toad
wed	weed	wood **	word *		

* 表示 2022 版新课标中二级词汇；** 表示 2022 版新课标中三级词汇。

/f/ as in fan

Words begin with /f/ sound in National Curriculum

face *	family *	fan *	far *	farm *	farmer *
farm *	fast *	father *	favorite *	feel *	film *
find *	fine *	fish *	floor *	flower *	fly *
food *	foot *	feet **	football *	for *	friend *
from **	fruit *	**ph**oto *	fact **	factory **	fail **
fair **	fall **	famous *	fantastic **	fat **	fear **
February **	feed **	feeling **	festival *	fever *	few *
field *	fifteen *	fifth *	fifty *	fight *	fill *
finally *	finger *	finish *	fire *	first *	fisherman *
fit *	five *	fix *	flag *	follow **	foot *
feet *	force **	foreign **	forest **	forget **	fork **
form **	forty **	four *	fourteen **	fourth **	France **
free *	fresh **	Friday **	fridge **	friendly **	from *
front *	fruit *	full ***	fun *	funny **	future **

/f/ represented by F in initial position

fad	fade	fail **	faint	fair **	fake
fall **	false	fame	fan *	far *	farm *
fast *	fate	feast	feather	fed **	feed **
feel *	fell	fence	few **	fib	fig
fight *	file	film *	fine *	fire *	first **
fish *	fist	fit **	five **	foam	foe
foil	fold	folk	fond	fool	foot *
football *	for *	force	fork **	form **	fort
four **	fowl	fox **	fun **	fur	fuse
fuzz					

/f/ represented by F in final position

beef	brief	chef	chief	deaf **	elf
goof	grief	hoof	if **	knife **	leaf **
loaf	off *	proof	reef	roof	scarf
shelf	spoof	wolf			

续表

/f/ represented by-ff in medial/ final position					
cliff	coffee	cuff	huff	puff	fluffy

/f/ represented by PH in initial position					
phone*	phoneme	phonics	photo*	photograph*	phrase
physics**	physical				

/f/ represented by PH in final position					
cough**	enough**	laugh**	rough	tough	photograph*

注：*表示 2022 版新课标中二级词汇；**表示 2022 版新课标中三级词汇。

/g/ as in gate

Words begin with /g/ sound in National Curriculum					
game*	girl*	get*	give*	go*	good*
goodbye*	grandpa*	grandfather*	grandma*	grandmother*	grass*
great*	green*	garden*	gate**	glad**	glass*
glove**	glue**	go*	gold**	government**	grade**
grammar**	granddaughter	grandparent	grandson	grape*	grey**
ground**	group**	grow**	guard**	guess**	guest**
guide**	guitar**	gun**			

/g/ represented by G in initial position					
gain	game*	gap	gasp	gate*	gave**
gear	geese	get*	gift*	gill	girl*
give*	go*	goal**	goat	goes**	gold**
golf	gone**	good*	goof	goose	guitar**
gum	gun**	gush	gust		

/g/ represented by G in the final position					
bag*	big*	bog	bug	chug	clog
dig**	dog*	drag	drug	dug**	fig
flag*	fog**	frog	hog	hug**	jig
jug	keg	lag	leg*	log	lug
meg	mug	nag	peg	pig*	plug
rag	rig	rug	sag	shag	shrug
smug	snag	snug	tag	tug	twig
wag	wig	zag	zig		

注：*表示 2022 版新课标中二级词汇；**表示 2022 版新课标中三级词汇。

/h/ as in hat

Words begin with /h/ sound in National Curriculum					
hair *	half *	hand *	happy *	have *	he *
head *	healthy *	hear *	heavy *	hello *	help *
her *	here *	hi *	high **	him *	his *
holiday *	home *	horse *	hospital *	hot *	hour *
house *	how *	hungry *	habit **	hall **	hamburger **
handbag	handsome **	hang **	happen **	hard *	hardly **
harmful	hat **	hate **	headache	heart **	heat **
helpful *	hen **	hero **	hers **	herself **	hide **
high **	hill *	himself **	history **	hit **	hobby **
hold **	hole **	home **	hometown *	homework **	honest **
hope **	horse **	hospital *	hotel **	however **	huge **
human *	humorous *	hundred *	hungry *	hurry *	hurt *
husband **					
/h/ represented by H in initial position					
hair *	half *	hall **	halt	ham	hammer
hand *	hang **	hard *	hare	has *	hat **
hate **	have *	hay	he *	head *	heal
hear **	heard *	heart *	heat	heel	help *
hen **	her *	here *	high **	hill *	him *
hip	his *	hit *	hive	hoe	hog
hold **	hole **	home *	hood	hoof	hook
hop	hope **	horn	horse *	hose	hot *
house *	how *	hum	hung **	hunt **	hurl
hurt *	husk	hut			

注：＊表示 2022 版新课标中二级词汇；＊＊表示 2022 版新课标中三级词汇。

/j/ as in jump

Words begin with /j/ sound in National Curriculum					
juice **	jump **	jacket *	January **	Japan **	Japanese **
job *	join **	joke **	journey **	July **	June **
just *					

续表

/j/ represented by J in initial position					
jab	jacket **	jade	jail	jam	jar
jaw	jay	jeans	jeep	jerk	jet
jig	job *	jog	join	joke *	jolt
joy **	jug	juice *	July *	jump **	jump rope
June **	junk	jury	just **		
/j/ represented by-DGE in final position					
badge	bridge **	budge	dodge	edge	fidget
fudge	gadget	grudge	ledge	lodge	nudge
ridge	smudge	wedge			
/j/ represented by GE, -GE and G					
garage	gee	gem	general **	generous	genius
geography *	George	geranium	germ	giant	ginger
gingerbread	giraffe *	gym **	gypsy	age *	change **
collage	courage **	damage	danger **	engineer **	forge
fringe	hinge	huge **	large **	magic **	manage **
message **	orange *	package	page **	passage **	pigeon
rage	stage **	singe	strange **	stranger	urgent
village **	wage				

注：＊表示 2022 版新课标中二级词汇；＊＊表示 2022 版新课标中三级词汇。

/k/ as in kite

Words begin with /k/ in National Curriculum					
kid *	kind *	kitchen *	kite *	cake *	call *
can *	candy *	cap *	car *	card *	cat *
class *	clean *	clever *	clock *	close *	clothes *
close *	cloud **	coat *	cold *	color *	come *
computer *	cook *	cool *	cousin *	cow *	crayon
cry *	keep *	key *	keyboard *	kick *	kill *
kilo *	kilometer *	king *	kiss *		
/k/ represented by K in initial position					
kale	keen	keep *	kelp	kettle	kept **

续表

/k/ represented by K in initial position					
key **	kid *	kill **	kilt	kind *	king **
kiss **	kit	kite *	kitten		
/k/ represented by K in medial/final position					
bank **	beak	bike *	bleak	book *	break **
cook *	desk *	fork **	hook	leak	look *
milk *	oak	pink *	peek	seek	shook **
sick **	silk **	sock *	speak *	think *	took **
weak **	week *				
/k/ represented by-CK in medial / final position					
back *	black *	block **	brick	buck	bucket
checkers	chick	chicken *	click **	clock *	crack
deck	dock	duck *	jack	kick **	lack
lick	lock **	locket	luck **	muck	neck **
nickel	pack **	packet **	pick **	pocket **	quack
quick **	rack	racket	rock *	rocket	sack
shack	shock	sick *	slack	slick	snack
sock *	socket	speck	stack	stick **	stock
stockings	stuck **	suck	tack	tick	ticket **
track	trick	truck **	thick **	wick	wreck
/k/ represented by C in initial position					
cap *	cake *	call *	came **	camp **	can *
Canada **	cap **	cape	car *	card *	care **
clock *	candy *	cartoon **	come *	cat *	color *
coal *	coast **	coat *	cook *	cool *	cover **
coin **	copy *	crayon **	corn *	cost *	cot
cough *	could **	count **	corner **	cover **	cow *
cup *	cry *	crazy	cross **	cut *	cute *

注：＊表示 2022 版新课标中二级词汇；＊＊表示 2022 版新课标中三级词汇。

/l/ as in leaf

Words begin with /l/ sound in National Curriculum

lake *	late *	left *	leg *	library *	light *
like *	listen *	little *	live *	long *	look *
love *	luck **	lab *	lady **	land **	language **
large **	last *	later **	laugh **	law **	lay **
lazy **	lead **	leader *	leaf **	learn *	least **
leave **	lemon **	lend	less **	letter *	level **
lie **	life **	lift **	line **	lion *	list **
litter **	lively **	local **	lock **	London **	lonely **
lose **	lot *	loud **	lovely **	low **	luck **
lucky	lab **				

/l/ represented by L in the initial position

lab **	lace	lack	lad	ladder	lag
laid	lake *	lamp	land **	lane	lap
lash	last *	latch	late *	leaf *	leak
lean	leap	least **	leaves **	left **	leg *
lemon *	lend	less *	lest	let *	lick
lie **	life **	lift **	light *	like *	limp
line **	link	lion *	lip	list **	lit **
live *	loaf	loan	local **	log	lose **
long *	look *	loose	lot *	love *	luck **
lug	lump	lunch *	lunchbox		

/l/ sound in the final position

bail	boil **	bowl **	cancel **	coal	coil
cool *	fail **	feel *	foil	girl *	hotel **
heal	heel	jail	mail	meal **	nail
national	oil **	pupil	pencil *	pool **	pretzel
rail *	sail	school **	seal	special *	soil
steal *	steel	tail *	tool **	towel	veal
veil	wheel **				

/l/ represented by-LL in final position

ball *	bill **	call *	dill	doll *	dull

续表

/l/ represented by-LL in final position					
fall **	fill **	ill *	hall **	hill *	kill **
mill	pill **	sell *	small *	still **	tell *
tall *	wall *	well *	will *	yell	

注：* 表示 2022 版新课标中二级词汇；** 表示 2022 版新课标中三级词汇。

/m/ as in mop

Words begin with /m/ sound in National Curriculum					
make *	man *	men **	many *	map *	math *
me *	meet *	milk *	minute *	Miss *	monkey *
month *	moon *	morning *	mother *	mouth *	Mr. *
Mrs. *	much *	music *	my *	machine **	mad **
magazine **	magic **	main **	manage **	manager	March **
mark **	market **	marry **	match **	matter **	may *
maybe **	meal **	mean **	meaning **	meat *	meeting **
member **	mention **	menu **	mess **	message **	method **
meter **	middle *	might **	mile **	milk *	mind **
mine **	miss **	missing *	mistake **	mix **	mobile **
model **	modern **	Monday **	money *	more **	most **
mum **	mountain **	mouse *	mouth *	move *	movie
museum	musician	must *	myself **		
/m/ represented by M in the initial position					
mad **	made **	maid	main **	make *	man *
mane	many *	map *	marble	march *	marry *
mask	mat	match **	may *	meal **	mean **
meat *	men **	mend	menu **	mess **	met **
mice	mild	mile **	milk **	mill	mind **
mine **	mirror *	miss **	mist	missing	mitten
mix **	moan	moat	monkey *	moon *	mop
more **	most **	motorcycle	mouse *	mouth *	move *
much *	music *	mud	mug	my **	must *

续表

/m/ represented by M in final position					
beam	bottom **	broom	clam **	dream **	drum
film **	farm *	firm	form **	from **	gram
gum	ham	him *	hum	jam	mum *
mom **	plum	ram	roam	room *	Sam
gem	scream	gloom	seam	seem	slam
storm **	swim *	steam	sum	team **	them *
term **	whom **	worm	warm *	yam	yum
zoom					

注：* 表示 2022 版新课标中二级词汇；** 表示 2022 版新课标中三级词汇。

/n/ as in nest

Words begin with /n/ sound in National Curriculum					
name *	near *	new *	next *	nice *	night *
no *	noodle *	nose *	not *	now *	nurse *
national	natural	nature **	nearly **	necessary **	neck **
need **	neither **	nervous **	never *	news **	newspaper **
nine **	nineteen **	ninety **	ninth **	nobody *	nod
noise **	noisy *	none **	noon **	nor **	north **
northern	nose *	not *	notebook **	nothing **	notice **
November **	number **				
/n/ represented by N in initial position					
name *	neck **	next *	nine **	not *	nature **
need **	nice *	no *	note **	nail	noodle *
nest	net	new *	newspaper **	next *	nice *
nine **	night *	nib	nip	ninth **	ninety **
no *	nod **	noise **	noon **	north **	nose *
not *	note **	now *	number **	nurse *	nut
/n/ represented by N in final position					
an *	balloon **	born **	bean **	been **	bin **
brain **	burn **	button	can *	cartoon **	clean *
cousin *	coin	corn **	den	down *	drain

续表

/n/ represented by N in final position					
fan *	fin	flown	fun **	gain	garden *
green *	grin	hen **	horn	in *	Jean
join **	lesson *	lemon **	lion *	learn *	man **
mean **	men *	noon **	moon *	pain **	pan
pen *	pain **	plan **	queen **	rain *	ran **

注：＊表示 2022 版新课标中二级词汇；＊＊表示 2022 版新课标中三级词汇。

/p/ as in pig

Words begin with /p/ sound in National Curriculum					
panda *	parent *	park *	party *	pen *	pencil *
people *	photo *	picture *	pig *	place *	plane *
planet **	plant *	play *	playground *	please *	police *
potato *	pupil	put *	pacific	page **	pain *
paint **	pair *	palace **	pale **	pancake **	panda *
paper *	pardon **	part **	pass **	passage **	passenger **
passport **	past **	patient **	pay **	peace **	pear **
perfect **	perhaps **	period **	person **	personal **	pet *
phone *	photograph *	physics **	pick **	picnic **	pie **
piece **	pilot **	pink *	pioneer **	pity **	plan **
plane **	planet **	player	playground *	pleasure **	plenty **
pocket **	poem **	point **	policeman **	policewoman **	polite **
pollute **	pollution	possible **	post **	postcard **	postman **
pound **	practise **	praise **	prepare **	present **	president **
pretty **	price **	pride **	primary *	print **	private **
prize **	probably **	problem **	produce **	product **	program **
progress **	project **	promise **	pronounce **	pronunciation	proper **
protect **	proud **	provide **	publish **	purple **	purpose **
push **	playground				
/p/ in initial position					
pack **	pad	page **	pail	pain **	paint **
pal	pale **	pan	pant	pass **	past **

续表

/p/ in initial position					
patch	paw	pay **	pea	peace **	peak
pear **	pedal	peel	peg	pen *	pencil *
penny	pet *	pickle	pie *	pig *	pike
pill	pillow	pin	pine	pint	pipe
pit	pod	point **	poke	pole	pond
pop	pork	port	post **	potato *	pour **
puddle	puff	pull **	pumpkin	punish **	puppet
purse	push **	put *	pull **	puzzle	
/p/ represented by P in final position					
cap *	camp **	cheap **	chop	clip	crop
cup *	deep **	dip	develop **	drop **	flap
flip	flop	help *	hip	hop	jump *
keep *	lamp **	lap	leap	lip	map *
mop	nap	peep	pep	pop	pup
rap	rip	sap	sheep *	sip	skip
sleep *	slip	soup *	soap	stamp **	step **
stop *	sweep *	tap *	tip	top *	trap
trip **	up *	weep	whip	wrap	whip
zip					

注：＊表示 2022 版新课标中二级词汇；＊＊表示 2022 版新课标中三级词汇。

/r/ as in rap

Words begin with /r/ sound in National Curriculum					
rain *	read *	red *	rice *	right *	river *
room *	ruler *	run *	rabbit *	race **	radio **
railway **	rainy	raise **	rapid **	reach **	ready **
real *	realize **	really **	reason **	receive **	recently
record **	refuse **	regret **	relationship **	relative **	relax **
remain **	remember **	repair **	research **	rest **	restaurant **
result **	return **	review **	rich **	ride **	ring **
rise **	risk **	river **	road **	robot *	rock **

续表

Words begin with /r/ sound in National Curriculum					
role **	rope **	rose **	round **	row **	rubbish **
rule **	rush **	Russia **	Russian **		
/r/ represented by R in the initial position					
rabbit *	ramp	rack	radio **	rag	rail
rain *	raise **	rake	ram	ramp	ranch
range	rank	rap	rat	rate	rattle
rave	raw	ray	real *	red *	rent
rib	rich **	ride **	rig	right *	rim
ring **	rink	rip	ripe	rise	road **
roast	rob	robe	rock **	rocket **	rod
roll	roof	room *	root	rope **	rose **
rot	round **	row **	rub	rude	rug
run *	rush **				
/r/ in final position					
bear *	car *	chair *	dear *	door *	finger **
four **	guitar **	hammer	her *	jar	later **
letter *	pear **	spider	zipper		
/r/ represented by WR					
wrap	wreck	wriggle	wrinkle	wrist	write *
wrote **	wreath	wrench	wrong *	writer	

注：＊表示 2022 版新课标中二级词汇；＊＊表示 2022 版新课标中三级词汇。

/s/ as in sun

Words begin with /s/ sound in National Curriculum					
sad *	say *	school *	schoolbag *	science *	season *
see *	sing *	sister *	sit *	skirt *	slow *
small *	snow *	sock *	some *	sometimes *	song *
sorry *	soup *	speak *	sport *	spring *	stand *
star *	stop *	story *	street *	strong *	study *
subject *	summer *	sun *	sunny *	supermarket *	sweater *
swim **	sing *	slow *	small *	song *	sorry *

续表

Words begin with /s/ sound in National Curriculum					
soup *	speak	sport *	spring *	stand *	star *
stop *	story *	storm **	street *	strong *	study *
safe *	salad **	sale **	salt **	same **	sand **
sandwich *	satisfy *	Saturday **	save **	say *	scarf **
scientist **	scissors **	score **	screen **	sea *	search **
season *	seat **	second **	secret **	secretary	seldom **
sell *	send **	sense **	sentence **	safety **	separate **
September **	serious **	serve **	service **	set **	seven **
seventeen *	seventh **	seventy **	several **	sick **	side **
sign **	silence	silent **	silk **	silly **	silver **
similar **	simple **	since *	sing *	single **	sir **
situation **	six **	sixteen **	sixth **	size **	skate **
skill **	skirt **	sky **	sleep *	sleepy	slow *
small *	smart **	smell **	smile **	smoke **	smooth **
snake **	so *	social **	sock *	sofa **	soft **
solve **	sometimes *	somewhere **	son **	song *	soon **
sorry *	sound **	soup *	south **	southern	space *
spare **	speak *	speaker *	special **	speech **	speed **
spell **	spend **	spirit **	spoon **	sport **	spread **
spring *	square **	stamp **	stand *	standard **	star **
start **	state **	station *	stay **	steal **	step **
stick **	still **	stomach **	stomachache	stone **	stop *
store **	straight **	strange **	strawberry **	student *	strict **
stupid	succeed **	success **	successful	such **	sudden **
suggest **	suggestion	support *	suppose *	surface *	sweet **
Sunday **	survey **				

/s/ represented by S in the initial position					
safe *	sad *	sage	said **	sail	sake
sale **	salt **	same **	sand **	sandwich **	sang **
sap	sat **	safety **	save **	saw **	sax
say *	sea *	seal	see *	seed	seek

续表

/s/ represented by S in the initial position					
seem *	seen **	sew	sick **	side **	sieve
sigh	sight	sign **	silk ***	sill	since **
sing *	sink	sip	sir **	sit *	six **
size **	so *	soak	soap	soar	sock *
sod	soft **	soil **	some *	son **	song *
soon **	soot	sore **	sort	soul	sound **
soup *	sour	south **	sow	sub	such *
sue	suit	sum	sun *	surf	
/s/ represented by S in the final position					
bus *	circus	gas **	octopus	this *	plus
us *	yes *				
/s/ represented by-SS in the final position					
boss **	class **	kiss **	less **	loss **	mess **
moss	pass **	toss			
other spellings					
/s/ represented by C in initial position by					
ceiling	celery	cell	cellar	cement	cent **
center **	cereal	cigar	cinch	cinder	circle **
circus	citizen **	city *	cycle	cylinder	celebrate **
central **	century **	certain **	certainly		
/s/ represented by-CE in final position					
ace	advice **	Alice	bounce	brace	Bruce
chance **	choice **	dance *	France **	face *	fence
force **	glance	grace	ice *	lace	mice
nice *	notice **	office **	ounce	pace	peace **
palace **	place *	piece **	practice **	race **	rice *
since **	slice	space *	spruce	twice **	voice **

注：* 表示 2022 版新课标中二级词汇；** 表示 2022 版新课标中三级词汇。

/t/ as in top

Words begin with /t/ sound in National Curriculum					
table **	take **	talk **	tall **	taxi **	tea **
teacher **	tell **	tiger **	time **	tired **	to **
today **	toilet **	tomato **	tomorrow **	too **	toy **
turn **	TV **	tennis *	tenth *	term *	terrible *
test *	text *	ticket *	tidy *	tie *	tiger *
time *	tiny *	to *	today *	together *	toilet *
tomato *	tomorrow *	ton *	tonight *	too *	tool *
tooth *	toothache *	top *	total *	touch *	tour *
tourist *	towards *	tower *	town *	toy *	twelfth *
twelve *	twentieth *	twice *	two *		

/t/ represented by T in the initial position					
table **	tail **	tape *	task *	tail *	take **
talk **	tall **	tame	taxi *	tea *	teen
telephone **	tell **	ten **	team *	tick	tide
tie *	ticket *	time **	tin	tip	tie *
to **	toad	toe	told *	tomato **	ton
tone	tool	toothbrush	top *	torn *	toss
tote	touch *	tough	tour *	tow	towel
town *	toy *	tub	tube	tuck	tug
tune	turn **	turtle			

/t/ represented by T in the final position					
bat	beat *	beast *	bit *	boat *	but **
cat **	carrot *	cheat	cent *	coast *	coat *
cost *	cut *	dot	eat *	fat *	feet *
fit *	fast *	first *	foot *	get **	goat
got *	great *	hat **	heat *	hit *	hot **
hurt *	jacket *	jet	let **	lot *	mat
meat *	meet *	met *	most *	neat	next *
net	not **	nut	paint *	pat	pet *
past *	pilot *	point *	pot	put *	quit
rat	rabbit *	rest *	right *	sat *	seat *

续表

/t/ represented by T in the final position					
set *	shut *	sit **	shout *	spot	sweet
test *	treat *	wait *	want *	wallet *	west *
wet *	what **	wheat	yet *	unit *	visit *

注：＊表示 2022 版新课标中二级词汇；＊＊表示 2022 版新课标中三级词汇。

/v/ as in vase

Words begin with /v/ sound in National Curriculum					
vegetable *	very *	visit *	vacation **	valuable *	value **
victory **	video **	village **	violin **	visit *	visitor
voice **	volleyball **				
/v/ represented by V in the initial position					
valentine	van	vase	violin **	vain	van
veal	vein	vet	vent	verse	very *
vest	view	vine	visit *	voice **	vote
/v/ represented by-VE in final position-					
active **	arrive **	brave **	cave	cove	dive
dove	drive *	drove **	five **	gave **	give *
glove	grave	grove	have *	hive	leave
live *	love *	move *	nerve	pave	prove
rave	save **	serve **	shave	sleeve	stove
wave **	weave	wove			

注：＊表示 2022 版新课标中二级词汇；＊＊表示 2022 版新课标中三级词汇。

/w/ as in wagon

Words begin with /w/ sound in National Curriculum					
wait *	walk *	want *	warm *	wash *	watch *
water *	way *	we *	wear *	weather *	week *
welcome *	well *	white *	window *	windy *	winter *
with *	woman *	women *	wonderful *	word *	worker *
worry *	write *	wrong *	wake *	wall *	wallet **
war **	warn **	waste **	weak **	wealth **	website **

续表

Words begin with /w/ sound in National Curriculum					
wednesday **	weekday **	weekend **	weigh **	weight **	welcome *
west **	western	wet **	wheel **	whether **	while **
white *	wide **	wife **	wild **	will *	win *
wind **	wing **	winner **	wise **	within **	wolf **
wish *	without **	wonder **	wood **	world *	worse **
worst **	worth **	would **	wound **	writer	
/w/ represented by W in the initial position					
wad	wade	wag	wage	wagon	waist
wait *	wake *	walk *	wall *	wand	want *
war *	ware	warm *	warn *	wash *	wasp
waste **	watch *	water *	wave **	wax	way *
we *	weak **	wealth **	wear *	weave	wet **
weak **	week **	weep	weigh **	weird	weed
well *	went **	west **	wet **	wick	wide **
wife **	wig	wild **	will *	wilt	win *
wind **	window *	wing **	wink	wipe	wire
wise **	wish *	wit	with *	woke **	wolf **
won **	wood **	wool	word *	work *	world *
worm	worry **	worst *	would **		

注：* 表示 2022 版新课标中二级词汇；** 表示 2022 版新课标中三级词汇。

/y/ as in yo-yo

Words begin with /y/ sound in National Curriculum					
year *	yellow *	yes *	yesterday *	you *	young *
your **	yard *	yet **	yours *	yourself **	
/y/ represented by Y in the initial position					
yacht	yak	yam	yank	yard	yarn
yawn	year *	yeast	yellow *	yes *	yield
yoke	you *	young	your **	yowl	yo-yo
yuck					

注：* 表示 2022 版新课标中二级词汇；** 表示 2022 版新课标中三级词汇。

/z/ as in zoo

Words begin with /z/ sound in National Curriculum					
zoo *	zero **				
/z/ represented by Z in the initial position					
zag	zap	zeal	zebra	zero **	zest
zinc	zing	zip	zipper	zone	zonk
zoo *	zoom				
/z/ represented by-ZZ in the mid and final position					
blizzard	buzzard	buzz	fizz	fuzz	
/z/ represented by-ZE in the mid and final position					
dozen	frozen	breeze	daze	doze	freeze
sneeze	wheeze	prize **	quiz	size **	sneeze
snooze	squeeze	whiz			
other spellings for /z/					
amuse	as **	because *	birds *	boys *	cars *
cheese **	chose **	close *	daisy	dogs **	easy *
excuse **	fuse	girls **	has *	hose	is **
noise *	nose **	pause	please **	raise *	rose *
shoes *	suppose **	tease	these *	those *	was **
wise **					

注：* 表示 2022 版新课标中二级词汇；** 表示 2022 版新课标中三级词汇。

/ch/ as in cheese

Words begin with /ch/ sound in National Curriculum					
chair *	chicken *	child *	China *	children *	Chinese *
chalk **	change **	cheap **	check **	cheer **	chess **
chocolate **	choice **	choose **	chopsticks **		
/ch/ represented by CH in the initial position					
chain	chair *	chalk **	change **	chap	chapter
charge	charm	chart	chase	chat	cheap **
cheat	check *	checker	checkup	cheer *	cheerful
cheese **	cheeseburger	cherry	chess **	chest	chestnut
chew	chick	chicken *	child *	children *	chilly

续表

/ch/ represented by CH in the initial position					
chime	chimney	chin	chip	chipmunk	chirp
chocolate *	choose **	chop	chose **	chow	chuckle
chum	chunk	churn			
/ch/ represented by CH in final position					
beach *	bench	branch	bunch	church	clinch
couch	crunch	each **	hunch	inch	lunch *
much *	munch	peach	perch	pinch	punch
quench	ranch	reach **	rich **	sandwich **	search **
such *	teach	touch *	trench		
/ch/ represented by-TCH in final position					
batch	catch *	clutch	crutch	ditch	fetch
hitch	hutch	itch	latch	match **	notch
patch	pitch	scratch	sketch	snatch	stitch
stretch	switch	watch *	witch		

注：＊表示 2022 版新课标中二级词汇；＊＊表示 2022 版新课标中三级词汇。

/sh/ as in shark

Words begin with /sh/ sound in National Curriculum					
she *	sheep *	ship **	shirt *	shoe **	shop *
short *	shorts **	shut **	shy **	shake **	shall **
shame **	shape **	shine **	should *	shoulder **	shout **
show *	shower **				
/sh/ sound in the initial position					
shack	shade	shadow	shake	shall **	shallow
shame **	shampoo	shape **	share *	shark **	shave
shake **	she *	shear	sheep *	sheet	shelf **
shell	shield	shift	shin	shine **	ship *
shirt *	shock **	shoe *	shoelace	shoot	shop *
shore	short *	shorts *	shot	should *	shoulder **
shout **	shove	shovel	show *	shower **	shuck
shut **	shy **				

续表

/sh/ represented by SH in the final position					
ash	blush	brush **	bush	cash **	clash
crash	crush	dash	dish	fish *	flash
fresh **	gash	gush	lash	leash	mash
mesh	mush	push **	rash	rush **	smash
splash	trash	wash *	wish *		
/sh/ represented by-TI in final position					
action **	addition	attention **	fraction	nation **	station **
vacation **	patient **				
/sh/ represented by-CI in final position					
social **	delicious **	musician	precious	suspicion	vicious

注：* 表示 2022 版新课标中二级词汇；** 表示 2022 版新课标中三级词汇。

/zh/ as in treasure

/zh/ sound in the medial position					
Asia	decision	casual	exposure	measure	occasion
pleasure **	television *	treasure	usual **	vision	

注：* 表示 2022 版新课标中二级词汇；** 表示 2022 版新课标中三级词汇。

Voiced /th/ as in th

Words begin with voiced /th/ sound in National Curriculum					
those *	that **	the **	their **	them **	then **
there **	these **	they **	this **	than *	though *
voiced /th/ sound in the initial position					
than *	the **	them **	there **	they **	those **
thus	that **	their **	then **	these **	this **
though *					
voiced /th/ sound in the final/middle position					
bathe	gather	smooth *	together *	whether *	weather *

注：* 表示 2022 版新课标中二级词汇；** 表示 2022 版新课标中三级词汇。

Voiceless /th/ as in thumb

Words begin with voiceless /th/ sound in National Curriculum					
thin *	think *	thank *	theatre **	thick **	thing **
thirsty **	thirteen **	third **	thought **	thousand **	three **
through **	throw **	Thursday **			
voiceless /th/ sound in the initial position					
thank *	Thanksgiving	theatre **	theme	thermometer	thick **
thermos	thief	thimble	thin *	thing **	think *
third **	thirsty **	thirteen **	thirty **	thread	through **
thorn	thought **	thousand **	three **	thump	thunder **
throw **	thumb	thief			
voiceless /th/ sound in the final position					
bath **	birth **	booth	both **	broth	cloth
death **	fifth **	fourth **	growth	length	math *
month *	moth	mouth *	north *	oath	path
sixth **	south **	teeth **	worth **	tooth *	

注：* 表示 2022 版新课标中二级词汇；** 表示 2022 版新课标中三级词汇。

/hw/ as in wheel

Words begin with /wh/ sound in National Curriculum					
what *	when *	where *	why *	whose *	who *
/hw/ sound in the initial position					
whale	what *	whatever **	wheat	whom **	why *
wheel **	wheelbarrow	wheelchair	when *	whenever **	where *
wherever **	which *	whisker	whisper	whistle	while *

注：* 表示 2022 版新课标中二级词汇；** 表示 2022 版新课标中三级词汇。

/ng/ as in ring

Words with /ng/ sound in National Curriculum					
angry *	bring *	evening *	interesting *	morning *	spring *
strong *	thank **	think *	wrong *		
/ng/ sound in the medial/ final position					
angry *	hang **	finger **	hung **	hunger	king **

续表

/ng/ sound in the medial/ final position					
long *	longer **	rang **	ring **	rung **	sang **
sing *	song *	thing **	wing **	strong *	strength
young *	bank **	drink *	drunk **	honk	ink
thank *	pink *	link	sank	sunk	junk
tank	wink	rank			

注：* 表示 2022 版新课标中二级词汇；** 表示 2022 版新课标中三级词汇。

第二部分　元音音素词汇表

（1）为了方便教学，2022 版本新课标所要求的单词已经按照字母顺序列出来。

（2）同时，单词列表也包括 Blevins（2017）和 Hepplewhite（2020）所列出来的词汇。

单词表的使用建议如下：

1）可供学习者进行拼读练习。

2）可供学习者造句和教师用来编撰可解码文本。

3）可用于词汇游戏。

4）可用于拼读练习和听写。

Long-A sound /ai/ as in cake

base	blade	brace	brake	brave **	cage
cake *	came **	case **	cave	chase	date **
face *	fade	flake	flame	game *	gate **
gave **	grace	grade **	grape *	lake *	late *
made **	make *	maze	male	name *	page **
place *	plate **	race **	rake	sale **	same **
save **	shame **	shake **	shape **	skate **	space *
state **	take *	tale	tape **	trace	trade **
vase (*AmE*)	wade	wake *	wave **	whale **	aid
aim	bait	braid	braille	brain **	chain
claim	drain	fail **	faint	faith	frail

续表

grain	jail	laid **	maid	mail	main **
nail	paid **	paint **	pain **	praise **	raid
rain *	rainy	raise **	sail	Spain **	stain
strain	tail *	trail	train *	vain	waist
wait *	bay	birthday *	clay	day *	gay
gray	hay	jay	lay **	may *	maybe **
pay **	play *	player	pray	ray	say *
spray	stay **	sway	today *	tray	way *

注：* 表示 2022 版新课标中二级词汇；** 表示 2022 版新课标中三级词汇。

Long-E sound /ee/ as in feet

be *	me *	we *	bee	beech	beef **
beep	beet	cheer **	cheep	cheese **	creep
deed	deep **	deer	fee	feed **	feel **
feet *	flee	free *	greed	green *	greet **
heed	jeep	keep *	knee **	meet *	need **
peek	peel	peep	queen **	reef	screech
screen **	see *	seed	seek	seem **	seen **
seep	sheep *	sheet	sleep *	sleet	speech **
speed **	steel	steep	street *	sweep *	sweet **
teen	teeth **	three **	tree *	weed	week *
weep	wheel **	beach *	bead	beak	beam
bean **	beat **	bleach	bleak	cheap **	cheat **
clean *	cream	deal **	dear *	dream **	each **
east **	eat **	feast	flea	gleam	heal
heap	heat **	jeans **	lead **	leaf **	leak
lean	leap	leash	least **	meal **	mean **
meat *	near *	pea	peach	peak	peace **
plead	reach **	read *	real **	scream	sea *
season *	seam	seat *	sneak	speak **	steal
steam	stream	tea *	teach **	team **	treat **
weak **	wheat	yeast	zeal	any *	baby *

续表

beauty	bunny	candy *	carry **	chilly	city *
county	daddy	daisy	dirty *	dizzy	dusty
duty	easy *	eighty *	family *	forty *	fifty *
funny **	fuzzy	gravy	happy **	jelly	kitty
lady **	lately	lobby	lucky	many *	mommy
muddy	navy	ninety *	only **	party *	penny
plenty **	pony	pretty **	puppy	quickly	sandy
seventy *	shiny	silly	sixty *	sleepy	slowly
smoothly	sticky	story *	strawberry *	sunny *	thirty **
thirsty **	tidy *	tricky	ugly **	windy *	belief
believe **	chief	brief	field **	fierce	grief
niece	thief	pierce	relief	shield	yield

注：＊表示 2022 版新课标中二级词汇；＊＊表示 2022 版新课标中三级词汇。

Long-I sound /igh/ as in bike

bike *	bite	bride	chime	chive	dime
dine	dive	drive	fine **	fire *	five **
grime	hike	hive	ice *	kite *	life **
like *	lime	line **	live *	mice	mile **
mine **	nice *	nine **	pike	pine	pipe
price **	rice *	ride **	ripe	rise **	shine **
side	spice	spike	splice	stride	strive
tide	time *	tire	twice	twine	whine
white *	wide **	wife	wise *	by *	cry *
dry **	fly *	fry	my *	pry	shy **
sky **	sly	spy	try *	why *	bind
blind **	child *	climb **	find *	grind	hind
kind *	mild	mind **	rind	wild *	wind **
die **	lie **	pie **	tie **	tight	thigh
bright **	fight *	flight	fright	high **	knight
light *	might **	night *	right *	sign **	sight

注：＊表示 2022 版新课标中二级词汇；＊＊表示 2022 版新课标中三级词汇。

Long-O sound /oa/ as in boat

bold	bolt	cold *	fold	go *	gold **
hold **	jolt	mold	no *	old *	poll
pro	roll	scold	scroll	so *	sold **
stroll	told **	toll	troll	volt	alone **
broke **	choke	chose **	close *	clothes *	code
dome	doze	drove **	froze **	globe	hole
home *	hope *	hose	joke **	nose *	note **
phone *	poke	pole	pose	robe	rode **
rope **	rose **	slope	smoke *	spoke **	stone **
stove	stroke	those *	tone	vote **	wrote **
yoke	zone	boat *	cloak	coal	coast **
coat *	croak	float	foam	goal **	goat
groan	Joan	load	moan	moat	oak
oat	road **	roam	roast	soak	soap
throat **	toad	toast	below **	blow **	bow
bowl **	crow	flow	flown **	glow	grow **
grown **	know *	known **	low **	mow	pillow
row **	shadow	show *	shown **	slow *	tow
snow *	sparrow	swallow	throw **	thrown **	willow
window *	yellow *	doe	foe	toe	

注：* 表示 2022 版新课标中二级词汇；** 表示 2022 版新课标中三级词汇。

Long-U sound /yoo/ as in cube

cube	cute *	fume	fuse	huge **	mule
muse	mute	puke	use *	bugle	community
future **	human **	humid	humor **	January **	menu
museum *	music *	pupil	regular	uniform **	union
unit **	united	university **	usually	usual ** ya	few *
view	review	argue	continue *	cue	fuel
rescue	value	beautiful *	beauty		

注：* 表示 2022 版新课标中二级词汇；** 表示 2022 版新课标中三级词汇。

Short-A /a/ as in cat

act **	add *	am **	as **	at *	back *
bad *	bag *	ban	bank **	basket **	bat **
batch	bath **	black *	blast	bamboo **	branch
brand	brass	cab	camp *	can *	cap *
cast	cat *	catch *	champ	clan	clap
clash	class * (*AmE*)	crack	craft	cramp	crash
dad	damp	dash	drag	fact **	fad
fan *	fast * (*AmE*)	fat **	flag **	flap	flash
flat **	gap	gas **	gasp	glad **	glass * (*AmE*)
grab	grand	grant	graph (*AmE*)	grass * (*AmE*)	had **
ham	hand *	has **	hat **	hatch	jack
jam	jazz	lack	lad	lag	lamp **
land **	lap	lash	last * (*AmE*)	latch	mad **
man *	map *	mash	mask (*AmE*)	mass	mast (*AmE*)
mat	match *	math **	nag	nap	pack **
pad	pal	pam	pant	pants	pass **
past **	pat	patch	path	plan **	plant *
quack	rack	rag	ram	ramp	ran **
rant	rap	rash	rat	sack	sad *
sag	sand **	sap	sat **	scratch	slab
slack	slam	slant	snap	span	splash
snack	stamp **	stand *	strand	tab	tack
tag	tan	tap	task * (*AmE*)	than **	that *
track	trap	van	vat	wag	yam

注：* 表示 2022 版新课标中二级词汇；** 表示 2022 版新课标中三级词汇。

Short-E sound /e/ as in bed

bed *	beg	bell **	belt **	bench	bend
bent	best **	bet	bled	blend	bless
cell	cent	check **	chess *	chest	crest
deck	den	desk *	dress *	egg *	elf
elm	end **	fed	fell *	fled	fresh **

续表

gem	get *	help *	hem	hen **	jet
kept **	led **	left *	leg *	lend **	less **
letter *	lemon *	let *	men *	mend	mesh
mess **	met **	neck **	nest	net	peck
peg	pen *	pest	pet *	press	red *
rest **	sell *	send *	sent **	set **	seven **
shelf **	shell	sled	slept **	smell **	spell **
spend **	spent **	west **	bless	end **	less **
press **	stem	wet **	when *	wreck	yell
yes *	yet **				
other spellings					
ahead	bread *	breakfast *	dead **	feather	head *
health **	heaven	heavy *	instead **	lead *	leather
meant **	read *	ready **	spread **	sweater *	thread
wealth **	wealthy	weather *	dense	fence	hedge
ledge	pledge	sense **	tense	wedge	

注：* 表示 2022 版新课标中二级词汇；** 表示 2022 版新课标中三级词汇。

Short-I /i/ as in fish

bib	bid	big *	bill	bit	blimp
blink	brick	chick	chill	chin	click
clip	crib	crisp	did **	dig *	dill
dim	dip	dish **	disk	drink *	drip
fib	fig	fill **	fin	fish *	fist
fit *	fix **	flick	flip	gift *	gig
gill	glint	hid	hill *	him *	hip
his *	hiss	hit **	in *	ink	inn
is **	it *	kick **	kin	kiss **	lick
lid	lift *	link	lip	list *	milk *
mill	miss **	mitt	mix **	nip	pick **
pig *	pill **	pin	pink *	pit	rib
rich **	rid	rig	rim	rip	shift

续表

ship *	sill	sink	sip	sit *	six **
skin	skip	skill **	slick	slid	slim **
slip	splint	sprint	stick	stink	swim *
thin *	think *	this *	tick	trim	trip **
twig	which **	whip	wick	wig	will **
win *	wink	wish *	wit	zip	

注：＊表示 2022 版新课标中二级词汇；＊＊表示 2022 版新课标中三级词汇。

Short-O sound /o/ as in lock

blob	block **	blot	bop	box *	chop
clock *	cob	cod	cot	crop	dock
doll *	dot	drop **	flock	flop	fog
fox **	frog	gob	got **	hog	hop
hot *	job *	jog **	knob	knock **	knot
lock **	log	lot *	mom *	mop	nod **
not *	on *	ox	plod	plop	plot
pod	pond	pop	pot	prop	rob
rock **	rod	rot	shock **	shot	shop *
slop	slot	sob	sock *	sod	spot
stop *	tock	top *	trot		

注：＊表示 2022 版新课标中二级词汇；＊＊表示 2022 版新课标中三级词汇。

Short-U sound /u/ as in duck

bluff	blunt	blush	brush	buck	bud
buff	bug	bum	bump	bunch	bunt
bus *	but *	buzz	chunk	club **	clump
clunk	clutch	crust	cub	cuff	cup *
cut *	drug	drum	duck *	dug **	dull
dump	dunk	dusk	dust	fluff	fun *
fuss	fuzz	glum	grub	gruff	gum
gust	hug	hum	hunt	hush	husk
hut	jug	jump *	just **	luck *	lunch *

续表

lump	much *	muck	mud	mug	mush
musk	must *	mutt	nut	pluck	plug
plum	plus	puff	pump	punt	pup
putt	rub	ruff	rug	run *	runt
rush **	rust	rut	shun	shrub	shut **
skunk	slug	slump	snub	snug	struck
strum	stub	stuck	stump	sub	such **
suds	sum	sun *	truck **	trust **	tub
tuck	tug	tusk	up *	us *	

注：* 表示 2022 版新课标中二级词汇；** 表示 2022 版新课标中三级词汇。

Diphthong /oi/ sound

/oi/ represented by OI					
avoid **	boil **	choice **	coil	coin **	foil
hoist	join **	joint	moist	moisture	noise **
oil **	point **	poison	rejoice	soil **	spoil
toil	voice **				
/oi/ represented by OY					
annoy	boy *	cowboy	coy	decoy	destroy
employ	enjoy **	joy **	joyful	loyal	ploy
royal	soy	toy *	voyage		

注：* 表示 2022 版新课标中二级词汇；** 表示 2022 版新课标中三级词汇。

Diphthong /ou/ sound

/ou/ represented by OU					
about *	bounce	bound	cloud **	couch	count **
crouch	doubt **	flour	foul	found **	grouch
ground *	hound	house **	loud *	mound	mouth *
noun	ouch	out *	pouch	pound	pout
proud *	round	scout	shout *	snout	sour
south *	spout	sprout	trout		

续表

/ou/ represented by OW					
allow **	bow	brown *	brow	chow	cow *
crowd	crown	down *	drown	fowl	frown
gown	growl	how *	howl	now *	owl
plow	powder	power	prowl	sow	towel
town **	vow	wow			

注：* 表示 2022 版新课标中二级词汇；** 表示 2022 版新课标中三级词汇。

Variant vowel sound long /oo/

long /oo/ sound represented by-OO					
balloon **	bloom	boo	boom	broom	coo
cool *	coop	doom	food *	fool	gloom
goose	groom	hoof	hoop	hoot	igloo
kangaroo	loom	loop	loose	loot	moo
mood	moon *	moose	noon **	ooze	pool **
proof	roof	room *	root	school *	scoop
scoot	scooter	shampoo	shoo	shoot	sloop
smooth **	snoop	soon **	spook	spooky	spool
spoon **	stool	too *	tool **	toot	tooth **
troop	zoo *	zoom			
long /oo/ sound represented by-UE					
blue *	clue	due	glue **	sue	true **
long /oo/ sound represented by-EW					
blew **	brew	chew	crew	dew	drew **
flew **	grew **	knew **	new *	news **	screw
shrew	stew	threw **			
long /oo/sound in U-E pattern					
crude	June **	prune	rude	reduce **	
long /oo/ sound represented by-U					
junior **	solution	July **			
in this category, when long-U sound loses its /y/ part in /yoo/, the letter U sounds like long /oo/.					

注：* 表示 2022 版新课标中二级词汇；** 表示 2022 版新课标中三级词汇。

Short-OO sound /oo/ as in book

short /oo/ sound represented by-OO					
afoot	book *	brook	cook *	cookie **	crook
foot *	football *	good *	goodbye *	hood	hoof
hook	look *	nook	notebook	rook	rookie
shook **	soot	stood **	took **	wood **	wooden
woof	wool				

注：＊表示 2022 版新课标中二级词汇；＊＊表示 2022 版新课标中三级词汇。

Variant vowel sounds: Broad-O sound /or/

broad-O sound /or/ represented by AU					
audience	August **	author	autumn *	because *	caught **
cause **	clause	daughter **	dinosaur	fault	fraud
haul	haunt	launch	laundry	Paul	pause
sauce	sausage	taught **	vault		
broad-O sound /or/ represented by AW					
awful **	bawl	brawl	bawl	caw	crawl
dawn	draw *	drawn	fawn	flaw	gnaw
hawk	jaw	law **	lawn	lawyer **	paw
pawn	raw	saw **	shawl	slaw	sprawl
straw	strawberry **	thaw	yawn		
broad-O sound /or/ represented by AL (L)					
chalk **	stalk	talk *	walk *	call *	ball *
fall **	hall	mall **	small *	stall	tall *
wall *	halt	malt	salt *		
words in this category are also defined as L-influenced or L-controlled spellings by Bear et al. (2015)					

注：＊表示 2022 版新课标中二级词汇；＊＊表示 2022 版新课标中三级词汇。

R-controlled vowel sound /air/

/air/ represented by AIR					
air *	chair *	fair **	flair	hair *	pair *
stair					

续表

/air/ represented by-ARE					
bare	blare	care **	dare	fare	flare
glare	hare	mare	pare	rare	scare
share *	spare **	square **	stare		
/air/ represented by-EAR					
bear *	pear **	tear	swear	wear *	

注：* 表示 2022 版新课标中二级词汇；** 表示 2022 版新课标中三级词汇。

R-controlled vowel sound /ar/

/ar/ represented by AR					
arch	Arctic	ark	arm *	art *	artist **
article **	bar	bark	barn	car *	card *
cart	charge	charm	chart	guard **	harm **
dark *	dart	far *	farm *	garden *	hard *
harp	jar	lard	large **	march	mart
park *	part **	scar	scarf **	shark **	sharp
smart *	spark	star *	start	starch	tar
tart	yard **	yarn			

注：* 表示 2022 版新课标中二级词汇；** 表示 2022 版新课标中三级词汇。

R-controlled vowel sound /ur/ as in bird, fern and burn

/ur/ represented by UR					
blur	burn *	burst	church	churn	curb
curl	curse	curve	fur	hurt *	nurse *
purple **	purr	purse	spur	surf	Thursday **
turkey	turn *	turtle	urge		
/ur/ represented by-IR					
thirst	twirl	squirm	whirl	bird *	birth **
birthday *	chirp	circle	circus	dirt	dirty *
fir	firm	first **	girl *	quirk	shirt *
sir *	skirt *	squirt	stir	swirl	third *

续表

/ur/ represented by-ER					
other **	over *	perch	perk	after *	better **
certain **	clerk	ever	fern	germ	her *
herd	jerk	letter *	merge	mother *	nerve
person **	river *	serve **	sister *	stern	swerve
term **	under *	verb	verge	verse	water *
winter *					

注：* 表示 2022 版新课标中二级词汇；** 表示 2022 版新课标中三级词汇。

R-controlled vowel sound /or/

/or/ represented by OR					
bore	born **	chore *	chord	core	cork
corn **	door *	dorm	for *	force **	fork **
form **	fort	forth **	horn	horse *	more **
morning *	north **	or *	porch	pore	pork **
port	scorch	score **	shore	short	snore
sore	sort	sport *	store **	stork	storm **
sword	swore	sworn	thorn	torch	tore *
torn **	wore **				
/or/ represented by OAR					
aboard **	board **	coarse	hoard	oar	roar
soar					

注：* 表示 2022 版新课标中二级词汇；** 表示 2022 版新课标中三级词汇。

Schwa /uh/ as in alarm

about *	above **	account **	adult **	afloat	afoot
afraid **	again *	ago *	agree **	ahead *	ajar
alarm **	alas	alone **	along **	American **	among **
anew	annoy	another **	apart	appear **	applause
ashamed	ashore	aside	asleep **	avoid **	await
awake **	aware **	away **	awhile		

注：* 表示 2022 版新课标中二级词汇；** 表示 2022 版新课标中三级词汇。

第三部分　拼读模块词汇表

目的：以下拼读模块（Fry et al，1993；Blevins Cites，2017）可供教师用于教学目的或者有选择性地根据教学需求挑选出运用在类比教学模式中，毕竟中国的很多主流教材都包括了拼读模块（Phonogram）。

来源：引自于下表按照字母顺序，包括了从元音派生的单音节词。字母顺序从单个辅音开始并过渡到辅音字母连缀和二合字母。

Long-A sound /ai/ Phonograms

Phonograms	word list				
-ace	face *	lace	mace	pace	brace
	grace	place *	space *	trace	
-ade	fade	jade	made **	wade	blade
	glade	grade	shade	spade	trade
-age	age *	cage	gage	page **	rage
	sage	wage	stage **		
-aid	laid **	maid	paid **	raid	braid
-ail	bail	fail **	trail	hail	jail
	mail	nail	pail	quail	rail
	sail	tail *	wail	flail	frail
	snail				
-ain	main *	pain **	rain *	vain	brain **
	chain	drain	grain	plain	slain
	Spain **	sprain	stain	strain	train *
-aint	faint	paint **	saint	quaint	
-aise	praise **	raise **			
-ait	bait	gait	wait *	strait	trait
-ake	bake	cake *	fake	jake	lake *
	make *	quake	rake	sake	take *
	wake *	drake	flake	shake **	snake **
	stake	brake			
-ale	bale	gale	male	pale	sale **
	tale	scale	stale	whale	

续表

Phonograms	word list				
-ame	came **	dame	fame	game *	lame
	name *	same **	tame	blame	flame
	frame	shame **			
-ane	cane	jane	lane	mane	pane
	sane	vane	wane	crane	plane *
-ange	range	change **	grange	strange **	
-ape	cape	gape	nape	tape	drape
	grape *	scrape	shape **		
-ase	base	case **	chase		
-aste	taste **	baste	haste	waste **	paste
-ate	date **	fate	gate **	hate **	Kate
	late *	mate	rate	crate	grate
	plate **	skate	state **		
-ave	cave	gave **	pave	rave	save **
	wave	brave **	crave	grave	shave
	slave				
-ay	bay	day *	gay	hay	jay
	lay **	may *	nay	pay **	ray
	say *	way *	clay	fray	gray
	play *	pray	slay	spray	stay **
	stray	sway	tray		
-aze	daze	faze	gaze	haze	maze
	raze	blaze	craze	glaze	graze
-eak	break **	steak			
-eight	neigh	weigh **	sleigh		
-ey	hey	grey **	prey	they *	whey

注：* 表示 2022 版新课标中二级词汇；** 表示 2022 版新课标中三级词汇。

Long-E sound /ee/ Phonograms

-e	be *	he *	me *	we *	she *
-ea	pea	sea *	tea *	flea	plea

续表

-each	beach *	leach	peach	teach **	bleach
	breach	preach			
-ead	bead	lead **	read **	knead	plead
-eak	beak	leak	peak	weak **	bleak
	creak	freak	sneak	speak *	squeak
	streak	tweak			
-eal	deal **	heal	meal **	peal	real **
	seal	teal	veal	zeal	squeal
	steal **				
-eam	beam	ream	seam	team *	cream
	dream **	gleam	steam	stream	
-ean	bean **	dean	jean	lean	mean **
	wean	clean *	glean		
-eap	-eap	leap	heap	reap	cheap **
-ear	dear *	fear	gear	hear *	near *
	rear	tear	year *	clear **	shear
	smear	spear			
-ease	cease	lease	crease	grease	
-east	beast	feast	least **	yeast	
-eat	beat **	feat	heat **	meat *	neat
	peat	seat **	bleat	cheat **	cleat
	pleat	treat **	wheat		
-eath	heath	sheath	wreath		
-eave	heave	leave **	weave	cleave	sheave
-ee	bee *	fee	knee **	see *	free *
	tee	wee	glee	flee	
	spree	three **	tree *		
-eech	beech	leech	breech	screech	speech **
-eed	deed	feed **	heed	need **	reed
	seed	weed	bleed	breed	creed
	freed	greed	speed **	tweed	
-eek	leek	meek			

续表

-eel	feel *	heel	kneel	peel	reel
	steel	wheel **			
-eem	deem	seem **	teem		
-een	keen	queen **	seen **	teen	green *
	screen **				
-eep	beep	deep **	jeep	keep *	peep
	seep	weep	cheep	creep	sheep *
	sleep *	steep	sweep *		
-eer	deer	jeer	peer	queer	sneer
	steer				
-eet	beet	feet *	meet *	fleet	greet
	sheet	skeet	sleet	street *	sweet **
	tweet				
-eeze	breeze	freeze	sneeze	squeeze	tweeze
	wheeze				
-iece	niece	piece **			
-ief	brief	chief	grief	thief	
-ield	field **	yield	shield		

注：* 表示 2022 版新课标中二级词汇；** 表示 2022 版新课标中三级词汇。

Long-I sound /igh/ Phonograms

-ibe	bribe	scribe	tribe		
-ice	dice	twice **	mice	nice *	rice *
	vice	price *	slice	splice	trice
-ide	hide **	ride **	side **	tide	wide **
	bride	glide	pride **	slide	snide
	stride				
-ie	die *	lie *	pie	tie **	vie
-ied	died **	lied **	cried **	dried **	fried
	spied	tried **			
-ier	brier	crier	drier	flier	

续表

-ies	dies **	lies **	pies	ties **	cries **
	dries **	flies **	skies **	spies	tries **
-ife	fife	knife **	life **	rife	wife **
	strife				
-igh	high **	nigh	sigh	thigh	
-ight	fight **	knight	light *	might **	night *
	right *	sight	tight	blight	bright **
	flight	fright	plight	plight	slight
-ike	bike *	pike	hike **	like *	spike
-ild	mild	wild **	child *		
-ile	file	mile **	smile **	pile	tile
	vile	while **			
-ime	dime	lime	mime	time *	chime
	grime	prime	slime		
-ind	bind	find *	hind	kind *	mind **
	rind	wind *	blind **	grind	
-ine	dine	fine *	line **	mine **	nine **
	pine	vine	shine **	shrine	spine
	swine	whine			
-ipe	pipe	ripe	wipe	gripe	snipe
	stripe	swipe			
-ire	fire *	hire	tire	wire	spire
-ise	guise	rise **	wise **		
-ite	bite	kite *	mite	quite **	rite
	site	white *	write *	sprite	
-ive	dive	five **	hive	jive	live *
	chive	drive **	strive	thrive	
-uy	buy *	guy			
-y	by *	my *	cry *	dry **	fry
	ply	pry	shy **	sky **	sly
	spy	try *	why *		
-ye	bye *	dye	eye *	lye	rye

注：* 表示 2022 版新课标中二级词汇；** 表示 2022 版新课标中三级词汇。

Long-O sound /oa/ Phonograms

-o	go *	no *	so *	pro	
-oach	coach	poach	roach	broach	
-oad	load	road **	toad		
-oak	soak	cloak	croak		
-oal	coal	foal	goal **		
-oam	foam	loam	roam		
-oan	loan	moan	groan		
-oast	boast	coast *	roast	toast	
-oat	oat	boat *	coat *	goat *	moat
	bloat	float	gloat	throat **	
-obe	lobe	robe	globe	probe	
-ode	code	lode	mode	node	strode
-oe	doe	foe	hoe	joe	toe
	woe				
-oke	coke	joke	poke	woke	yoke
	broke **	choke	smoke **	spoke **	stoke
-old	old *	cold *	fold	gold **	hold *
	mold	sold **	told **	scold	
-ole	dole	hole *	mole	pole	role
	stole **	whole **			
-oll	poll	roll	toll	droll	knoll
	scroll	stroll	troll		
-olt	bolt	colt	jolt	molt	volt
-ome	dome	home *	chrome		
-one	bone	cone	hone	lone	tone
	zone	clone	drone	phone *	prone
	shone	stone *			
-ope	cope	dope	hope **	mope	nope
	pope	rope **	scope	slope	
-ose	hose	nose *	pose	rose **	chose *
	close *	prose	those *		
-ost	host	most **	post **	ghost	

续表

-ote	note **	quote	rote	vote	wrote **
-ove	cove	wove	clove	drove	grove
	stove	trove			
-ow	bow	know *	low **	mow	row **
	sow	tow	blow **	crow	flow
	glow	grow **	show *	slow *	snow *
	stow				
-own	known **	mown	sown	blown **	flown **
	grown **	shown **	thrown **		

注：* 表示 2022 版新课标中二级词汇；** 表示 2022 版新课标中三级词汇。

Long-U sound /yoo/ phonograms

-ew	dew	few **	knew **	pew	
-ude	dude				
-ue	due	hue			
-uke	duke	puke			
-une	dune	tune			
-ube	cube	tube			
-ule	mule				
-ume	fume				
-ure	cure	pure			
-use	use	fuse	muse		
-ute	cute *	mute			

注：* 表示 2022 版新课标中二级词汇；** 表示 2022 版新课标中三级词汇。

在英式英语中，dude，tube，due，dune，tune，mute 和 duke 这一类单词被归于长元音 Long-U 组中，可是在美式英语中，根据语音解码规则，虽然它们也被归于长元音 Long-U 组中，但是它们的发音确实存在长元音/oo/，如同在单词 goose 中一样。

Short-A sound / a/ Phonograms

-ab	cab	dab	gab	jab	lab
	nab	tab	blab	crab	drab
	flab	grab	scab	slab	stab

续表

-ack	back *	hack	Jack	knack	lack
	Mack	pack	quack	rack	sack
	tack	black *	clack	crack	shack
	slack	smack	snack	stack	track
	whack				
-act	fact **	pact	tact	tract	
-ad	bad *	dad *	fad	had **	lad
	mad **	pad	sad *	tad	clad
	glad **				
-aft	daft	raft	waft	craft	draft
	graft	shaft			
-ag	bag *	gag	jag	lag	nag
	rag	sag	tag	wag	brag
	crag	drag	flag	shag	snag
	stag				
-am	dam	ham	jam	ram	tam
	scam	scram	yam	clam	gram
	sham	slam	swam		
-amp	camp	damp	lamp	ramp	vamp
	champ	clamp	cramp	scamp	stamp
	tramp				
-an	ban	can *	fan *	man *	pan
	ran **	tan	van	bran	clan
	plan **	scan	span	than **	
-ance	dance *	lance	chance **	France **	glance
	prance	stance	trance		
-anche	ranch	blanch	branch		
-and	band **	hand *	land **	sand **	bland
	brand	gland	stand *	strand	
-ang	bang	fang	gang	hang **	pang
	rang **	sang **	clang	slang	sprang **

续表

-ank	bank **	lank	rank	sank **	tank
	yank	blank	clank	crank	drank *
	flank	plank	prank	spank	thank *
-ant	pant	rant	chant	grant	plant *
	scant	slant			
-ap	cap *	gap	lap	map *	nap
	rap	sap	tap	yap	chap
	clap	flap	scrap	slap	snap
	strap	trap	wrap		
-ash	bash	cash	dash	gash	hash
	lash	mash	rash	sash	brash
	clash	flash	slash	smash	stash
	thrash	trash			
-ask	ask *	cask	mask	task **	flask
-asm	chasm	plasm	spasm		
-asp	gasp	hasp	rasp	clasp	grasp
-ast	cast	fast *	last *	mast	past *
	vast	blast			
-at	bat	cat *	fat **	gnat	hat **
	mat	pat	rat	sat **	vat
	brat	chat **	flat	scat	slat
	slat	spat	that **		
-atch	batch	catch *	hatch	latch	match **
	patch	scratch	snatch		
-ath	bath **	math *	path	wrath	
-ax	lax	tax	wax	flax	

注：* 表示 2022 版新课标中二级词汇；** 表示 2022 版新课标中三级词汇。

Short-E sound /e/ phonograms

-ead	dead **	head *	lead **	read **	bread *
	dread	spread **	thread	tread	
-ealth	health **	wealth **	stealth		

续表

-eck	deck	heck	neck **	peck	check **
	fleck	speck	wreck		
-ed	bed *	fed **	led **	red *	wed
	bled	bred	fled	shed	shred
	sled	sped			
-edge	hedge	ledge	wedge	dredge	pledge
	sledge				
-eft	left *	cleft	theft		
-eg	beg	keg			
-eld	held **	meld	weld		
-elf	self	shelf **			
-ell	bell **	cell	dell	fell	jell
	sell *	tell *	well *	yell	
	dwell	shell	smell **	spell **	swell
-elp	help *	kelp	yelp		
-elt	belt	felt **	knelt	melt	pelt
	welt	dwelt			
-em	gem	hem	stem	them *	then *
-en	den	hen **	pen *	men *	ten **
	when *				
-ence	fence	hence	pence	whence	
-end	end **	bend	fend	lend **	mend
	send **	tend	vend	blend	spend **
	trend				
-ength	length	strength			
-ense	dense	sense **	tense		
-ent	bent	cent	dent	gent	
	lent **	rent	sent *	tent **	vent
	went **	scent	spent **		
-ep	pep	rep	prep	step	
-ept	kept **	wept **	crept	slept **	swept **
-esh	mesh	flesh	fresh		

续表

-ess	guess **	less **	mess **	bless	chess
	dress *	press	stress **		
-est	best *	jest	lest	nest	pest
	rest **	test **	vest	zest	blest
-et	bet	get *	jet	let *	met **
	net	pet *	set *	wet **	yet **
	fret				
-etch	fetch	sketch	wrench		
-ext	next *	text **			

注：* 表示 2022 版新课标中二级词汇；** 表示 2022 版新课标中三级词汇。

Short-I Phonograms

-ib	bib	fib	rib	crib	glib
-ick	kick **	lick	pick **	quick **	sick **
	tick	wick	brick	chick	click **
	flick	slick	stick **	thick **	trick
-id	bid	did **	hid *	kid *	lid
	mid	rid	grid	skid	slid
	squid				
-iff	cliff	sniff	stiff	whiff	
-ift	gift *	lift **	rift	sift	drift
	shift *	swift	thrift		
-ig	big *	dig **	fig	jig	pig *
	wig	brig	sprig	swig	twig
-ilk	milk *	silk **			
-ill	ill *	bill	dill	fill **	gill
	hill *	kill **	mill	pill **	quill
	sill	till	will *	chill	drill
	frill	grill	skill **	spill	still **
	thrill	trill	twill		
-ilt	kilt	tilt	wilt	quilt	stilt

续表

-im	dim	him *	rim	brim	grim
	prim	slim **	swim *	trim	whim
-imp	limp	blimp	chimp	crimp	primp
	skimp				
-in	bin	fin	kin	pin	tin
	win *	chin	grin	shin	skin
	spin	thin *	twin		
-ince	mince	since **	prince **		
-inch	inch	cinch	finch	pinch	clinch
	flinch				
-ing	bing	ding	king **	ping	ring **
	sing *	wing **	bring *	cling	fling
	sling	spring *	sting	string	swing
	thing *	wring			
-is	is **	his *			
-ish	dish	fish *	wish *	swish	
-isk	disk	risk **	brisk	frisk	whisk
-isp	lisp	wisp	crisp		
-iss	hiss	kiss **	miss **	bliss	Swiss
-ist	fist	list **	mist	wrist	twist
-it	bit	fit **	hit **	kit	knit
	lit **	pit	quit	sit *	wit
	flit	grit	skit	slit	spit
	split				
-itc	ditch	hitch	pitch	witch	switch
-ive	give *	live *			
-ix	fix **	mix **	six **		

注：＊表示 2022 版新课标中二级词汇；＊＊表示 2022 版新课标中三级词汇。

Short-O phonograms

-ob	cob	gob	job *	knob	lob
	mob	rob	sob	blob	glob
	slob	snob	throb		

续表

-ock	dock	hock	knock **	lock **	mock
	rock **	sock *	tock	block **	clock *
	crock	flock	frock	shock **	smock
	stock				
-od	cod	mod	nod	pod	rod
	sod	clod	plod	prod	trod
-oft	loft	soft			
-og	bog	cog	dog *	fog	hog
	jog **	log	clog	flog	frog
	smog				
-omp	pomp	romp	chomp	stomp	
-ond	bond	fond	pond	blond	
-op	bop	cop	hop	mop	pop
	sop	top *	chop	crop	drop **
	flop	plop	prop	shop *	slop
	stop *				
-ot	cot	dot	got **	hot *	jot
	knot	lot *	not *	pot	rot
	tot	blot	clot	plot	shot
	slot	spot	trot		
-otch	botch	notch	blotch	crotch	
-ough	cough **	trough			
-ox	ox	box *	fox **	lox	pox

注：* 表示 2022 版新课标中二级词汇；** 表示 2022 版新课标中三级词汇。

Short-U sound /u/ Phonograms

-ome	come *	some *			
-on	son **	ton	won **		
-ough	rough	tough	slough		
-ove	love *	glove **	shove	above **	
-ub	cub	dub	hub	nub	rub
	sub	tub	club	flub	grub
	scrub	shrub	snub	stub	

续表

-uch	much *	such **			
-uck	buck	duck	luck **	muck	puck
	suck	tuck	cluck	pluck	stuck
	struck **	truck **			
-ud	bud	cud	dud	mud	crud
	spud	stud	thud		
-uge	budge	fudge	judge **	nudge	drudge
	grudge	sludge	smudge	trudge	
-uff	buff	cuff	huff	puff	ruff
	bluff	fluff	gruff	scuff	sluff
	snuff	stuff			
-ug	bug	dug **	hug **	jug	lug
	mug	rug	pug	tug	chug
	drug	plug	shrug	slug	smug
	snug	thug			
-ulk	bulk	hulk	sulk		
-ull	cull	dull	gull	hull	lull
	mull	skull			
-um	bum	gum	hum	mum *	sum
	chum	drum	glum	plum	scum
	slum	strum	swum **		
-ump	bump	dump	hump	jump *	lump
	pump	rump	chump	clump	frump
	grump	grump	plump	stump	thump
	trump				
-un	bun	fun **	gun **	pun	run *
	sun *	shun	spun	stun	
-unch	bunch	hunch	lunch *	munch	punch
	brunch	crunch	scrunch		
-ung	hung **	lung	rung **	sung **	clung
	flung	sprung **	stung	strung *	swung **

续表

-unk	bunk	dunk	hunk	junk	sunk *
	chunk	drunk **	flunk	plunk	shrunk
	skunk	slunk	spunk	stunk	trunk
-unt	bunt	hunt	punt	runt	blunt
	grunt	stunt			
-up	cup *	pup	sup		
-us	bus *	plus	thus		
-ush	gush	hush	mush	rush **	blush
	brush **	crush	flush	plush	slush
	thrush				
-ust	bust	dust	gust	gust	just **
	must *	rust	crust	thrust	trust **
-ut	but *	cut *	gut	hut	jut
	nut	rut	glut	shut **	strut
-utch	hutch	clutch	crutch		
-utt	butt	mutt	putt		

注：* 表示 2022 版新课标中二级词汇；** 表示 2022 版新课标中三级词汇。

Diphthong /oi/ Phonograms

-oil	oil **	boil **	coil	foil	toil
	broil	spoil			
-oin	coin **	join *	loin	groin	
-oint	joint	point **			
-oise	noise **	poise			
-oist	foist	hoist	moist		
-oy	boy *	coy	joy **	toy *	soy

注：* 表示 2022 版新课标中二级词汇；** 表示 2022 版新课标中三级词汇。

Diphthong /ou/ Phonograms

-ouch	couch	pouch	vouch	crouch	grouch
	slouch				
-oud	loud **	cloud **	proud **		

续表

-ounce	bounce	pounce	trounce		
-ount	count **	mount			
-ound	bound	found **	hound	mound	pound
	round **	sound **	wound **	ground **	
-our	our *	hour *	sour	flour	scour
-ouse	house *	louse	mouse *	blouse **	spouse
-out	out *	about *	gout	tout	clout
	scout	snout	spout	sprout	stout
	trout				
-outh	mouth *	south **			
-ow	bow	cow *	how *	now *	vow
	brow	chow	plow		
-owl	fowl	howl	growl	prowl	scowl
-own	down *	gown	town **	brown *	clown
	crown	drown	frown		

注：* 表示 2022 版新课标中二级词汇；** 表示 2022 版新课标中三级词汇。

Variant vowel sound broad-O sound /or/ Phonograms

-all	all *	ball *	call *	fall **	mall **
	tall *	wall *	small *	squall	stall
-alk	balk	talk **	walk *	chalk **	stalk
-alt	halt	malt	salt **		
-aught	caught **	naught	taught **	fraught	
-aunch	haunch	launch	paunch	staunch	
-aunt	daunt	gaunt	haunt	jaunt	taunt
	taunt	flaunt			
-ault	fault	vault			
-aw	caw	gnaw	jaw	law **	paw
	raw	saw **	claw	draw *	flaw
	slaw	squaw	straw		
-awl	bawl	brawl	crawl	drawl	scrawl
	shawl				

续表

-awn	dawn	fawn	lawn	pawn	yawn
	brawn	drawn	prawn		
-ong	bong	dong	long	song	tong
	prong	strong *	wrong *		
-oss	boss	loss	moss	toss	cross
	cross	floss	gloss		
-ost	cost	lost **	frost		
-oth	moth	broth	cloth	froth	sloth
-ought	ought	bought **	fought **	sought **	brought **
	thought **				

注：* 表示 2022 版新课标中二级词汇；** 表示 2022 版新课标中三级词汇。

Variant vowel sound short /oo/ Phonograms

-ood	good *	hood	wood *	stood **	
-ook	book *	cook *	hook	look *	nook
	brook	crook	shook **		
-oot	foot *	soot			
-ould	could **	would **	should **		
-ull	bull	full **	pull **		
-ush	bush	push **			

注：* 表示 2022 版新课标中二级词汇；** 表示 2022 版新课标中三级词汇。

Variant vowels long /oo/ sound Phonograms

-ew	blew **	brew	crew	grew **	screw
-o	do *	to *	who *		
-oo	boo	coo	goo	moo	too *
	woo	zoo *	shoo		
-ood	food *	mood	brood		
-oof	goof	roof	proof	spoof	
-ool	cool *	fool *	pool	tool *	drool
	school *	spool	stool		

续表

-oom	boom	doom	loom	room *	zoom
	bloom	broom	gloom	groom	
-oon	boon	loon	moon *	soon *	croon
	spoon **	swoon			
-oop	coop	hoop	loop	droop	scoop
	sloop	snoop	stoop	swoop	troop
-oose	goose	loose	moose	noose	
-oot	boot	hoot	loot	moot	root
	toot	scoot	shoot		
-ooth	booth	tooth **			
-ooze	ooze	snooze			
-oup	soup *	croup	group **		
-ube	lube				
-uce	spruce	truce			
-ude	rude	crude			
-ue	blue *	clue	glue	true **	
-uke	fluke				
-ule	rule **				
-ume	plume				
-une	June **	prune			
-ure	lure	sure			
-use	ruse				
-ute	jute	lute	brute	chute	flute

注：* 表示 2022 版新课标中二级词汇；** 表示 2022 版新课标中三级词汇。

在英式英语中，dude，tube，due，dune，tune，mute 和 duke 这一类单词被归于长元音 Long-U 组中，可是在美式英语中，根据语音解码规则，虽然它们也被归于长元音 Long-U 组中，但是它们的发音确实存在长元音/oo/，如同在单词 goose 中一样。

R-controlled sound /air/ phonograms

-air	air *	fair **	hair *	lair	pair *
	chair *	flair	flair	stair *	

续表

-are	bare	care *	dare	fare	hare
	mare	pare	rare	ware	blare
	flare	glare	scare **	spare **	snare
	square **	stare *			
-ear	bear *	pear **	wear *	swear	

注：* 表示 2022 版新课标中二级词汇；** 表示 2022 版新课标中三级词汇。

R-controlled vowel sound /ur/ phonograms

-earn	earn	learn *	yearn		
-erb	herb	verb			
-erge	merge	serge	verge		
-erk	jerk	clerk			
-erm	germ	term **			
-en	fern	stern			
-erve	nerve	serve	swerve		
-ir	fir	sir **	stir	whir	
-ird	bird *	third **			
-irk	quirk	shirk	smirk		
-irl	girl *	swirl	twirl	whirl	
-irt	dirt	flirt	shirt *	skirt *	
-irst	first **	thirst			
-irth	birth **	girth			
-ur	fur	blur	slur	spur	
-urb	curb	blurb			
-urge	urge	purge			
-url	curl	furl	hurl		
-urn	burn **	turn *	churn	spurn	
-urk	lurk	murk			
-urse	curse	nurse	purse		
-urt	curt	hurt *	blurt	spurt	

注：* 表示 2022 版新课标中二级词汇；** 表示 2022 版新课标中三级词汇。

R-controlled vowel sound /ar/ phonograms

-ar	bar	car *	far *	jar	mar
	par	tar	char	scar	spar
	star *				
-ard	card *	guard **	hard *	lard	yard
-arge	-barge	large **	charge		
-ark	bark	dark **	hark	lark	mark **
	park *	shark **	spark	stark	
-arm	arm *	farm *	harm **	charm	
-arn	barn	darn	yarn		
-arp	carp	harp	tarp	sharp	
-art	cart	chart	mart	part **	tart
	chart	smart **	start **		

注：＊表示 2022 版新课标中二级词汇；＊＊表示 2022 版新课标中三级词汇。

R-controlled vowel sound /or/ phonograms

-oar	boar	roar	soar		
-oor	door *	floor *			
-orch	porch	torch	scorch		
-ord	cord	ford	lord	chord	sword
-ore	bore	core	fore	gore	more **
	pore	sore	tore	wore	chore
	spore	force **	sore **	score **	store **
	gore	tore	shore	swore	
-ork	cork	fork **	pork **	stork	
-orm	dorm	form **	dorm	storm **	
-orn	born *	corn *	horn *	morn	torn *
	worn *	scorn	sworn	thorn	
-ort	fort	port	sort	short *	snort
	sport *				
-our	four *	pour			

注：＊表示 2022 版新课标中二级词汇；＊＊表示 2022 版新课标中三级词汇。

第四部分 视觉词汇

The most Frequent 150 words

(in order of frequency according to American Heritage Word Frequency Book)

the *	could **	they *	use *	of *
no *	at *	may *	and *	make *
be *	water **	an *	than **	this *
go *	to *	first **	from **	good *
in *	been **	I *	new *	is **
long *	have *	write *	you *	little *
or *	our *	that *	very *	by *
used *	it *	after *	one **	me *
he *	word *	had **	man *	for *
called **	not *	too *	was **	just **
will *	any *	on *	his *	each **
day *	are *	most *	about *	same **
but *	know *	how *	right *	what *
get *	up *	look *	all *	through **
out *	think *	where *	back *	them *
such **	when *	much *	then *	here *
we *	before *	she *	take *	there *
also *	many *	why *	can *	around *
some *	thing **	find *	another *	so *
help *	your *	came **	these *	put *
which *	come *	would **	year *	their *
work *	other **	different *	said **	three **
its *	away **	if **	word *	who *
again *	do *	must *	now *	off *
into **	because *	people *	went **	has **
does **	my *	old **	more **	part **
made **	number **	her *	even **	over *
two **	place *	did **	like *	well *
down *	him *	as **	only **	see *
with *	way *	time *		

注：* 表示 2022 版新课标中二级词汇；** 表示 2022 版新课标中三级词汇。

Dolch Basic Sight Words 220				
a *	don't	in *	pick *	those **
about *	down **	into **	play **	three **
after *	draw *	is **	please **	to **
again *	drink **	it **	pretty *	today **
all *	eat *	its *	pull **	together **
always *	eight *	jump *	put *	too **
am *	every *	just **	ran **	try **
an *	fall **	keep *	read **	two **
and *	far *	kind *	red **	under *
any *	fast *	know *	ride *	up *
are *	find *	laugh **	right **	upon **
around *	first **	let *	round *	us *
as **	five **	light *	run **	use *
ask *	fly *	like *	said *	very *
at *	for *	little *	saw *	walk *
ate **	found **	live *	say *	want *
away **	four **	long *	see **	warm *
be *	from *	look *	seven **	was **
because *	full **	made **	shall *	wash *
been **	funny **	make *	she *	we *
before *	gave **	many *	show *	well *
best *	get *	may *	sing *	went **
better **	give *	me *	sit **	were **
big *	go *	much *	six *	what *
black *	goes **	must *	sleep *	when *
blue *	going	my *	small *	where *
both **	good *	myself **	so *	which *
bring *	got **	never *	some	white *
brown *	green *	new *	soon *	who *
but *	grow **	no *	start *	why *
buy *	had **	not *	stop *	will *
by *	has **	now *	take **	wish *